Also by Wolfgang Puck

The Wolfgang Puck Cookbook
Wolfgang Puck's Modern French Cooking

WOLFGANG PUCK

ADVENTURES IN THE KITCHEN

WOLFGANG PUCK

ADVENTURES IN THE KITCHEN

Foreword by Calvin Trillin

RANDOM HOUSE   NEW YORK

Tableware courtesy of Tesoro, Cottonwood, and Sue Fisher.

Library of Congress Cataloging-in-Publication Data
Puck, Wolfgang.
Adventures in the kitchen: 175 new recipes from Spago, Chinois
on Main, Postrio, and Eureka / Wolfgang Puck.
p.   cm.
Includes index.
ISBN 0-394-55895-2
1. Cookery. 2. Spago (Restaurant) 3. Chinois (Restaurant)
4. Postrio (Restaurant) 5. Eureka (Restaurant) I. Title.
TX714.P83   1991
641.5—dc20   91-16018

Manufactured in the United States of America

I dedicate this book to Judy Gethers.

Without her tenacity, hard work, and patience, this
would still be a manuscript on the back burner of my kitchen.

I'd like to be able to say that Wolfgang Puck won my heart with a pizza made with peppered Louisiana shrimp, sun-dried tomatoes, and leeks. He has certainly won a lot of hearts with pizzas and chopped Chino Farm vegetable salads and sautéed shrimp cakes and Chinois chicken salad. In fact, whenever I'm in California, I eat as much of his food as I can, just to make sure my affection doesn't stray.

But the realization that Wolfgang was my sort of chef didn't come when I was at table. It came at an industry association dinner in New York at which distinguished chefs were to demonstrate that light and inventive dishes could be made with beef. Just before the dinner, the Manhattan public relations person in charge seemed even more nervous than usual, and I discovered that Wolfgang, wearing his most solemn expression, had just told her how upset he was to learn that everyone involved in the presentation was a vegetarian.

In my experience, Wolfgang tends to wear a solemn expression only for the sake of a prank. He always seems to be having a good time, although I'll admit that I have never been around when the dishwasher breaks down on the same night that three waitresses have decided to take an unannounced beach trip to Baja.

The tone of someone having a good time is reflected in his cooking. People who go to Spago for the first time are sometimes surprised that it isn't fancy. Over the years, I've written occasionally about the evenings I've endured in fancy restaurants—the American rooftop spinner I used to call La Maison de la Casa House, Continental Cuisine, for instance, and the English country inn serving the complicated concoctions I always thought of as stuff-stuff with heavy. I can't imagine Wolfgang Puck running that sort of place or cooking that sort of food. It wouldn't be any fun.

Calvin Trillin

ACKNOWLEDGMENTS

With sincere thanks . . .

To Jason Epstein, my editor, because he has more patience than any saint I know.

To Rochelle Udell, the most talented book designer in the world, who took only five minutes to understand what I like.

To Audrey and Barry Sterling, and Joy Sterling and Forest Tancer at Iron Horse Vineyards, who are not only our good friends, but also lent us their beautiful home to take photographs in and made our efforts easier by serving us their wonderful sparkling wine.

To all the chefs at Spago, Chinois on Main, Postrio, Eureka, and Granita, who inspire me as much as I hope that I inspire them.

And since this is a cookbook from our restaurants, I must say I feel that we have some of the best people working in our restaurants . . .

To our manager and partner at Spago, Tom Kaplan, managers Bella Lantsman at Chinois on Main, Richard Coraine at Postrio, Micky Kanolzer at Eureka, and Pam Brunson at Granita, who all do their best to run things smoothly so that I have time to cook.

To our maitre d's: Bernard Erpicum, Jannis Swerman, and Anita Austin at Spago, who make everyone feel as welcome as in their own home; to Lisa Brady, Kathleen Beaton, and Charlie Pucket, who make Chinois run like clockwork; to Doug Washington and Teri Esensten at Postrio, who represent us well in San Francisco; and to Fernand Poitras and Elaine Woo, who keep up with the lively pace at Eureka.

With these recipes, you can certainly experience the food of our restaurants, but you will miss the friendly and professional service given by our great dining room staff. So cheers to all of them!

To my partner and wife, Barbara, and my son, Cameron, who inspire me every day, and always encourage me to do my best.

CONTENTS

I have loved food since I was a very young boy. The smells of the kitchen are as aromatic to me as the finest perfume—the pungent tomato sauces bubbling in an Italian kitchen, the fragrant spices of an Indian household, or the earthy aroma of fresh bread baking in the oven. I consider eating good food one of the great pleasures of life. Whether it is an informal meal cooked at home for family and friends, or an elaborate feast served in one of our restaurants, I enjoy the planning as well as the preparation and eagerly look forward to nods of approval from my guests.

I like to think of this book as a big adventure, taking you from Spago to Chinois to Postrio to Eureka and back again to Spago, each with its own individual setting and distinctive flavor. This is a collaborative effort; the chefs have been with me for years, helping me develop and perfect recipes for each of the restaurants. These recipes have been tested and retested, tasted and retasted, so that our customers can experience something new and unusual.

It is almost ten years since we opened Spago, with the other restaurants spaced a few years apart, like a well-planned family. I am often asked to what I attribute the success of our restaurants. I think about this often, too, and have come up with a few reasons. In general, people feel comfortable in our restaurants, almost like eating in their own homes. The service is friendly. Many of our guests are frequent diners and are well known by all the staff. And we take great pride in the food we serve. Only the best ingredients are used, whether it is for a pizza, a hamburger, or foie gras.

Not too long ago a restaurant had to serve French food to be great. Today, restaurants have become much more eclectic and so has the taste of the public. When looking for new food trends, one does not have to travel further than one's own backyard. This country is a melting pot of different peoples and cultures, and out of this mixture, a new cuisine has evolved. Professional chefs and home cooks alike have experimented with a variety of foods, using spices from the Far East, chiles from South America, pastas from Italy, sashimi from Japan, and techniques from France. Emphasis is on simpler and healthier foods—less red meat, more fish and poultry, salads of every description, and lots of fresh vegetables. Sauces are lighter, grilling and roasting have replaced heavier types of cooking.

Creating an interesting menu is not as difficult as you might expect, but it does require some thought. If you are serving many appetizers, a light main dish is in order. If you are aware of certain preferences, for religious or dietary reasons, adjust your menu accordingly. Prepare as much as possible earlier in the day so that you are able to spend the evening in the living room with your friends, not in the kitchen with your pots and pans.

I have always considered myself lucky. Not only is cooking my vocation, it is my favorite avocation. I am happiest when spending a few hours behind the stove in one of my kitchens. I think it is important to enjoy yourself, whether it is peeling potatoes, seasoning a roast, whisking a sauce, or creating an elegant dessert.

WOLFGANG PUCK'S PIZZAS (PAGE 178-183)

CHICKEN LASAGNA
(PAGE 189)

STUFFED CABBAGE BALLS
(PAGE 77)

BARBECUED SHRIMP
"BLT" SANDWICH
(PAGE 36)

ROASTED DUNGENESS CRAB WITH PICKLED GINGER SAUCE
(PAGE 29)

FRANK'S LOBSTER SALAD
(PAGE 36)

PORK LOIN WITH THAI SAUCE
AND PAPAYA SALAD
(PAGE 96)

BRAISED MOROCCAN LAMB
(PAGE 89)

ROASTED SALMON WITH BLACK PEPPER
AND GINGER ON CELERY ROOT PUREE
(PAGE 66)

FRANÇOIS' SEAFOOD RISOTTO
WITH CRISP GINGER
(PAGE 200)

SAUTÉED SHRIMP
WITH TOMATO-BASIL VINAIGRETTE
(PAGE 18)

CHINOIS ROASTED SQUAB
ON PAN-FRIED NOODLES
WITH SPICY MUSHROOM SAUCE (PAGE 86)

SOFT-SHELL CRAB TEMPURA
WITH CILANTRO
(PAGE 26)

ROASTED RED SNAPPER
WITH NEW POTATO CRUST
AND RED ONION SAUCE (PAGE 67)

APRICOT-COCONUT MACAROONS
(PAGE 232)

HOLIDAY PANCAKES
WITH SMOKED FISH (PAGE 159)

CHOCOLATE CHIP COOKIES
(PAGE 233)

APRICOT PINE NUT TART
(PAGE 205)

WHISKEY FUDGE CAKE
(PAGE 218)

CHRISTMAS APPLE PIE
(PAGE 206)

STRAWBERRY SHORTCAKE
(PAGE 221)

WHITE CHOCOLATE
CHEESE CAKE
(PAGE 219)

THREE-CHOCOLATE FROZEN MOUSSE
(PAGE 225)

Butterscotch Pudding
(page 222)

WOLFGANG PUCK

ADVENTURES IN THE KITCHEN

APPETIZERS, FIRST COURSES, AND SALADS

Beef Saté with Spicy Szechuan Sauce

Chicken Saté with Mint Vinaigrette

Shrimp Skewers with Almond Pesto

Goat Cheese and Black Olives in Puff Pastry

Goat Cheese and Eggplant Crisps

Roasted Potatoes with Sour Cream and Caviar

Duck Liver Pâté (Foie Gras Terrine)

Duck Liver (Foie Gras) with Sautéed Cabbage and Green Onion

Passover Gefilte Fish

Grilled Santa Barbara Shrimp with Sweet Maui Onion and White Truffle Oil
Vinaigrette

Gulf Shrimp Salad with Spicy Jalapeño Sauce

Sautéed Shrimp with Tomato-Basil Vinaigrette

Sea Scallop Salad with Cold Cucumber Sauce

Sizzling Calamari Salad with Potato Strings

Red Snapper with Spring Vegetable Vinaigrette

Spago's Tuna Sashimi

Tempura Sashimi with Uni Sauce

Soft-shell Crab Tempura with Cilantro

Sautéed Crabcakes with Sweet Red Pepper Sauce

Roasted Dungeness Crab with Pickled Ginger Sauce

Broiled Quail with Persimmon Relish

Chinois Minced Garlic Chicken in Radicchio Cups

Chino Chopped Vegetable Salad

Frank's Lobster Salad

Barbecued Shrimp "BLT" Sandwich

When I entertain at home, informal parties are my favorite—guests can just mingle and talk. I like to prepare a variety of appetizers and small portions of main courses, creating a lively meal. Spicy foods like Chicken and Beef Satés, Sea Scallop Salad with Cold Cucumber Sauce, Grilled Shrimp with Sweet Maui Onion and White Truffle Oil Vinaigrette add excitement to the menu.

A combination of luxurious treats like Roasted Potatoes with Sour Cream and Caviar with an inexpensive appetizer such as Goat Cheese and Black Olives in Puff Pastry or phyllo dough can be popped into the oven as needed. And when I feel really extravagant, I prepare my Foie Gras Terrine.

Appetizers should be served in small portions, well seasoned, to stimulate the appetite. Dinner for many of my customers consists of two or three appetizers. They like the idea of many tastes but smaller portions.

The weather should also influence your choice of appetizers. In the winter, nothing is more satisfying than a bowl of tasty, steaming hot soup, but in the summer a fresh shrimp or lobster salad is far more welcome.

But whether it is a simple green salad, Soft-shell Crab Tempura, or Foie Gras with Sautéed Cabbage and Green Onion, always make something you are comfortable doing, and then do it well.

BEEF SATÉ WITH SPICY SZECHUAN SAUCE

Makes 24 skewers

¾ pound trimmed
  New York or fillet
  steak

MARINADE
½ cup soy sauce
1 tablespoon honey
1 teaspoon chili flakes
½ teaspoon ground
  cumin
½ teaspoon turmeric

SZECHUAN SAUCE
6 tablespoons (3
  ounces) unsalted
  butter
2 blanched garlic
  cloves, chopped fine
  (about 1 tablespoon)
1 green onion, chopped
  fine
1 cup Brown Veal or
  Chicken Stock (see
  pages 42, 43)
¼ cup soy sauce
1 teaspoon chili flakes

24 6-inch bamboo
  skewers
Large platter
Small bowl
Small skillet
Strainer
Small pan
Whisk

Soak the skewers in cold water and refrigerate for one hour, then skewer the steak and continue with the recipe.

① Cut the steak into 24 3 × 1-inch strips, each weighing about ½ ounce. Using 24 6-inch bamboo skewers, stick a skewer into each strip lengthwise and arrange on a large platter or baking pan. Refrigerate until needed.

② *Prepare the marinade:* In a small bowl, combine all the marinade ingredients and pour over the meat, turning to coat all sides. Let marinate, unrefrigerated, about 15 minutes.

③ Preheat the grill or broiler while the steak is marinating.

④ *Prepare the sauce:* In a small skillet, melt 2 tablespoons butter. Add the garlic and green onion and sauté over medium-high heat until soft, about 2 minutes. Pour in the stock, soy sauce, and chili pepper flakes, and cook 1 or 2 minutes longer. Strain into a clean pan and whisk in the remaining 4 tablespoons butter. Keep warm.

⑤ Arrange the skewers of steak on the grill or under the broiler,* being careful that the bare ends of the skewers are not directly over (or under) the flame. Grill until medium rare, about 30 to 40 seconds each side.

Presentation: Pour the sauce into a small bowl and set in the center of a large serving platter. Arrange the skewers around the bowl and serve immediately.

To prepare ahead: Through step 1 earlier in the day. Through step 4 about 20 to 30 minutes before you are ready to serve.

*Bring your broiler tray directly under the flame for best results.

CHICKEN SATÉ WITH MINT VINAIGRETTE

Makes 24 skewers

INGREDIENTS

About 10 ounces
   boned and skinned
   chicken breast

MARINADE
1 ½ teaspoons curry
   powder
1 teaspoon freshly
   ground pepper
½ teaspoon salt
½ teaspoon ground
   cumin
1 ½ to 2 tablespoons
   peanut oil

MINT VINAIGRETTE
2 egg yolks
¼ cup rice wine
   vinegar
2 tablespoons (about
   ½ bunch) plus 2
   teaspoons finely
   chopped mint leaves
1 tablespoon soy sauce
½ teaspoon ground
   coriander
½ cup peanut oil
¼ teaspoon salt
¼ teaspoon freshly
   ground pepper

Satés can be readied early in the day and grilled or broiled as your guests arrive. These saté recipes can be increased as necessary and are frequently served at cocktail parties at Spago.

1 Soak 24 6-inch bamboo skewers in cold water and refrigerate for 1 hour.

2 Cut the chicken breast into 24 3 × 1-inch strips. Stick one skewer into each chicken strip, lengthwise, and arrange on a large platter or baking tray.

3 *Prepare the marinade:* In a small cup or bowl, combine the curry powder, pepper, salt, and cumin. Spoon the oil over the chicken, turning to coat well, and then sprinkle the dry ingredients on both sides. Let marinate for 1 hour, refrigerated.

4 *Prepare the vinaigrette:* In a blender, combine the egg yolks, vinegar, 2 tablespoons mint leaves, soy sauce, coriander, and a little oil. With the motor running, slowly pour in the remaining oil and blend until smooth. Transfer to a small bowl and stir in the remaining 2 teaspoons chopped mint leaves. Season with salt and pepper to taste and refrigerate, covered, until needed.

5 Preheat the grill or broiler.

6 Arrange the skewers of chicken on the grill or under the broiler,* careful that the bare ends of the skewers are not directly over (or under) the flame. Grill the chicken until golden brown, 1 ½ to 2 minutes on each side.

24 6-inch bamboo
  skewers
Large platter or baking
  tray
Small bowls
Blender

Presentation: Pour the vinaigrette into a small serving bowl. Arrange the skewers around the bowl and serve immediately. Let your guests help themselves.

To prepare ahead: Through step 4, removing the chicken and the vinaigrette from the refrigerator 15 minutes before grilling.

*Bring your broiler tray directly under the flame for best results.

SHRIMP SKEWERS WITH ALMOND PESTO

Makes 24 skewers

INGREDIENTS

24 large peeled (about
  ¾ pound) uncooked
  shrimp

MARINADE
¼ cup olive oil
1 teaspoon salt
1 teaspoon freshly
  ground white pepper
¼ cup chopped fresh
  basil leaves
1 tablespoon blanched
  chopped garlic

Soaking the bamboo skewers in cold water and refrigerating for 1 hour decreases the possibility of the skewers catching on fire, but still watch carefully when grilling.

1 Using 24 6-inch bamboo skewers, straighten each shrimp and stick a skewer through. Arrange on a large platter or baking pan. In a small bowl, combine the marinade ingredients and mix well. Pour over the shrimp, turning to coat well. Refrigerate 2 to 3 hours.

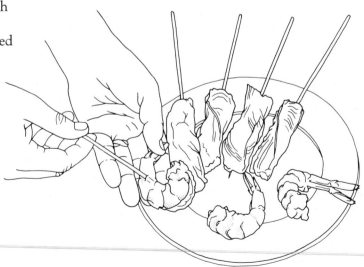

(Continued)

PESTO SAUCE

1 cup loosely packed
   parsley, washed,
   large stems removed
1 cup firmly packed
   basil leaves
2 tablespoons chopped
   blanched garlic
1 tablespoon finely
   ground almonds
¾ cup olive oil
1 teaspoon salt
1 teaspoon freshly
   ground white pepper
2 tablespoons lemon
   juice

EQUIPMENT

24 6-inch bamboo
   skewers
Large platter or baking
   pan
Small bowls
Blender

② *Prepare the sauce:* In a blender, combine the parsley, basil, garlic, almonds, and a little of the oil and puree. With the motor running, slowly pour the remaining oil through the opening and blend until smooth. Season with salt, pepper, and lemon juice and correct seasoning to taste. Scrape into a small serving bowl and set aside.

③ Preheat the grill or broiler.*

④ Arrange the skewers of shrimp on the grill or under the broiler, being careful that the bare ends of the skewers are not over (or under) the flames. Grill about 2 minutes on each side. Do not overcook.

Presentation: Place the dipping sauce in the center of a serving platter. Arrange the skewers around the sauce and serve immediately. Let your guests help themselves.

To prepare ahead: Through step 2.

*Bring your broiler tray directly under the flame for best results.

GOAT CHEESE AND BLACK OLIVES IN PUFF PASTRY
Makes 36 pieces

INGREDIENTS

1 pound Puff Pastry
   (see page 237) or 3
   sheets of phyllo
   dough
About 4 ounces fresh
   goat cheese, at room
   temperature
1 ounce (about ¼ cup)
   finely chopped pitted
   niçoise olives*

Sometimes the goat cheese is seasoned already. If so, you can eliminate the thyme and continue with the recipe.

① Roll out the puff pastry to a 15-inch square, about ⅛ inch thick. (See note on use of phyllo dough.) Cut the pastry into 36 squares, approximately 2½ inches each, and arrange on a baking tray lined with parchment or wax paper. Refrigerate until needed.

½ teaspoon chopped
    fresh thyme
Freshly ground pepper
About ¼ cup milk

A few fresh greens

EQUIPMENT

Rolling pin
Baking tray
Parchment or wax
    paper
Small bowl
Pastry brush

②　In a small bowl, combine the goat cheese, olives, thyme, and pepper to taste. Mix well and correct seasoning to taste.

③　Preheat oven to 375°F.

④　Remove the pastry from the refrigerator. Spoon a heaping ½ teaspoon of the cheese mixture in the center of each square. With a pastry brush, lightly brush milk along 2 adjacent edges and fold the dry corners of the dough onto the moistened ones, forming a triangle. Press the edges together, being careful that the dough isn't pressed too thin. Repeat with the remaining squares, cheese mixture, and milk.

⑤　With the tip of a small, sharp knife, poke 3 holes into the top of each triangle and brush lightly with milk. Arrange on one or two baking trays, spaced about 2 inches apart.

⑥　Bake until golden brown and puffy, 25 to 30 minutes. The seams may pop open during baking, but that's okay.

Presentation: Arrange triangles on a bed of greens and serve immediately as an hors d'oeuvre.

To prepare ahead: Through step 6, baking about 15 minutes and finishing when ready to serve.

Note: If using phyllo dough, lay out one sheet and brush lightly with melted butter. Lay the second sheet directly on top and again brush with butter. Repeat with the third sheet. (You will use about 2 tablespoons of melted butter.) Cut into 36 squares and mound the cheese in the center. Fold into triangles and brush with melted butter. Bake until golden brown.

*To make it easier to pit the olives, roll a rolling pin over the olives, then remove the pits.

GOAT CHEESE AND EGGPLANT CRISPS

Makes 24 eggplant crisps

¾ pound (4 or 5
  medium) Japanese
  eggplants, unpeeled*
Salt
Freshly ground white
  pepper
About ⅓ cup olive oil
6 ounces goat cheese
¼ cup finely chopped
  black olives
About 1 cup
  all-purpose flour
3 or 4 eggs, lightly
  beaten
About 1 cup fresh
  bread crumbs
Peanut oil for deep
  frying

Large skillet
Small bowls
Deep, heavy saucepan
  or deep fryer
Deep-fat thermometer
Slotted spoon
Wooden skewers,
  optional

Not only are these crisps delicious served as an hors d'oeuvre, but they add flavor and texture to a green salad. Toss the salad greens with a simple dressing and then scatter a few goat cheese crisps around the greens.

1 Trim the ends of the eggplants and cut each one into lengthwise slices, about ¼ inch thick and 6 or 7 inches long, to make 24 slices. Season lightly with salt and pepper.

2 In a large skillet, heat 2 tablespoons olive oil. Sauté the eggplant slices until tender and lightly golden on both sides, 3 to 4 minutes. Do not overcrowd the pan and use additional oil as necessary. Drain on a clean towel and cool.

3 In a small bowl, combine the goat cheese and olives and mix well. Using 1 teaspoonful of the mixture for each crisp, make 24 small balls, about ¼ ounce each. Place a cheese ball in the center of a slice of eggplant and wrap the slice around, forming a large ball. Repeat with the remaining eggplant slices and cheese.

4 In a deep, heavy saucepan or deep fryer, heat about 3 inches of oil to 350°F.

5 Place the flour, eggs, and bread crumbs in separate bowls. Lightly coat each eggplant ball with flour, shaking off the excess. Dip into the egg and finally the bread crumbs. Gently place in the hot oil and cook until golden brown, about 30 seconds. Remove with a slotted spoon and drain on a clean towel.

Presentation: Poke a wooden skewer, if desired, into each eggplant crisp and arrange on a platter. Serve immediately.

To prepare ahead: In step 5, after coating with bread crumbs, arrange on a small tray sprinkled lightly with bread crumbs and refrigerate until needed. You can prepare this earlier in the day.

*Japanese eggplants are small purple eggplants that can be found in many food markets, especially those that carry oriental produce. They are sweeter than the larger American eggplant.

ROASTED POTATOES WITH SOUR CREAM AND CAVIAR

Makes about 32 slices

INGREDIENTS

1 pound small (about 8) red or white rose potatoes, scrubbed well
2 to 3 tablespoons unsalted butter, melted
Salt
Freshly ground white pepper

About ½ cup sour cream or crème fraîche
About ½ cup whitefish or sevruga caviar

EQUIPMENT

Baking tray
Pastry brush

I often serve these potatoes with a glass of fine champagne.

1 Preheat oven to 400°F.

2 Cut away the ends of the potatoes and use for another meal. Cut each potato into ½-inch rounds.

3 Brush a baking tray with a little melted butter and arrange the potato slices on the tray. Brush the tops with melted butter and season lightly with salt and pepper. Roast 15 to 20 minutes, turn, brush with the melted butter and season lightly with salt and pepper. Roast 15 minutes longer, or until the potatoes are very tender and golden brown. Drain on paper towels and correct seasoning to taste. Keep warm in a low oven.

Presentation: Arrange slices of potatoes on a serving tray. Spread a little sour cream on each slice and spoon ¼ teaspoon caviar in the center. Serve immediately.

To prepare ahead: In step 3, roast the potatoes about 10 minutes on each side and reserve until serving time. Then continue with the recipe.

Note: The cut potato ends are delicious sautéed in a little olive oil with garlic.

DUCK LIVER PÂTÉ (FOIE GRAS TERRINE)

Serves 20

2½ pounds fresh duck liver

MARINADE

½ cup good port, like Fonseca

2½ tablespoons Jack Daniels, or any good bourbon

2 teaspoons salt

1½ teaspoons white pepper

1½ teaspoons sugar

13 strokes fresh grated nutmeg

ASPIC*

2 cups Chicken Stock (see page 41)

¼ cup Brown Duck Stock (see page 42)

½ medium onion, cut into thin slices

1 egg white

1 sprig fresh thyme

3 gelatin leaves**

¼ pound unsalted butter, clarified

Mixed greens
Country bread

Small and large mixing bowls

4-cup porcelain terrine

For special occasions, this is an impressive first course but be sure to start several days in advance. Foie gras refers to the liver of ducks that have been force-fed, resulting in a liver at least three times the size of a regular duck liver. Foie gras can be purchased in specialty meat markets and probably will have to be ordered in advance. Whole nutmeg, freshly grated, is preferable, for flavor and fragrance, but if it is unavailable, use a pinch of ground nutmeg.

1 Scrape off the thin layer of skin from the duck liver and then remove the major veins, leaving the duck livers in as large pieces as possible. (To do this more easily, gently break off pieces, and using a clean towel, carefully pull out the veins.) Place the pieces in a large mixing bowl.

2 *Prepare the marinade:* In a small bowl, combine the port, bourbon, salt, pepper, sugar, and nutmeg. Pour over the duck livers and gently mix. Cover and place on the lowest rack of your refrigerator for 36 hours, turning the livers morning and night.

3 Preheat the oven to 200°F. Remove the bowl with the livers from the refrigerator and bring to room temperature.

4 Remove the livers from the marinade, carefully wiping away as much liquid as possible without bruising the livers. Arrange in a 4-cup porcelain terrine, fitting the pieces together, somewhat like a jigsaw puzzle. Wrap the entire terrine in plastic wrap, then in aluminum foil, to keep it airtight. Place the terrine in a baking pan and fill the baking pan with water that comes two thirds up the sides of the terrine. Place the pan on the stove and heat the water to a temperature of 80°F. Transfer to the oven and cook until a thermometer inserted into the center of the pâté

Plastic wrap
Aluminum foil
Baking pan large
   enough to hold the
   terrine
Kitchen thermometer
Cardboard
Medium saucepan
Fine strainer

reaches 100°F, about 2 hours. (To test, remove the pan from the oven, unwrap the terrine, and insert the thermometer. If the reading is less than 100°F, rewrap well and return to the oven.)

5 Measure a piece of cardboard to fit on top of the pâté, with little or no clearance around the edges. Wrap the cardboard in plastic wrap, and then in aluminum foil. Press down on the pâté so that the fat and the juices will rise. Pour into a small bowl and reserve, refrigerated. Repeat this procedure as necessary. (Potatoes sautéed in this will be delicious.) Return the cardboard to the top of the pâté and place a 1- to 2-pound weight (two cans evenly spaced) on the cardboard. Refrigerate the pâté, overnight, until firm.

6 *Prepare the aspic:* In a medium saucepan, heat the chicken and duck stocks. In a small bowl, combine the onion, egg white, and thyme, and stir into the hot liquid. Bring barely to a boil and then simmer for about 30 minutes, which will clarify the stock. Strain through a fine sieve. Soften the gelatin leaves in a little cold water, 3 to 4 minutes. Remove the leaves from the water and stir into the hot stock—the leaves will dissolve almost instantly. Cool but use before the liquid actually gels.

7 Remove the pâté from the refrigerator and carefully loosen from the sides of the terrine by slipping a sharp knife around the pâté. Invert onto a clean, flat surface, tapping the top of the terrine a few times to make it easier for the pâté to slip out. Wipe away any moisture and hardened fat that have accumulated.

8 Clean the terrine and pour in some of the cooled liquid aspic to a depth of ½ inch. Return the pâté to the terrine, bottom side down, and pour in a little more aspic to form a thin layer on top. Refrigerate until the aspic is firm. Pour the clarified butter over the aspic and refrigerate for two days to develop the flavor. The pâté tastes better after two days or longer, but can be eaten as soon as the butter hardens.

(*Continued*)
....

9 When ready to serve, remove all the hardened butter (save to make fried or mashed potatoes). Loosen the pâté from the sides of the terrine by running a sharp knife dipped in hot water around the edges. Place the terrine on its side and cut into ¼-inch slices.

Presentation: Mound a few mixed greens that have been tossed in a light vinaigrette on a small plate. Arrange 2 slices of pâté on top and serve with toasted country bread.

For a cocktail party, you can mound the greens on a flat platter large enough to hold the pâté. Loosen the pâté, turn the terrine upside down, and unmold on top of the greens. (If you have difficulty unmolding, place a warm towel over the terrine for 1 or 2 minutes, then unmold.)

To prepare ahead: Through step 5 or 8.

*The pâté can be made without the aspic. Follow the directions through step 5 and refrigerate. Pour the clarified butter over the pâté and return to the refrigerator. When ready to serve, remove the hardened butter and let your guests spoon the pâté onto slices of country bread.
**Gelatin leaves can be purchased in specialty food shops.

Duck Liver (Foie Gras) with Sautéed Cabbage and Green Onion

Serves 2*

INGREDIENTS

4 ounces foie gras, cut
  into 4 long slices
Salt
Freshly ground pepper
All-purpose or rice
  flour
3 tablespoons peanut
  or vegetable oil
6 ounces white
  cabbage, thinly sliced
1 tablespoon rice wine
  vinegar

SAUCE
¼ cup rice wine
¼ cup plum wine
2 tablespoons (1 ounce)
  reduced Brown Duck
  Stock (see page 42)
1 tablespoon (½
  ounce) unsalted
  butter

1 green onion, cut into
  diagonal slices, for
  garnish

EQUIPMENT

Medium and small
  skillets
Small saucepan

The crispness of the cabbage seasoned with vinegar and the moist richness of the foie gras sweetened with plum wine makes this a perfect combination.

1 Season the sliced liver with salt and lots of pepper. Dust lightly with flour and reserve.

2 In a medium skillet, heat 2 tablespoons oil. Over high heat, sauté the cabbage for 1 minute, tossing as it cooks. Season with salt and pepper, pour in the vinegar and sauté for 1 minute longer. Keep warm.

3 In a small skillet, heat the remaining 1 tablespoon oil. Over high heat, brown the liver on both sides. (It should be crisp on the outside and medium inside.) Keep warm.

4 Meanwhile, prepare the sauce. In a small saucepan, combine the rice wine, plum wine, and the stock. Reduce just until the sauce thickens. Stir in the butter and season to taste with salt and pepper.

Presentation: Divide the cabbage and mound in the center of 2 heated plates. Arrange 2 slices of liver on each mound and spoon the sauce over. Garnish with the green onion and serve immediately.

To prepare ahead: Through step 1, refrigerating, covered, until needed.

*Recipe can be increased as desired.

PASSOVER GEFILTE FISH

Serves 12

1 head (about 2½ pounds) green cabbage

6 slices brioche or egg bread, cut ½ inch thick, crusts removed

1 quart Fish Stock (see page 54)

1 tablespoon olive oil

½ medium (5 ounces) onion, minced

2 pounds whitefish fillets, such as pike, carp, or whitefish, cut into chunks

3 eggs, separated

½ cup chopped Italian parsley

2 tablespoons (6 or 7 sprigs) chopped fresh tarragon leaves

2 to 3 teaspoons salt

½ teaspoon freshly ground white pepper

Cayenne pepper to taste

1 medium carrot, peeled and cut into julienne

1 medium leek, white part only, cut into julienne

On the second night of Passover, Spago closes to the general public and we prepare a special Seder dinner for those of our customers who would like to share the evening with us. Long tables are set up throughout the restaurant, providing the atmosphere of a large family gathering. The meal begins with gefilte fish.

1 Preheat the oven to 375°F.

2 Blanch the head of cabbage in boiling salted water, about 5 minutes, then place in a basin of cold water. Remove the whole leaves and cut away the tough core. As you peel off the outer leaves, you may have to return the head of cabbage to the boiling water to soften the inner leaves. Dry on a clean towel and reserve.

3 Break the slices of bread into small pieces and place in a small bowl. Cover with 1 cup of stock and let soak until needed.

4 In a small skillet, heat the olive oil. Over medium heat, sauté the onion until wilted, 4 to 5 minutes. Do not brown. Cool.

5 In a wooden bowl or on a chopping board, chop the fish fine with a chopper or a large knife. Add the bread with the stock, the cooled onions, 3 egg yolks, the chopped parsley and tarragon, 2 teaspoons salt, white pepper, and cayenne, and continue to chop until well combined. In a clean, medium bowl, whisk the egg whites until firm but not stiff. Stir a little into the fish mixture, then, quickly but gently, fold in the remaining whites. To test for flavor, bring a little fish stock to a simmer, add a small ball of the fish mixture and cook for about 5 minutes. Taste and correct seasoning.

Large pot
Small and medium
   bowls
Small skillet
Chopping bowl or
   board
Chopper or large knife
Whisk
11-×-17-inch baking
   pan
Aluminum foil

6 Heat the remaining fish stock and spoon a little into an 11-×-17-inch baking pan. Divide the fish mixture into twelve portions, about 4 ounces each, and enclose each portion in one or two cabbage leaves. You will find that when the leaves get smaller, you will have to use two leaves to wrap the fish. As each package is formed, place in the prepared baking pan, seam-side down. This size pan holds the 12 packages comfortably. Pour the remaining stock over the fish and top with the julienned carrots and leeks. Cover the pan with foil and bake for 30 minutes. Let cool in the stock and refrigerate until needed.

Presentation: Place one package of fish on each of 12 plates, garnishing with some of the julienned carrots and leeks. Serve with homemade horseradish, white or red.*

To prepare ahead: Through step 6.

*To make white horseradish, finely grate peeled fresh horseradish into a small bowl, cover with plastic wrap, and refrigerate until needed.
   To make red horseradish, boil ½ pound red beets until tender. Peel and then finely grate into a medium bowl. Add about ½ cup grated horseradish, or to taste, and combine thoroughly. Refrigerate, covered, until needed.

GRILLED SANTA BARBARA SHRIMP WITH SWEET MAUI ONION AND WHITE TRUFFLE OIL VINAIGRETTE

Serves 4

INGREDIENTS

16 large shrimp, such
   as Santa Barbara
   shrimp
3 tablespoons olive oil
Salt
Freshly ground white
   pepper

TRUFFLE OIL VINAIGRETTE

½ cup white truffle oil
¼ cup lemon juice
2 tablespoons chopped
   sweet Maui or
   Vidalia onion
2 tablespoons chopped
   fresh Italian parsley,
   chervil, or chives, or
   a combination
Salt
Freshly ground white
   pepper

EQUIPMENT

Shallow dish
Small bowls
Whisk

Truffle oil is a delicacy that can be purchased at many food shops that carry gourmet products.

1 Preheat the grill.*

2 Break off the heads and butterfly** the shrimp. Place the shrimp in a shallow dish and sprinkle with olive oil. Refrigerate until needed. When ready to serve, season lightly with salt and pepper.

3 *Prepare the vinaigrette:* In a small bowl, whisk together the oil, lemon juice, chopped onion, and herbs. Season to taste with salt and pepper. Set aside. Whisk again when ready to serve.

4 Grill the shrimp just until the flesh turns opaque, about 2 minutes on one side and 1 minute on the other.

Presentation: Arrange the shrimp, split side up, on a plate. Drizzle with a little of the vinaigrette and pass the remaining vinaigrette in a small bowl.

To prepare ahead: Through step 3, seasoning the shrimp when ready to serve.

*Shrimp also can be seared in a nonstick pan over high heat, about 2 minutes on one side and 1 minute on the other side.
**To butterfly shrimp, cut down the length of the back of each shrimp and gently spread open. Remove any black vein, rinse, and dry. *Do not cut completely through the flesh.*

GULF SHRIMP SALAD WITH SPICY JALAPEÑO SAUCE

Serves 4

Kazuto is the head chef at Chinois on Main. He has worked with me at Ma Maison, Spago, and now at Chinois, where he developed this tasty salad.

① *Prepare the sauce:* In a blender or food processor fitted with the steel blade, puree the tomatoes, jalapeño peppers, garlic, and tomato paste. Transfer to a medium bowl. Chop the cilantro leaves very fine and fold into the sauce. Season with salt and pepper to taste and set aside.

② Peel the shrimp, leaving the tails intact. Season lightly with salt and pepper. In a large skillet, heat the peanut oil. Without crowding the pan, cook the shrimp, about 1½ minutes on each side. If necessary, do it in batches.

Presentation: Set the radicchio leaves on one half of a large serving platter. Toss the greens with the vinaigrette and spoon equal amounts into each of the radicchio leaves. Place the endive attractively around the radicchio. Spoon the sauce over the remaining half of the platter and arrange the shrimp on the sauce. Garnish with the garlic chives and julienne of peppers. Serve immediately. (You can also do this on individual platters, placing one radicchio leaf on each plate, dividing the remaining ingredients equally.)

To prepare ahead: Through step 1. In step 2, peel the shrimp and refrigerate, covered, until needed. Continue with the recipe at serving time.

Sautéed Shrimp with Tomato-Basil Vinaigrette

Serves 4

16 large shrimp, such
   as Santa Barbara
   shrimp
Salt
Freshly ground pepper

TOMATO-BASIL
VINAIGRETTE
6 ripe plum tomatoes
   (about 1 pound),
   peeled, seeded, and
   diced
2 medium shallots,
   minced
2 garlic cloves,
   blanched and cut
   into julienne
3 tablespoons chopped
   fresh basil plus 4
   whole sprigs for
   garnish
1 tablespoon minced
   fresh parsley
Salt
Freshly ground pepper
1 tablespoon good
   wine vinegar
1 tablespoon lime juice
½ cup plus 2
   tablespoons
   extra-virgin olive oil

EQUIPMENT

Small bowl
10-inch skillet

Santa Barbara shrimp, found in the Pacific Ocean, are most prized for their taste and their size. They are usually sold with head and tail intact. However, Gulf shrimp make a good substitute.

1 Remove the heads of the shrimp and peel the shell, leaving the tail intact. Season lightly with salt and pepper and set aside.

2 *Prepare the vinaigrette:* In a small bowl, combine the tomatoes, shallots, garlic, basil, and parsley. Season with salt and pepper. Stir in the vinegar, lime juice, and ½ cup olive oil, and mix well.

3 Heat a 10-inch skillet and pour in the remaining 2 tablespoons olive oil. Over medium-high heat, cook the shrimp, in batches, if necessary, about 1½ minutes per side. Do not crowd the pan. Do not overcook—well-done shrimp will become dry.

Presentation: Spoon some vinaigrette into the center of each of 4 plates. Arrange 4 shrimp on the vinaigrette and garnish with basil sprigs. Serve immediately.

To prepare ahead: Through step 2, but season the shrimp when ready to serve.

Sea Scallop Salad with Cold Cucumber Sauce

Serves 2

1 green onion, minced
1 garlic clove, minced
½-inch piece fresh
  ginger, peeled and
  minced
Pinch of chili pepper
  flakes
2 tablespoons unsalted
  butter
¼ pound (4 large) sea
  scallops, small,
  white, rounded
  protuberances on the
  sides removed, cut in
  half horizontally
Salt
1 tablespoon peanut or
  vegetable oil
1 cup mixed salad
  greens (radicchio,
  endive, watercress,
  etc.), cut or torn into
  bite-size pieces
2 tablespoons Chinois
  Vinaigrette (see page
  132)
Freshly ground pepper

¼ cup Cucumber
  Sauce (see page 137)

EQUIPMENT

Small bowls
Small skillet
Small dish

*In the wintertime, I replace sea scallops with bay scallops from Nantucket. Bay scallops are smaller and sweeter. This salad is perfect for a light luncheon. As a main dish, it will serve one person.**

1 In a small bowl, combine the green onion, garlic, ginger, and chili pepper flakes. In a small skillet, melt the butter and stir in the green onion mixture. Over medium-high heat, cook for 30 seconds.

2 Place the scallops in a small dish and season lightly with salt. Pour the butter mixture over, turning to coat all sides, and let marinate until the mixture cools.

3 In a clean skillet, heat the oil. Over medium-high heat, sauté the scallops until golden brown, about 1 minute per side. The scallops should be slightly undercooked.

4 Toss the salad with the dressing and season with salt and pepper to taste.

Presentation: Spoon the cucumber sauce in the center of 1 or 2 plates and arrange the scallops on the sauce. Mound the salad on one side of the sauce and serve immediately.

To prepare ahead: Through step 2, about ½ hour before cooking. Have the salad greens ready and toss with the dressing at serving time.

*This recipe can be increased easily by doubling, tripling, etc., the amounts. Just make sure that the skillet(s) you use can hold the scallops in one layer so that they cook evenly.

SIZZLING CALAMARI SALAD WITH POTATO STRINGS

Serves 4

INGREDIENTS

SALAD DRESSING
About ⅓ cup Chinois
   Vinaigrette (see page
   132)
Juice of 1 medium lime
1 teaspoon Chili Oil
   (see page 145)
Pinch of togarashi
   (Japanese pepper
   mixture),** optional

½ pound calamari,
   cleaned and cut into
   ¼-inch strips
Salt
Freshly ground pepper
About ¼ cup rice
   flour**
Peanut oil for deep
   frying
¼ pound red rose or
   new potatoes, peeled,
   and cut into julienne
3 cups assorted greens
   (radicchio, endive,
   watercress leaves,
   etc), cut or torn into
   bite-size pieces
½ cup enoki
   mushrooms,**
   trimmed

4 whole radicchio
   leaves

This is an oriental version of the famous calamari fritti served in Italy. Calamari are inexpensive and everyone loves this dish. The calamari can be cleaned by your fishmonger, but is not difficult to do yourself.*

1 *Prepare the salad dressing:* Pour the vinaigrette into a small bowl and whisk in the lime juice, chili oil, and a dash of togarashi. Set aside. Whisk again at serving time.

2 Season the calamari strips lightly with salt and pepper and toss with the rice flour to coat lightly.

3 In a wok, heat about 3 inches of oil. (Oil must be very hot, about 400°F.) Deep fry the potatoes until golden, 1 to 2 minutes. Remove from the oil and reserve. Deep fry the calamari 1 to 2 minutes, then add the potatoes just to reheat. (The easiest way to do this is to use a fine mesh basket or strainer, place the potatoes, then the calamari into the basket and gently ease the basket into the oil.) Drain on clean paper toweling.

4 In a large mixing bowl, combine the salad greens, enoki mushrooms, calamari, and potatoes. Toss with the salad dressing. Correct seasoning to taste, adding more chili oil if desired.

Presentation: Arrange the radicchio in a circle, leaves touching, on a large round or oval platter. Spoon the salad into the center of the circle and garnish with the julienned peppers and the cilantro. Or you can place one radicchio leaf on each of 4 salad plates and fill. Serve immediately.

10 to 12 julienned
  slices of red pepper
  for garnish
Sprig of cilantro

EQUIPMENT

Small and large mixing
  bowls
Whisk
Wok
Deep-fat thermometer
Fine mesh basket or
  strainer

To prepare ahead: Through step 2, cutting the calamari and refrigerating, covered, until needed. Cut the potatoes, place in a small bowl, cover with cold water, and refrigerate. *Dry thoroughly* before frying. Have the salad greens ready and continue with the recipe at serving time.

Note: When calamari is not available, substitute shucked clams or bay scallops. The clams and scallops can be kept whole.

*To clean calamari, wash in cold running water. Pull out the head, the tentacles and the cartilage found inside. Discard. Cut away the flaps from each side and scrape off the dark skin.
**Can be purchased in markets that carry fine produce and/or oriental products.

RED SNAPPER WITH SPRING VEGETABLE VINAIGRETTE

Serves 4

INGREDIENTS

4 red snapper fillets,
  skin on, 3 to 4
  ounces each
2 or 3 tablespoons
  olive oil
½ bunch fresh basil,
  chopped
½ medium red onion,
  thinly sliced
Salt
Freshly ground white
  pepper

I created this recipe for a wine dinner at the Rainbow Room in New York City. A crisp sauvignon blanc was the wine that accompanied the salad. If you can find small whole red snappers, this would be a perfect entree for a warm-weather luncheon. Stuff the cavity with a few sprigs of parsley or tarragon and watch out for bones when eating.

1 Score the fillets with a sharp knife (they will absorb the marinade better), arrange on a plate, and spoon over the olive oil. Sprinkle with the basil and red onion, and let marinate for 1 hour, refrigerated. Just before cooking, season lightly with salt and pepper.

2 Preheat the oven to 450°F.

3 *Prepare the vegetable vinaigrette:* In a small bowl, whisk together the ⅓ cup olive oil, vinegar, and lime juice. Set aside.

(Continued)

VEGETABLE VINAIGRETTE

⅓ cup olive oil

⅓ cup balsamic vinegar

2 teaspoons fresh lime juice

½ pound asparagus

1 carrot (about 4 ounces), peeled and diced

4 ounces small broccoli florets

1 small (3 ounces) red bell pepper, cored, seeded, and diced

½ pound (about 2) tomatoes, peeled, seeded, and diced

2 large shallots, diced

1 tablespoon diced sun-dried tomatoes*

2 teaspoons olive oil

2 cups assorted greens, cut into bite-size pieces

EQUIPMENT

Small bowl and larger bowl

Whisk

Vegetable peeler

Fine strainer

Ovenproof skillet

④ With a vegetable peeler, peel away any rough scales on the asparagus spears, cut off the hard bottoms, and dice. Blanch the asparagus, carrot, broccoli, and red pepper separately. (You can do this most easily by placing each vegetable in a fine strainer and plunging into boiling salted water for about 2 minutes per vegetable.) Cool and transfer to a mixing bowl. Add the tomatoes, shallots, and sun-dried tomatoes. Whisk the dressing and, reserving a little for the greens, toss the vegetables with the dressing and season with salt and pepper to taste.

⑤ Heat an ovenproof skillet large enough to hold the fillets in one layer. Add the 2 teaspoons of olive oil and when it almost begins to smoke, lay the fillets in the pan and sear on one side for 1 minute. Transfer to the oven and continue to cook 3 to 4 minutes longer. The fillets do not need to be flipped. (Fish should be cooked on the outside and a little underdone on the inside.)

⑥ Toss the greens with the reserved dressing.

Presentation: Divide the greens and mound in the center of 4 large serving plates. Arrange a layer of the vegetable vinaigrette on one side of the greens and top with one of the fillets, skin-side down. Serve immediately.

To prepare ahead: Have the fish marinating, the salad greens cleaned and ready, the vegetables blanched, and continue with the recipe at serving time.

*To reconstitute sun-dried tomatoes, steep in boiling water to cover until tender, 3 to 5 minutes.

SPAGO'S TUNA SASHIMI

Serves 4

INGREDIENTS

½ pound very fresh
  loin of tuna

GINGER SAUCE
1 small shallot, minced
½ teaspoon finely
  grated fresh ginger
Freshly ground pepper
⅓ cup soy sauce
⅓ cup lime juice
⅓ cup olive oil

1 medium ripe avocado
2 cups mixed greens
  (radicchio, endive,
  watercress, etc.), in
  bite-size pieces
12 thin slices red onion
½ package daikon
  sprouts,* trimmed
1 medium tomato,
  peeled, seeded, and
  diced
1 teaspoon caviar,
  optional

EQUIPMENT

Small bowl
Whisk

Years ago, raw tuna was served only in Japanese restaurants, but now it has become very popular and is on the menu of many restaurants. Even my father, who would never eat raw fish, loves this salad. The tuna must be very fresh.

1 With a very sharp knife, cut the tuna into very thin slices, 6 to 8 slices per serving (24 to 32 slices). Or have your fishmonger cut the fish loin for you.

2 *Prepare the sauce:* In a small bowl, combine the shallot, ginger, a few grinds of pepper, soy sauce, and lime juice. Slowly whisk in the olive oil and set aside. When ready to serve, whisk to thoroughly combine.

3 Peel, pit, and quarter the avocado. Then cut each quarter into 4 thin slices.

Presentation: Divide the greens and mound in the center of each of 4 large salad plates. Arrange 6 or 8 slices of tuna on the greens, one slice overlapping the other. Place 4 avocado slices just below, 3 slices of onion on one side, a few sprouts on the other, and top with some of the chopped tomato. Pour a generous amount of the sauce over the tuna and around the greens and garnish with a little caviar, if desired. Serve immediately.

To prepare ahead: Through step 2, refrigerating the tuna, covered, until ready to serve.

*An oriental radish sprout that can be bought, packaged, in markets that carry fine produce.

TEMPURA SASHIMI WITH UNI SAUCE

Serves 4

1 pound very fresh
  tuna fillet
4 pieces sushi seaweed*
  (4 × 6 inches)
4 thin asparagus spears,
  scraped and
  blanched

UNI SAUCE
1 tablespoon (½
  ounce) unsalted
  butter
1 large shallot, minced
1 cup dry champagne
  or white wine
1 cup heavy cream
3 ounces uni (sea
  urchin),* about 12
  pieces
½ teaspoon wasabi*
  (dry mustard), mixed
  with just enough
  cold water to make a
  paste

If baby asparagus are in season, two or three are used for each roll. If not, use the thinnest asparagus you can find. This has been on the menu at Chinois since opening night. After a few years, I decided to take it off. A customer called me over to his table and, quite dismayed, asked why it was not on the menu. I told him that it had been on so long, I was getting bored cooking it. His reply was, "I come to Chinois very often and eat this all the time. I don't get bored eating it and you shouldn't get bored cooking it." We aim to please our customers—it went back on the menu.

1 Using a very sharp, wet knife, cut the tuna fillet into 12 thin slices, each about 2 × 7 inches. (Or have your fishmonger slice the tuna for you.)

2 Lay the seaweed pieces, shiny side up, on a flat surface. For each roll, arrange 3 tuna slices, in overlapping layers, to cover about half of the seaweed, making the tuna layer thicker at the top. (The tuna will extend out of the seaweed, but that's okay.) Lay 1 asparagus spear across the center of the tuna and roll the seaweed and tuna very tightly around the asparagus (the asparagus will be in the center of the finished roll). Moisten the remaining half of the seaweed to seal. Refrigerate until needed.

*Roll the seaweed and tuna
tightly around the asparagus*

*Cut the roll in half
before dipping in batter*

½ teaspoon chili
   pepper flakes
½ teaspoon soy sauce
Salt
Freshly ground white
   pepper

TEMPURA BATTER
2 eggs
½ cup milk
2 tablespoons sake*
1 tablespoon ground
   ginger
1 green onion, minced
½ cup all-purpose
   flour
Japanese hot pepper (7
   flavors)*

Peanut oil for deep
   frying
Red and green
   seaweed, presoaked
   in water, as garnish

EQUIPMENT

Medium saucepan
Blender
Medium bowl
Whisk
Wok or deep, heavy
   saucepan

3 *Prepare the uni sauce:* In a medium saucepan, melt the butter. Sauté the shallot over medium heat for 2 minutes. Pour in the champagne and cook until about ¼ cup remains. Add the cream and reduce by half. Transfer to a blender and add the uni, the wasabi, chili pepper flakes, and soy sauce, and blend until well mixed. Season with salt and pepper to taste and set aside.

4 *Prepare the tempura batter:* In a medium bowl, whisk together the eggs, milk, sake, ginger, and green onion. Slowly whisk in the flour until the batter is slightly thick. Flavor with the hot pepper to taste and set aside.

5 In a wok or deep, heavy saucepan, heat 3 inches of oil until a drop of batter dropped into the oil will sizzle and quickly float to the surface. Cut each roll in half and dip into the batter, coating thoroughly. Carefully place in the hot oil and fry until golden brown, about 30 seconds. *Do not overcook* (fish should be uncooked).

Presentation: Spoon some uni sauce in the center of 4 warm plates. Cut each half roll into 6 circular slices and arrange attractively on the sauce, cut side up. Garnish with the red and green seaweed and serve immediately.

To prepare ahead: Through step 4, refrigerating the batter until needed and then whisking it when ready to use.

*All these ingredients can be found in markets that sell oriental ingredients.

SOFT-SHELL CRAB TEMPURA WITH CILANTRO

Serves 4

INGREDIENTS

4 large soft-shell crabs
1 large or 2 small
   jalapeño peppers,
   seeded and minced
Leaves of 4 or 5 sprigs
   cilantro, chopped
Juice of 2 medium
   limes
Salt

TEMPURA BATTER
1 cup all-purpose flour
1 tablespoon baking
   powder
1 ¼ cups water
2 tablespoons sesame
   seeds
1 to 1 ½ teaspoons
   cayenne pepper
Salt
¼ cup cilantro leaves,
   chopped fine

Peanut oil for frying
1 bunch spinach, leaves
   only (see Fried Spin-
   ach Leaves, page 126)

EQUIPMENT

Large platter
Small bowl
Sifter
Whisk
Deep, heavy saucepan
Deep fat thermometer
Slotted spoon

Soft-shell crabs are in season from late spring through August. You should buy them alive and use the same day.

1 *Prepare the crab:* Remove the lungs and tail and arrange the crab on a large platter. Sprinkle with the minced jalapeño and the chopped cilantro. Pour the lime juice over and let marinate for at least 30 minutes, refrigerated. When ready to cook, season lightly with salt.

2 *Prepare the batter:* In a small bowl, sift together the flour and baking powder. Whisk in the water until the batter is smooth, then add the remaining ingredients, seasoning with cayenne and salt to taste. If made earlier in the day, set the bowl into an ice bath.

3 At serving time, in a deep, heavy saucepan, wok, or deep-fat fryer, heat 3 inches of oil to 350°F.

4 Dip each crab into the batter and coat well. Carefully place one or two in the hot oil and cook until golden brown, about 2 minutes. Remove with a slotted spoon or a flat strainer and drain on paper or clean toweling. Keep warm while preparing the remaining crab and the spinach.

6 In the same oil, cook the spinach. Drain on clean toweling and season lightly with salt.

Presentation: Arrange a few fried spinach leaves on half of each of 4 plates. Place 1 crab on the other half and serve immediately.

To prepare ahead: Through step 2, the fish can be marinating, the batter ready. Heat the oil at serving time and continue with the recipe.

Note: Shrimp can be substituted for the crab. If using shrimp, peel, leaving the tail intact.

Sautéed Crabcakes
with Sweet Red Pepper Sauce

Makes 12 crabcakes

CRABCAKES

2 tablespoons olive oil
½ medium (about 4 ounces) red bell pepper, cored, seeded, and diced
½ medium (about 4 ounces) yellow bell pepper, cored, seeded, and diced
½ medium (about 4 ounces) red onion, diced
1 cup heavy cream
½ teaspoon diced jalapeño pepper
2 teaspoons chopped fresh chives
2 teaspoons chopped fresh dill
2 teaspoons chopped Italian parsley
Leaves from 2 sprigs fresh thyme
½ teaspoon salt
⅛ teaspoon cayenne pepper
1 extra-large egg, lightly beaten
1 cup fresh bread crumbs
1 cup almond meal*
1¼ pounds fresh crabmeat, any shells removed

I ate crabcakes for the first time in Chesapeake Bay. To my dismay, I tasted more potato than crab in the crabcakes. I decided to take home a few pounds of fresh lump crabmeat, experimented with it, and finally came up with this recipe which we serve at Spago. If you have difficulty finding fresh crabmeat, you can make this with uncooked shrimp.

1 *Prepare the crabcakes:* In a 10-inch skillet, heat the olive oil. Sauté the red and yellow peppers and the onion until the onion is translucent and the peppers are tender, 10 to 15 minutes. Transfer to a large bowl and let cool.

2 In a small saucepan, reduce the cream with the jalapeño until ½ cup remains. Cool and add to the onion mixture. Stir in the chives, dill, Italian parsley, thyme, salt, and cayenne pepper. Stir in the egg and ½ cup each bread crumbs and almond meal. Gently fold in the crabmeat. Mixture will be lumpy. Correct seasoning to taste. Divide the mixture into 12 crabcakes, about 2½ ounces each.

3 Combine the remaining ½ cup each breadcrumbs and almond meal on a flat plate. Dip both sides of each crabcake into the mixture and coat well. Place on a tray and refrigerate, covered, 2 to 3 hours, up to 6 hours.

4 *Prepare the sauce:* In a 10-inch skillet, melt 3 tablespoons of butter. Sauté the pepper, onion, garlic, and thyme until the onion is translucent, about 10 minutes. Deglaze with the wine and cook until 3 tablespoons liquid remain. Pour in the cream and bring to a boil.

5 Scrape the contents of the skillet into a blender and puree until smooth. Strain, return to a clean pan, and

(Continued)

RED BELL PEPPER SAUCE

5 tablespoons (2½ ounces) unsalted butter

½ medium (about 4 ounces) red pepper, cored, seeded, and diced

½ medium (about 4 ounces) red onion, diced

2 garlic cloves, mashed

Leaves from 2 sprigs thyme

½ cup dry white wine

1 cup heavy cream

Juice of ½ medium lemon

Salt

Freshly ground white pepper

2 tablespoons (1 ounce) unsalted butter

About 2 tablespoons vegetable oil

3 cups mixed greens of your choice, cut or torn into bite-size pieces

EQUIPMENT

10-inch skillet
Large bowl
Small saucepan
Blender
Strainer
Extra skillet
Whisk

reheat. Whisk in the remaining 2 tablespoons of butter and the lemon juice and season to taste with salt and pepper. Keep warm.

6 When ready to serve, in 1 or 2 skillets, melt the 2 tablespoons butter with the vegetable oil. Over medium-high heat, sauté the crabcakes until golden brown, about 4 minutes on each side, using additional oil as necessary. Drain on paper towels.

Presentation: Divide the salad greens among 6 large plates. Arrange 2 crabcakes on the greens, drizzle sauce around the greens and on top of the crabcakes. Serve immediately.

To prepare ahead: Through step 4. In step 5, return the sauce to a clean pan but reheat over a low flame and continue with the recipe when ready to serve.

Note: Coarsely ground or chopped uncooked shrimp can be substituted for the crabmeat.

*To make almond meal, grind blanched almonds in a food processor, being careful that you don't overgrind—you want the texture of fine bread crumbs.

ROASTED DUNGENESS CRAB WITH PICKLED GINGER SAUCE

Serves 2

INGREDIENTS

SAUCE

2 tablespoons peanut oil

3 garlic cloves, chopped

Peel from 1 ounce fresh ginger root, chopped

2 green onions, chopped

1 tablespoon curry powder

½ cup plum wine or port

¼ cup dry white wine

½ cup Fish Stock (see page 55)

1 cup heavy cream

2 tablespoons Chinese black vinegar*

½ teaspoon chili pepper flakes

2 tablespoons (1 ounce) unsalted butter

1 teaspoon Chili Oil (see page 145)

Salt

Freshly ground pepper

½ ounce fresh ginger root, peeled and cut into a fine julienne

1 cup plum wine

¼ cup rice wine vinegar

This is a Thai-inspired recipe that we prepare in Postrio, in San Francisco. In the winter months, crab is readily available and not too expensive.

1 Preheat the oven to 450°F.

2 *Prepare the sauce:* In a medium saucepan, over medium-high heat, heat the peanut oil. Sauté the garlic, ginger root, and green onion until wilted, 1 to 2 minutes. Stir in the curry powder and cook 2 minutes longer. Deglaze the pan with the plum and white wine and reduce by half. Add the stock and the cream and simmer over low heat for 30 minutes. Strain and return to a clean pan. Stir in the black vinegar and chili flakes, then whisk in the butter and the chili oil and correct seasoning with salt and pepper to taste. Reserve.

3 In a small skillet, combine the ginger, plum wine, and rice wine vinegar. Simmer over low heat for 10 minutes. Strain, reserving the ginger and liquid in separate bowls.

4 *Prepare the crab:* In an ovenproof 10-inch skillet, heat the 2 tablespoons oil. Set the crab in the pan and place in the oven. Roast about 12 minutes, turning the crab after about 6 minutes.

5 Transfer the crab to your work surface. Remove the tail and then the shell in one piece, being careful to save the liquid in the shell. Discard the lungs and cut the body into 4 quarters. Detach the legs and crack them with the back of a large chef's knife.

6 Pour out the oil from the 10-inch skillet and deglaze with the ginger liquid. Pour in the liquid remaining in the crab shell plus the reserved sauce. Stir in the body

(Continued)

2 tablespoons plus 1
  teaspoon peanut oil
1 whole Dungeness
  crab, about 1½
  pounds, lungs
  removed
1 green onion, white
  part only, cut into
  julienne

EQUIPMENT

Medium saucepan
Strainer
Whisk
Small skillet
Small bowls
Ovenproof 10-inch
  skillet

of the crab, the tail and the legs, and simmer for 4 to 5 minutes, coating well with the sauce.

Presentation: Place the 4 quarters of the body in the center of a large oval platter. Arrange the legs and tail around the crab to resemble the whole crab and spoon the sauce over all. Sprinkle with the green onion and reserved ginger. Brush the shell with the remaining 1 teaspoon oil and place on top of the body. Serve with steamed rice and a good French bread to sop up the sauce.

To prepare ahead: Through step 3, reheating the sauce and the ginger liquid over a low flame.

*Ingredients can be purchased in markets that sell oriental products.

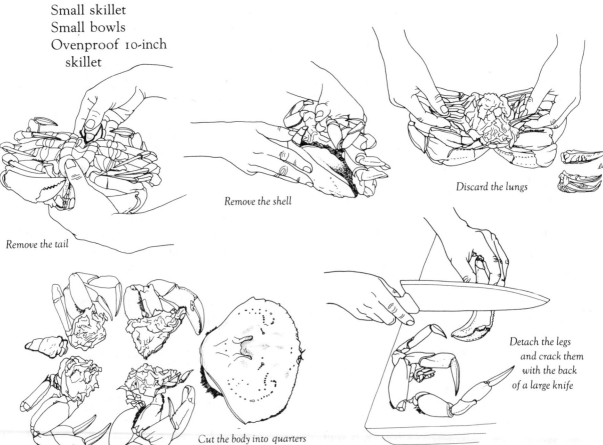

Remove the tail

Remove the shell

Discard the lungs

Cut the body into quarters

Detach the legs
and crack them
with the back
of a large knife

BROILED QUAIL WITH PERSIMMON RELISH

Serves 6 as appetizer

6 boned quail, about 3
 ounces each
1 very ripe persimmon
 (about 4 ounces),
 pulp pureed
Juice of 1 lemon
Pinch of ground cumin
Salt
Freshly ground white
 pepper

RELISH
1 cup diced (about 2
 medium) very ripe
 persimmons
½ cup diced onion
½ jalapeño pepper,
 cored, seeded, and
 diced
2 tablespoons lime
 juice
3 teaspoons chopped
 cilantro
Pinch of cayenne
 pepper
Salt

1 tablespoon cooking
 oil
Cilantro leaves

Toothpicks or skewers
Large dish or pan
Small bowl
Ovenproof skillet

Persimmons must be very ripe for the best flavor. If not in season, mango or papaya can be substituted.

① Split each quail down the back, flatten, and skewer the legs into the body with toothpicks or small skewers.

② In a dish large enough to hold the quail in one layer, combine the pureed persimmon, lemon juice, cumin, and salt and pepper to taste. Marinate the quails, turning to coat all sides, for about 2 hours, refrigerated.

③ *Prepare the relish:* In a small bowl, combine all the ingredients and season with salt to taste.

④ Preheat the oven to broil.

⑤ Heat the oil in an ovenproof skillet large enough to hold the quails in one layer. Remove the quail from the marinade and arrange in the pan, opened side down. Sauté for 2 minutes and then transfer to the broiler for 2 to 3 minutes, until nicely browned.

Presentation: Spoon some of the relish on each of 6 plates. Set 1 quail in the center of the relish, open side down, and garnish with a few cilantro leaves. Serve immediately.

To prepare ahead: Through step 3, refrigerating, covered, until needed.

CHINOIS MINCED GARLIC CHICKEN
IN RADICCHIO CUPS

Serves 4

INGREDIENTS

¾ pound uncooked
  chicken meat, white
  or dark, ground
3 green onions,
  trimmed and minced
Salt
Freshly ground pepper

SALAD

2 tablespoons rice wine
  vinegar
1 tablespoon soy sauce
1 tablespoon peanut oil
1 tablespoon sesame oil
1 teaspoon sherry wine
  vinegar
1 cup watercress leaves,
  densely packed
½ cup julienned celery
½ cup julienned
  carrots
½ cup julienned onion
Salt
Freshly ground pepper
8 to 12 whole radicchio
  leaves, depending
  upon size

2 tablespoons peanut
  oil
1 ½ tablespoons finely
  chopped garlic
1 tablespoon finely
  chopped fresh ginger

*The idea originated with the minced squab recipe that can
be found in the better Chinese restaurants. But chicken also
is delicious. Using radicchio rather than iceberg lettuce,
brings not only color but an interesting flavor to this
appetizer.*

1 In a small bowl, combine the chicken and green
onion. Season lightly with salt and pepper and set
aside.

2 *Prepare the salad:* In a medium bowl, whisk together
the rice wine vinegar, soy sauce, peanut and sesame
oils, and the sherry wine vinegar. Add the watercress,
celery, carrot, and onion, and toss and season with salt
and pepper to taste. Using 2 large or 3 small radicchio
leaves for each serving, form 4 cups and arrange on a
large serving platter. Divide the salad among the 4 cups.

3 In a 10-inch skillet, heat the peanut oil over high
heat until smoking. Form the chicken into one large
patty and carefully set into the pan. Let brown on one
side, then stir in the garlic, ginger, and chili pepper
flakes, breaking up the patty, and continue to stir until
the chicken is browned. Pour in the rice wine vinegar,
plum wine, soy sauce, and stock, and reduce until most
of the liquid has evaporated. Correct seasoning to taste.

¼ teaspoon chili
  pepper flakes
¼ cup rice wine
  vinegar
¼ cup plum wine
2 tablespoons soy
  sauce
¼ cup Brown Stock
  (Chicken, Duck, or
  Veal) (recipe pages
  42 or 43)
2 tablespoons chopped
  fresh mint or
  cilantro

EQUIPMENT

Small and medium
  bowls
Whisk
Large serving platter
10-inch skillet

Presentation: Divide the chicken mixture and spoon equal amounts into the radicchio cups. Sprinkle with the chopped mint or cilantro. Or you can set 1 cup on each of 4 salad plates and fill with the salad. To eat, roll softly like a taco and eat with your hands.

To prepare ahead: In step 2, prepare the dressing and the radicchio cups and refrigerate. At serving time, finish the salad and continue with the recipe.

CHINO CHOPPED VEGETABLE SALAD

Serves 4

INGREDIENTS

MUSTARD VINAIGRETTE

1 tablespoon Dijon
   mustard
3 tablespoons sherry
   wine vinegar
½ cup extra-virgin
   olive oil
½ cup almond or
   safflower oil
Salt
Freshly ground white
   pepper

SALAD

1 tablespoon olive oil
½ cup diced fresh
   artichoke bottoms
Salt
Freshly ground white
   pepper
½ cup diced carrots
½ cup diced green
   beans
½ cup diced red onion
½ cup diced radicchio
½ cup fresh corn
   kernels

No one I know grows better vegetables than the Chino family on their farm in Rancho Santa Fe. What tastes better on a hot summer day than a fresh vegetable salad!

1 *Prepare the vinaigrette:* In a small bowl, combine the mustard and vinegar. Slowly whisk in the oils. Season to taste with salt and pepper and set aside. Whisk again when ready to serve.

2 *Prepare the salad:* In a small skillet, heat the olive oil. Season the diced artichokes lightly with salt and pepper and sauté until al dente, about 3 minutes. Transfer to a large bowl and let cool.

3 Blanch the carrots and beans by placing each into a fine mesh basket. Set the basket into a pot of boiling salted water and cook until al dente, 2 to 3 minutes. Plunge into cold water to stop the cooking process. Drain, cool, and add to the artichokes. Add the onion, radicchio, corn, and celery.

4 When ready to serve, dice the avocado and the tomato and add to the other vegetables. Reserving a little vinaigrette, toss the vegetables with the vinaigrette, sprinkle with the grated cheese, and toss again. Correct seasoning to taste.

½ cup diced celery

½ cup diced ripe
avocado

¼ cup peeled, seeded,
and chopped tomato

4 teaspoons grated
Parmesan cheese

1 cup mixed greens of
your choice (curly
endive, chicory, baby
lettuce), cut or torn
into bite-size pieces

EQUIPMENT

Small and large bowls
Whisk
Small skillet
Fine mesh basket
Medium saucepan

5 Toss the greens with the reserved vinaigrette and season with salt and pepper to taste.

Presentation: Divide the salad greens among 4 salad plates. Mound the chopped salad on the greens and serve immediately.

To prepare ahead: Through step 3, refrigerating until needed.

Note: You can be creative as to the vegetables you want to include or exclude in your salad. For example, you can use baby peas in season, or diced Chinese pea pods, or diced Italian squash, etc.

FRANK'S LOBSTER SALAD

Serves 8

INGREDIENTS

Spago House Salad
    Dressing (see page
    131)
½ pound cooked fresh
    lobster meat, tails or
    claws, cut into thin
    slices
4 cups packed Chino
    Chopped Vegetable
    Salad (see page 34)
2 cups assorted greens
    (curly endive, baby
    lettuce, chicory, etc.)
Fresh caviar, optional

EQUIPMENT

Pastry brush
8 ¾-cup ramekins

Maine lobster is available almost everywhere. This is a splendid appetizer for an elegant dinner party. Lobster is not cheap, but in this salad, a small amount serves many.

❶ Lightly brush eight ¾-cup ramekins with Spago salad dressing. For each portion, arrange a few pieces (about 1 ounce) of lobster on the bottom. Fill with ½ cup chopped salad and pat down well to fill the cup and level the top.

Presentation: Toss the greens with just enough dressing to coat the leaves. Divide equally and arrange in the center of each of 8 salad plates. Invert a cup of salad onto the greens and rap gently as necessary to unmold. Spoon a little caviar on top, if desired. Serve immediately.

To prepare ahead: Through step 1, refrigerating until serving time.

Note: Shrimp, scallops, or crabmeat can be substituted for the lobster.

BARBECUED SHRIMP "BLT" SANDWICH

Makes 4 triple-decker sandwiches

INGREDIENTS

LEMON-BUTTER
SAUCE
1 teaspoon vegetable
    oil
3 ounces (about 5
    large) shallots, peeled
    and sliced

You would prepare this sandwich for a special luncheon and for someone with a hearty appetite. Lobster can be substituted for the shrimp. At Eureka, we serve this with freshly made potato chips.

❶ Preheat the barbecue or grill.

½ cup dry white wine
1 tablespoon
   champagne vinegar
½ cup heavy cream
½ cup (4 ounces)
   unsalted butter, cut
   into small pieces
Juice of ½ lemon
Salt
White pepper

3 tablespoons vegetable
   oil
½ pound (about 20
   medium) peeled
   shrimp

About ½ cup
   mayonnaise,
   preferably
   homemade
12 thin slices
   sourdough bread
2 cups baby lettuce or
   8 nice pieces
   romaine or iceberg
   lettuce
½ pound tomato, cut
   into 12 thin slices
6 ounces (12 thick
   slices) bacon, cooked
   and drained
Salt
Pepper

EQUIPMENT

Barbecue or grill
Medium saucepan
Whisk
Strainer

2 *Make the sauce:* In a medium saucepan, heat the oil. Sweat the shallots for about 2 minutes. Do not brown. Deglaze the pan with the wine and vinegar and reduce slightly. Pour in the cream and reduce the sauce by half. Whisk in the butter and strain into a clean pan. Season with lemon juice and salt and pepper to taste. Keep warm.

3 Sprinkle the vegetable oil over the shrimp. Grill the shrimp, about 1½ minutes on each side. Do not overcook. Drain and cut each shrimp in half lengthwise.

4 *Make the sandwiches:* For each sandwich, spread a little mayonnaise on one slice of bread and arrange a little lettuce (or 1 piece) on the bread. Top with 3 slices of tomato, season lightly with salt and pepper, and arrange the bacon on the tomatoes. Top with the second slice of bread, a thin layer of mayonnaise and a little lettuce. Heat the shrimp (10 halves) in the lemon butter and arrange on the lettuce. Top with the third slice of bread and cut in half. Serve immediately.

To prepare ahead: Through step 2, keeping the sauce warm.

STOCKS AND SOUPS

Chicken Stock

Brown Chicken Stock

Brown Veal Stock

Court Bouillon

Lobster Stock

Vegetable Stock

Mushroom Stock

Postrio's Golden Lentil Soup with Lamb Meatballs

Corn Chowder with Jalapeño Cream

Fennel Soup

Soup of Pistou with Basil Oil

Fish Soup with Aioli

Potato Spinach Soup

Annie's Garlic Soup

Warm Tomato Soup

Gazpacho with Crabmeat

Green Gazpacho

STOCKS

In years past, a stockpot simmered on the stove for days; today veal, beef, or duck stock is cooked for five to six hours, chicken stock even less, and fish stock is best when cooked for only twenty-five or thirty minutes.

For the home cook, stock making does not have to be a daily activity. Fortunately, stocks can be prepared in advance, frozen, and used as needed. Chicken giblets and bones or meat bones can be accumulated, frozen, and when enough has been collected, time can be set aside to make the stock.

The foundation of any good soup or sauce, as much attention should be given to the stock as to any other dish.

SOUPS

My native Austria is a haven for soup lovers; no meal starts without it. When I was growing up, I always knew when it was Sunday because that was the day that my grandmother made beef bouillon with one of three garnishes—kreplach, liver, or semolina dumplings. During the week, a meal might consist of a hearty potato soup with a splash of vinegar or a wonderful fresh vegetable soup flavored with smoked pork shank and barley.

Soup is one of the most versatile dishes, served in small portions as an appetizer or in large bowls as a full meal; a heartier one in the wintertime, a cool, refreshing gazpacho in the summer. It is especially helpful for the home cook, since it is always prepared in advance. If you make something when you have the time instead of at the last minute, it is much easier to make it well.

CHICKEN STOCK

Makes about 2 quarts

INGREDIENTS

5 to 6 pounds chicken
  bones, including
  necks and feet,
  coarsely chopped
About 3½ quarts cold
  water
1 medium carrot,
  peeled and sliced
1 medium onion,
  quartered
1 small celery stalk,
  sliced
1 small leek, sliced
3 sprigs parsley with
  stems
1 bay leaf
½ teaspoon whole
  white peppercorns

EQUIPMENT

6-quart pot
Ladle for skimming
Strainer
Large bowl

1 Place the chicken bones in a 6-quart pot, pour water over to cover, and bring to a rolling boil. Skim off the scum that collects on the top.

2 Add the remaining ingredients, lower the flame, and simmer about 2 hours, skimming as necessary. Strain into a clean bowl and cool. Refrigerate in a covered container for up to 3 days, discarding hardened layer of fat before using or freezing.

To prepare ahead: Through step 2. The stock can be frozen in small quantities and reheated and used as needed.

Brown Chicken Stock*

Makes 6 cups (1 ½ quarts)

INGREDIENTS

7 pounds chicken
  bones (backs, legs,
  breast)
2 large (about 1 ½
  pounds) onions
2 large (about ½
  pound) carrots
3 (about ½ pound)
  celery stalks
1 cup tomato paste

EQUIPMENT

Large roasting pan
Large stockpot
10- to 12-cup pot
Ladle for skimming
Strainer

Many people do not eat meat or meat stock. This then is a very effective substitute for brown veal stock, and a lot less expensive to make.

1 Preheat the oven to 400°F.

2 Arrange the chicken bones in a large roasting pan and roast until brown, turning to brown all sides. When golden, add the vegetables to brown. This entire procedure should take about 1 ½ hours.

3 Transfer the bones and vegetables to a large stockpot and stir in the tomato paste. Pour the grease out of the roasting pan and deglaze the pan with water, scraping up any bits clinging to the pan. Pour into the stockpot with just enough additional water to cover the bones. Bring to a boil, lower the heat, and simmer for 4 to 5 hours, skimming off any scum that forms on the top.

4 Strain into a clean pot, pressing down on the bones and vegetables to extract all the juices. Cook over a low flame until 6 cups remain, about 1 hour longer. Cool and refrigerate in a covered container up to 3 days, discarding any hardened layer of fat before using or freezing.

To prepare ahead: Through step 4. The stock can be frozen and reheated and used as needed. Brown Chicken Stock can be used in place of Duck Stock and, if necessary, in place of Brown Veal Stock.

*Using the same process, you can make brown duck or brown squab stock.

Brown Veal Stock

Makes 2 quarts

INGREDIENTS

8 pounds veal bones
(or veal and beef
bones), cut into
2-inch chunks
2 medium onions,
coarsely chopped
2 medium carrots,
coarsely chopped
1 celery stalk, coarsely
chopped
1 leek, coarsely
chopped
2 large tomatoes,
quartered*
1 teaspoon whole
peppercorns
2 bay leaves
2 sprigs fresh thyme
About 8 garlic cloves,
smashed, optional

EQUIPMENT

Large roasting pan
10-to 12-quart stockpot
Ladle for skimming
Strainer
Large pot

If you want to make lamb stock, substitute lamb bones for the veal and beef bones and continue with the recipe.

❶ Preheat the oven to 450°F.

❷ Arrange the bones in a roasting pan, large enough to hold them in a single layer. Roast in the oven until dark golden brown, about 1½ hours, turning to brown all sides. After one hour, add the remaining ingredients to brown. Transfer the bones and vegetables to a large stockpot, 10- to 12-quarts.

❸ Pour off the fat from the roasting pan and deglaze the pan with 2 cups of water, scraping up any particles that stick to the bottom of the pan. Pour into the stockpot with enough additional water to cover the ingredients by 2 inches. Bring the water to a boil, reduce the heat, and simmer, uncovered, 4 to 6 hours, skimming the foam as it accumulates on top, and adding water as needed to keep the bones and vegetables covered at all times.

❹ Strain the liquid into a clean pot, pressing down to extract all the juices. Reduce, over medium heat, until 2 quarts remain.

❺ Cool and refrigerate in a covered container up to 3 days, discarding any hardened layer of fat before using or freezing.

To prepare ahead: Through step 5. The stock can be frozen in small quantities and used as needed.

Note: To make demi-glace, in step 4 reduce the liquid until 1 quart remains.

*In the winter, when tomatoes are not at their best, you can use ½ cup tomato paste.

Court Bouillon

Makes about 2 quarts

INGREDIENTS

2 medium carrots,
  peeled
2 celery stalks
1 leek, white part only
1 sprig fresh thyme or
  a pinch of dried
  thyme
1 bay leaf
1 teaspoon salt
½ teaspoon freshly
  ground white pepper
2 quarts water
2 cups dry white wine

EQUIPMENT

6-quart pot
Ladle for skimming
Large bowl
Strainer

I find this excellent for poaching or steaming fish.

① Cut the carrots, celery, and leek into ½-inch pieces and place in a 6-quart pot. Add the remaining ingredients and bring to a boil. Lower heat and simmer for 20 minutes, skimming as necessary. Strain into a clean bowl and cool. Refrigerate in a covered container, up to 3 days, and use as needed.

To prepare ahead: Through step 1, this can be frozen in small quantities and reheated as needed.

LOBSTER STOCK

Makes about 5 cups

INGREDIENTS

3 live lobsters, each
   about 1¼ pounds
¼ cup plus 2
   tablespoons
   vegetable oil
½ pound white
   onions, coarsely
   chopped
1 medium carrot,
   coarsely chopped
¼ pound celery,
   coarsely chopped
¼ pound leeks,
   coarsely chopped
1 bunch tarragon
20 whole peppercorns
5 garlic cloves
2 bay leaves
½ cup Madeira
½ cup dry white wine
½ cup tomato paste

EQUIPMENT

1½- to 2-gallon
   stockpot
10-inch skillet
Tongs
Fine strainer
Large bowl

Lobster stock enriches many sauces served with fish. The lobster needed to make the stock can be reserved for another meal (see below).

1 Cut off the tails and claws from the live lobsters and reserve along with the bodies.

2 In a 1½- or 2-gallon stockpot, heat ¼ cup oil. Over medium-high heat, sauté the onions, carrots, celery, and leeks until the onions are translucent and slightly brown, about 10 minutes. Add the tarragon, peppercorns, garlic, bay leaves, and the lobster tails and claws, cover, and cook until the lobster meat is chalky white rather than translucent, barely 10 minutes. Remove the lobster and reserve for another meal (see Barbecued Shrimp "BLT" Sandwich and Frank's Lobster Salad, page 36).

3 Meanwhile, heat a 10-inch skillet and add the remaining 2 tablespoons oil. Cut the reserved lobster bodies in half and arrange in the skillet, cut-side down. Over medium heat, cook until golden red on both sides, turning with tongs. Transfer the lobster bodies to the stockpot and pour the grease from the skillet. Deglaze the skillet with the Madeira and white wine, and reduce by half. Pour into the stockpot and stir in the tomato paste. Add enough water to barely cover the lobster (about 1½ quarts), bring to a boil, then lower the heat and simmer about 45 minutes. During the last 15 minutes, smash down on the shells to get all the flavor possible into the stock. Strain through a fine strainer into a clean bowl. Cool and refrigerate in a covered container, discarding any hardened layer of fat before using or freezing.

To prepare ahead: Through step 3, the stock can be frozen and reheated and used as needed.

VEGETABLE STOCK

Makes 2 quarts

INGREDIENTS

1 pound (1 large)
   onion, coarsely
   chopped
¾ pound (2 large)
   carrots, cut into large
   chunks
½ pound (3 or 4
   stalks) celery, cut
   into large chunks
2 ounces (about 1
   head) garlic, coarsely
   smashed
1 ounce fresh ginger,
   peeled and sliced
1½ teaspoons whole
   peppercorns
1 bay leaf
3 quarts water

EQUIPMENT

Large stockpot
Strainer

*For the vegetarian, this can be very useful as a base for
soups and sauces.*

1 In a large stockpot, combine all the ingredients and
bring to a boil. Lower the heat and simmer until 2
quarts remain, about 3 hours. Strain, pressing down on
the vegetables to extract all the juices. Cool and
refrigerate until needed.

To prepare ahead: The stock can be frozen and
reheated over a low flame as needed.

MUSHROOM STOCK

Makes about 2 cups

INGREDIENTS

Stems of ½ pound
   wild mushrooms
3 cups Chicken or
   Vegetable Stock (see
   pages 41, 46)
1 or 2 sprigs Italian
   parsley
3 garlic cloves,
   smashed
Salt
Freshly ground pepper

EQUIPMENT

Medium saucepan
Strainer
Large pot

1 In a medium saucepan, combine all the ingredients except salt and pepper, and bring to a boil. Lower the heat and simmer 30 to 35 minutes. Strain into a clean pot, pressing down on the mushrooms to extract all the juices. Reduce until 2 cups remain. Season with salt and pepper to taste.

2 Cool and refrigerate in a covered container.

To prepare ahead: Through step 2. The stock can be frozen and used as needed.

POSTRIO'S GOLDEN LENTIL SOUP WITH LAMB MEATBALLS

Serves 8 to 10

SOUP

3 tablespoons olive oil
1½ cups chopped
    onion
½ cup chopped carrot
5 garlic cloves,
    chopped
½ celery stalk
1 branch fresh parsley
1 branch fresh thyme
1 tablespoon turmeric
2 teaspoons cumin
1 pound golden lentils
    (or regular lentils, if
    not available)
10 cups Chicken Stock,
    heated (see page 41)
Salt
Freshly ground pepper
Juice of ½ lemon

MEATBALLS

1 pound ground lamb
1 cup blanched
    almonds, toasted and
    ground
½ cup fresh bread
    crumbs
⅓ cup chopped onion
⅓ cup raisins, chopped
1 egg, lightly beaten
3 garlic cloves, minced
2 tablespoons chopped
    fresh parsley

The relatively short cooking time of these lentils makes this soup simple to prepare. Golden lentils have a bright orange color and can be found in many health food stores. Your family and friends will be delighted with the result and may be a little surprised to find that they are eating lentil soup.

1 *Prepare the soup:* In a large saucepan, heat the olive oil. Add the onion, carrot, garlic, a bouquet of celery, parsley, and thyme tied together, the turmeric, and the cumin. Sauté over high heat until the onions are glassy, about 5 minutes. Stir in the lentils and the chicken stock, season lightly with salt and pepper, and bring to a boil. Reduce the heat and simmer for 25 to 30 minutes, until the lentils are tender. Skim as necessary.

2 Remove the celery bouquet and transfer two-thirds of the soup to a blender. Blend until smooth and return to the saucepan. Stir in the lemon juice and correct seasoning to taste. Set aside until serving time.

3 Preheat the oven to 500°F.

4 *Meanwhile, prepare the meatballs:* In a mixing bowl, combine the lamb, almonds, bread crumbs, onion, raisins, egg, garlic, parsley, cilantro, and chili pepper flakes. Season lightly with salt and pepper. Divide the mixture into 40 meatballs, each approximately 1 inch in diameter and weighing 1 ounce. Wrap each meatball in caul fat, if desired.

5 Heat 2 tablespoons olive oil in a large ovenproof skillet or sauté pan. Arrange the wrapped meatballs, seam side down, in one layer in the pan and place in the oven. Cook until the meatballs are well browned and firm to the touch, turning to brown all sides, 8 to 10 minutes.

1 tablespoon chopped
  fresh cilantro
¼ teaspoon chili
  pepper flakes
Salt
Freshly ground pepper
1 pound caul fat,
  optional
2 tablespoons olive oil

GARNISH
1 cup plain yogurt
1 tablespoon chopped
  fresh mint leaves
½ teaspoon lemon zest

EQUIPMENT

Large saucepan
Ladle for skimming
Blender
Medium and small
  mixing bowls
Large ovenproof skillet

6 *Prepare the garnish:* In a small bowl, combine the yogurt with the mint and lemon zest. Refrigerate until serving time.

Presentation: Heat the soup and spoon into 8 or 10 soup bowls. Divide the meatballs among the soup bowls and drizzle the yogurt mixture over. Serve immediately.

To prepare ahead: The soup can be prepared through step 2 earlier in the day. The meatballs can be formed as in step 4 and refrigerated, covered. The garnish can be prepared and refrigerated. At serving time, continue with the recipe as in step 5.

CORN CHOWDER WITH JALAPEÑO CREAM

Serves 6 to 8

INGREDIENTS

CORN CHOWDER

3 cups Chicken Stock
   (see page 41)
1 cup dry white wine
1 garlic clove
2 sprigs fresh thyme
3 pounds (about 6
   dozen) littleneck
   clams in the shell,
   scrubbed clean
4 tablespoons (2
   ounces) unsalted
   butter
1 cup diced (1 medium)
   onion
½ cup diced (1
   medium) leek, white
   part only
½ cup diced (½ large)
   carrot
¼ cup diced (½
   medium stalk) celery
6 or 7 ears fresh sweet
   corn, shucked,
   kernels removed,
   reserving cobs
1½ cups heavy cream
Salt
Freshly ground white
   pepper
Juice of ½ small lemon

JALAPEÑO CREAM

½ cup heavy cream,
   whipped
¼ cup sour cream

It is important to get fresh corn, preferably corn picked the same day that you make the soup. If the corn is too old, it turns starchy and the soup will not have the same sweetness.

1 *Prepare the chowder:* In a large saucepan, bring the chicken stock and white wine to a boil with the garlic and thyme. Add the clams, bring back to a boil, cover, and steam until the clams are just opened, 3 to 4 minutes. Strain the liquid into a bowl and discard any unopened clams. Remove the clams from their shells and set aside.

2 In a 3-quart saucepan, melt the butter. Sauté the onion, leek, carrot, and celery over moderate heat, until al dente, about 10 minutes. Pour in the clam liquid and bring to a boil. Add the corncobs and the corn kernels, reserving 1 cup kernels for garnish. Simmer for 30 minutes.

3 Remove the cobs and strain the soup into a clean saucepan. Transfer the strained vegetables to a blender or food processor, pour in the cream, and process until pureed, still retaining a little texture. Stir back into the soup and season lightly with salt and pepper. Bring the soup to a boil, add the reserved clams, and simmer for 1 minute. Season to taste with salt, pepper, and lemon juice.

4 *While the soup is cooking, prepare the jalapeño cream:* In a small bowl, combine all the ingredients, seasoning to taste with salt, pepper, and lemon juice.

Presentation: Ladle the soup into heated bowls, making sure that there are clams in each bowl. Spoon a little of the jalapeño cream in the center, passing the remaining cream in a small bowl. Garnish with the reserved 1 cup corn kernels and serve immediately.

1 jalapeño pepper,
cored, seeded, and
minced
2 tablespoons chopped
cilantro
Salt
Freshly ground white
pepper
Lemon juice

EQUIPMENT

Large saucepan
Strainer
Medium and small
bowls
3-quart saucepan
Blender or food
processor

To prepare ahead: In step 3, puree the soup, return to
the saucepan and at serving time, reheat over a low
flame. Continue with the recipe. Have the ingredients
for the jalapeño cream ready, whipping the cream as
the soup reheats.

FENNEL SOUP

Serves 8

INGREDIENTS

5 to 5½ pounds (about
8) fennel bulbs,
trimmed, reserving
some leaves
¼ cup olive oil
½ cup (2 ounces)
chopped shallots
2 garlic cloves,
smashed
Leaves from 5 or 6
large sprigs of fresh
thyme
6 cups Chicken Stock,
heated (see page 41)
Salt
Freshly ground white
pepper

*Fennel bulbs generally are used in salads, grilled, or
marinated. However, if you like the flavor of fennel, try this
soup and it may well become a permanent addition to your
repertoire.*

1 *Prepare the soup:* Peel the fennel bulbs and cut into
small cubes. In a 2½- to 3-quart saucepan, heat the
olive oil. Sweat the fennel, shallots, garlic, and thyme
for about 5 minutes, stirring to coat with the oil. Pour
in the stock and season lightly with salt and pepper.
Bring to a boil, lower the heat, and simmer until the
fennel is very tender, about 20 minutes.

2 Transfer to a blender and blend to a smooth puree
(you will have to do this in batches). Strain through a
fine strainer into a clean saucepan. Stir in the lemon
juice and correct seasoning to taste. Keep warm.

(Continued)

Juice of 1 medium
   lemon

ITALIAN PARSLEY OIL

½ cup Italian parsley
   leaves
1 cup olive oil

HERBED CROUTONS

2 cups 1-inch cubes of
   country bread
3 to 4 tablespoons
   olive oil
2 to 3 tablespoons
   finely chopped
   fennel leaves
½ cup Italian parsley
   leaves, chopped

EQUIPMENT

2½- to 3-quart
   saucepan
Blender
Fine strainer
Baking tray
Medium skillet

③ *Meanwhile, prepare the parsley oil:* In the blender, combine the parsley and the olive oil and blend until pureed. Set aside.

④ *Prepare the herbed croutons:* Arrange the croutons on a baking tray in one layer. Toast in a preheated 400°F oven, turning to toast all sides, about 5 minutes. In a medium skillet, heat the oil. Stir in the herbs and the croutons and toss to just coat the croutons with the oil and the herbs; you don't want to cook the croutons.

Presentation: Ladle the soup into 8 heated bowls. Spoon a little of the parsley oil into the center and scatter some of the croutons over the top. Serve immediately. Any remaining parsley oil and croutons can be placed in small bowls and passed for your guests to help themselves.

To prepare ahead: Through step 3. Reheat the soup over a low flame. The croutons can be toasted, but continue with step 4 at serving time.

SOUP OF PISTOU WITH BASIL OIL

Makes about 2 quarts
Serves 8

INGREDIENTS

2 tablespoons olive oil
2 cups (1 whole) thinly
  sliced leek
1 cup (1 large) diced
  carrot
1 cup diced celery
1 large yellow squash,
  trimmed and diced
½ cup diced green
  beans
½ cup peeled and
  diced tomatoes
6 cups Chicken Stock,
  heated (see page 41)
1 tablespoon minced
  garlic
1 teaspoon salt
½ teaspoon freshly
  ground white pepper
Juice of ½ lemon

PISTOU SAUCE
⅔ cup olive oil
½ cup basil leaves
4 garlic cloves
2 tomatoes (about 5
  ounces), peeled and
  seeded

BASIL OIL
½ cup olive oil
12 fresh basil leaves

8 slices country bread

EQUIPMENT

4-quart saucepan
Blender or processor
Baking tray

Though many people think this is a cold weather soup, I believe this represents all the wonderful flavor of summer—the rich, ripe tomatoes, pungent olive oil, and fragrant basil leaves.

1 In a heavy 4-quart saucepan, heat the olive oil. Over medium-high heat, sauté the leek, carrot, and celery for 2 to 3 minutes, stirring occasionally. Add the squash, green beans, and tomatoes, and cook 2 minutes longer. Pour in the stock and add the garlic. Season with salt, pepper, and lemon juice and cook over medium heat 25 to 30 minutes.

2 *Meanwhile, prepare the pistou sauce:* In a blender, combine all the ingredients and puree. Stir into the finished soup and correct seasoning to taste.

3 *Prepare the basil oil:* In a blender or food processor, combine the olive oil and basil and puree. Pour into a small bowl.

4 Brush one side of each slice of bread with a little of the basil oil and arrange on a baking tray. Watching carefully so that the bread does not burn, toast in the oven.

Presentation: Ladle the soup into 8 heated bowls and serve with the toasted bread. Pass the remaining basil oil. Serve immediately.

To prepare ahead: Through step 3, reheating the soup at serving time. Toast the bread when ready to serve.

FISH SOUP WITH AIOLI

Serves 8

INGREDIENTS

FISH STOCK

3 tablespoons olive oil

Bones from 5 pounds of fish (turbot, rock cod, sea bass, halibut, red snapper, or striped bass), fish fillets reserved

1 heaping cup (1 large) coarsely chopped onion

1 cup (1 large stalk) coarsely chopped celery

1 cup (about ½ large) coarsely chopped fennel bulb

1 cup (1 large) coarsely chopped leek, white part only

1¼ pounds (4 medium) tomatoes, coarsely chopped

½ cup (½ large) peeled, coarsely chopped carrot

2 tablespoons diced garlic

2 teaspoons salt

1 teaspoon freshly ground white pepper

½ teaspoon saffron threads

¼ teaspoon chili pepper flakes

2 cups dry white wine

When making the stock, if you are using freshwater fish, a few clams or mussels added to the stock will give more flavor. You can use one whole fish or a combination for this recipe. On the West Coast, rock cod (not particularly good grilled or sautéed) is perfect for this soup.

1 *Prepare the stock:* In a 4-quart saucepan, heat the olive oil. Sauté the bones for a few minutes, stir in the onion, celery, fennel, leek, tomatoes, carrot, and garlic and cook 15 minutes, stirring occasionally. Season with salt, pepper, saffron, and chili pepper flakes. Pour in the wine and cook for 5 minutes. Pour in the water, bring to a boil, skim, and lower heat to a simmer. Add the mussels, if desired, the basil and thyme, and continue to simmer 20 minutes longer. Strain and reserve.

2 *Prepare the soup:* In a 4- to 6-quart stockpot, heat the olive oil. Add all the vegetables and simmer over a low flame, 5 to 8 minutes, stirring occasionally. Pour in the strained stock and simmer about 20 minutes longer. Cut the fish fillets into 1½-inch chunks, add to the soup, and cook until tender, about 5 minutes. Stir in the fennel seed and correct seasoning to taste.

3 *While the soup is cooking, prepare the aioli:* In a blender or food processor, combine the egg yolk, tomato, basil, garlic, and saffron. With the machine running, slowly pour in the oil and process until smooth. Season with salt, pepper, and lemon juice to taste. Scrape into a small bowl and reserve.

4 Brush the olive oil over one side of each slice of bread and rub with the garlic clove. Toast or bake in a preheated oven until crisp and lightly browned.

7 cups water

½ pound (11 or 12) mussels, optional

2 teaspoons chopped fresh basil

1 teaspoon chopped fresh thyme

FISH SOUP

¼ cup olive oil

½ cup (½ large) diced leek

½ cup diced fennel bulb

½ cup (about ½) diced celery root

½ cup (½ large) peeled, diced carrot

1 tablespoon minced garlic

½ teaspoon saffron threads

Pinch of fennel seed

AIOLI

1 egg yolk

1 tomato, peeled and diced

2 tablespoons coarsely chopped fresh basil

½ tablespoon chopped garlic

Pinch of saffron

¼ cup olive oil

Salt

Freshly ground white pepper

Juice of ½ lemon

About ¼ cup olive oil

16 slices country bread

1 garlic clove

Presentation: Spoon the soup into 8 heated bowls, making sure to include chunks of fish in each bowl. Pass the aioli and the garlic toast.

To prepare ahead: The stock can be prepared the day before and refrigerated until needed. In step 2, prepare the soup, adding the fish when ready to serve. The aioli also can be prepared earlier in the day and refrigerated, covered.

EQUIPMENT

4-quart saucepan
Strainer
4- or 6-quart stockpot
Blender or food
  processor
Small bowl
Pastry brush

POTATO SPINACH SOUP

Serves 8

INGREDIENTS

¼ cup olive oil

2 very large (14 ounces) leeks, white part only, coarsely chopped, plus 1 small leek, white part only, for garnish

2 large (1 pound) russet potatoes, peeled and coarsely chopped

1 ounce (about 11 medium cloves) garlic, blanched

5 to 6 cups Chicken Stock, heated (see page 41)

¾ pound spinach, washed well and trimmed

¼ cup crème fraîche

1 tablespoon salt

½ tablespoon lemon juice

¾ teaspoon white pepper

Freshly grated nutmeg

Vegetable oil for frying

All-purpose flour

This is an ideal soup for the cold winter months. Many times, at home, I serve this for lunch as a main course by adding lamb meatballs (see Postrio's Golden Lentil Soup, page 48) or sautéed and sliced link sausages.

❶ In a 4-quart saucepan or stockpot, heat the olive oil. Over medium-high heat, sweat the coarsely chopped leeks for about 5 minutes. Add the potatoes and garlic and continue to sweat 2 or 3 minutes longer, stirring occasionally.

❷ Pour in 5 cups stock, lower the heat, and simmer until the potatoes are very tender, 20 to 25 minutes.

❸ Blanch the spinach, drain, and chop coarsely. Transfer the spinach to a clean linen napkin and squeeze out the juice. Reserve the spinach.

❹ Puree the soup in a blender, strain through a medium strainer, and return the soup to a clean pot. If the soup is too thick, add the remaining 1 cup of stock. Place the crème fraîche in a small bowl. Whisk some of the hot soup into the bowl until the crème fraîche is completely dissolved and then whisk back into the pot. Break up the spinach and stir into the soup. Season with the lemon juice, pepper, and nutmeg to taste. Correct seasoning as necessary. Heat over a low flame.

4-quart saucepan or
   stockpot
Linen napkin
Blender
Medium strainer
Large pot
Small bowl
Whisk
Medium saucepan
Flat strainer

5 Meanwhile, in a medium saucepan, heat about 1 inch of vegetable oil to 325°F. Cut the remaining leek into julienne and lightly coat with flour, shaking off any excess. Carefully place the julienned leek into the hot oil and cook until golden, 1 or 2 minutes. Remove with a flat strainer and drain on a clean towel.

Presentation: Ladle the soup into heated bowls. Sprinkle some of the fried leeks into each bowl and serve immediately.

To prepare ahead: Through step 4. Reheat the soup over a low flame and continue with the recipe when ready to serve.

ANNIE'S GARLIC SOUP

Serves 4 to 6

INGREDIENTS

2 cups (about ¾
   pound) peeled garlic
1 large (about ¾
   pound) baking
   potato, peeled and
   cut into 1-inch cubes
2 cups Chicken Stock,
   heated (see page 41)
Salt
Freshly ground white
   pepper
¾ cup heavy cream

BASIL OIL
¼ cup fresh basil
   leaves
¼ cup Italian parsley
   leaves
1 cup olive oil

2 thin slices prosciutto
   ham, cut into strips

EQUIPMENT

Medium saucepan
Blender
Strainer

Many people who can't tolerate garlic will be able to eat this soup. Since the garlic is blanched and then cooked, it is easier to digest. By blanching the garlic, you get the full flavor without any noticeable aftereffects.

1 *Blanch the garlic:* In a medium saucepan, combine the garlic and water to cover. Bring to a boil, lower the heat, and simmer 5 minutes. Drain and return the garlic to the pan. (Blanching the garlic will soften and also decrease the strong taste of the garlic.) Add the potatoes and chicken stock and season lightly with salt and pepper. Bring to a boil, lower the heat, and simmer until the potatoes are tender, about 20 minutes.

2 Pour in the cream and just bring to a boil.

3 *Meanwhile, prepare the basil oil:* In a blender, puree the basil, parsley, and the olive oil until smooth. Strain and reserve. Clean the blender.

4 Pour the garlic soup into the blender (it may have to be done in two batches) and puree until smooth. Scrape into a clean saucepan and reheat over a low flame. Correct seasoning to taste.

Presentation: Ladle some soup into heated bowls. Arrange strips of prosciutto around the top and drizzle the basil oil over the soup. Serve immediately.

To prepare ahead: Through step 4, reheating the soup when ready to serve.

WARM TOMATO SOUP

Serves 6

INGREDIENTS

2 tablespoons olive oil
½ pound onions, cut
   into mirepoix
¼ pound carrots,
   peeled, trimmed, and
   cut into mirepoix
¼ pound celery, cut
   into mirepoix
¾ ounce (about 6
   cloves) garlic,
   coarsely chopped
4 pounds tomatoes,
   seeded and coarsely
   chopped
2 teaspoons salt
¾ teaspoon white
   pepper
1 cup Chicken Stock,
   heated (see page 41)
1 ounce (about 1
   bunch) chervil,
   chopped
¾ ounce chopped
   fresh basil
1 cup heavy cream

GARNISH
Crème fraîche
Chopped chives

EQUIPMENT

4-quart saucepan or
   stockpot
Blender
Medium strainer

Tomato soup, a favorite of mine, is welcome at any time of the year, but especially when tomatoes are at their peak.

1 In a 4-quart saucepan or stockpot, heat the olive oil. Over medium-high heat, sweat the onion, carrot, celery, and garlic for about 5 minutes, stirring occasionally.

2 Lower the heat, add the tomatoes, salt, and pepper, and simmer for 15 minutes. Pour in the stock and the herbs and continue to simmer another 10 minutes.

3 Puree in a blender, return to the heat, and stir in the cream. Simmer for 5 minutes. Strain through a medium strainer into a clean pot.

Presentation: Ladle the soup into heated bowls. Top with a dollop of crème fraîche, sprinkle with some chopped chives, and serve immediately.

To prepare ahead: Through step 3. Reheat over a low flame and continue with the recipe.

GAZPACHO WITH CRABMEAT

Serves 8

2 ½ pounds very ripe
 (7 or 8) medium
 tomatoes, cored and
 quartered
About 1 ¼ pounds (2
 medium) cucumbers,
 peeled and seeded
½ pound (1 medium)
 bell pepper (red,
 yellow, or green),
 cored, seeded, and
 cut into 1-inch
 chunks
2 large celery stalks,
 cut into 1-inch pieces
3 tablespoons tomato
 paste
2 teaspoons salt
½ teaspoon freshly
 ground pepper
½ teaspoon cayenne
 pepper
¼ cup olive oil
1 tablespoon sherry
 wine vinegar
2 cups Vegetable Stock
 (see page 46) or
 tomato juice
½ pound fresh lump
 crabmeat, at room
 temperature

EQUIPMENT

Large bowl
Food processor

Gazpacho, red or green, is a refreshing and healthy beginning to a warm weather meal. Family and friends, vegetarian or not, will welcome this deliciously simple way to get your daily vitamin supply.

1 In a large stainless steel, glass, or ceramic bowl, combine the tomatoes, 1 ½ cucumbers, bell peppers, celery, tomato paste, salt, pepper, and cayenne. Pour over the olive oil and vinegar, cover and refrigerate 6 to 8 hours, up to overnight, stirring occasionally.

2 Using a food processor fitted with a steel blade, process the vegetables until they are minced, still retaining some texture. (This will have to be done in 2 or 3 batches.) Return to the bowl and pour in the stock or tomato juice. Correct seasoning to taste and chill until serving time.

3 When ready to serve, cut the remaining half of cucumber into thin slices.

Presentation: Ladle the gazpacho into 8 soup bowls. Garnish with the cucumber slices and top with crabmeat.

To prepare ahead: Through step 2.

Note: Cooked lobster or sautéed shrimp may be substituted for the crabmeat.

GREEN GAZPACHO

Serves 8 to 10

INGREDIENTS

1 pound (about 4)
zucchini, trimmed
1 pound (1 large)
cucumber, peeled
and seeded
½ pound (1 medium)
green bell pepper,
cored and seeded
2 large stalks celery,
trimmed
4 ounces (½ large)
yellow onion
3 garlic cloves
1 jalapeño pepper,
cored and seeded
½ bunch parsley,
leaves only
½ bunch basil leaves
1 cup plus 2
tablespoons olive oil
½ cup sherry vinegar
¼ cup lemon juice
4 dashes Tabasco
Salt
½ pound tomatillos
(about 5)
1 avocado, peeled,
pitted, and diced
¼ cup fine vinegar
3 to 4 cups Vegetable
Stock (see page 46)

EQUIPMENT

1 or 2 very large bowls
Small baking dish
Food processor
Meat grinder

① Coarsely chop ½ pound zucchini, half the cucumber, the green pepper, celery, onion, garlic, and jalapeño, and place in a large bowl. Stir in the parsley and basil and toss with 1 cup olive oil, the vinegar, 2 tablespoons lemon juice, Tabasco, and salt to taste. Refrigerate, covered, overnight, tossing occasionally.

② The next day, place the tomatillos in a baking dish and roast in a preheated 450°F oven until tender, about 10 minutes. Cool, remove the husk, and rinse.

③ In a food processor fitted with the steel blade, puree the tomatillos, the remaining 2 zucchini, and the remaining half cucumber. Stir into the large bowl of vegetables and continue to marinate 2 hours longer.

④ In the food processor, puree the avocado with the vinegar and the remaining 2 tablespoons lemon juice. Stir into the marinated vegetables and combine well.

⑤ Using the large attachment of a meat grinder, grind all the marinated ingredients into a large bowl. (If you don't have a meat grinder, grind in the food processor in batches, being careful that you keep some texture.) Add 3 or 4 cups of vegetable stock, depending upon the consistency you like. Correct seasoning to taste and refrigerate, covered, until needed.

Presentation: Ladle the gazpacho into 8 or 10 bowls. Serve with slices of country bread sprinkled with grated Parmesan cheese and toasted.

To prepare ahead: Through step 5.

Main Dishes

Roasted Salmon with Black Pepper and Ginger on Celery Root Puree

Roasted Red Snapper with New Potato Crust and Red Onion Sauce

Grilled Striped Bass on Red and White Cabbage with Chinois Tomato Sauce

Grilled Halibut with Tomatoes and Sweet Peppers

Grilled Swordfish with Tomatillo Vinaigrette

Seared Tuna Steak au Poivre

Grilled Scallops with Chili-Persimmon Lobster Butter

Shrimp Fricadella with Dill and Caper Sauce

Sautéed Chicken Breast with White Truffles and Port Wine Glaze

Stuffed Cabbage Balls

Stir-fried Chicken with Cashews and Pine Nuts

Turkey Picatta on Pumpkin Puree

Grilled Quail with Wild Rice Risotto

Crisp Quail with Pineapple and Green Onion

Grilled Squab with Huckleberry Sauce and Potato Parsnip Pancakes

Chinois Roasted Squab on Pan-fried Noodles with Spicy Mushroom Sauce

Roasted Leg of Baby Lamb with Black Bean Ragout

Braised Moroccan Lamb

Roasted Lamb Balls on Mashed Potatoes with Brown Onions

Meat Loaf on Vegetable Puree with Mushroom Sauce

Mandarin Noodles with Sautéed Tenderloin and Vegetables

Quesadilla Eureka

Pork Loin with Thai Sauce and Papaya Salad

Billy Wilder's Calves' Liver

Grilled Calves' Liver with Pancetta Sauce

Grilled Veal Tongue on Warm White Bean Salad with Basil Vinaigrette

Veal Medallions on Apple Compote with Black Pepper Cider Sauce

Braised Veal Shanks with Red Wine Sauce

Eureka Venison (Lamb, Beef, Duck, or Chicken) and Black Bean Chili

Almost anything can be considered a main course, even appetizers, served in larger portions. Gone are the days when a twenty-ounce porterhouse steak or a one-pound pork chop was considered a normal helping. Today, people want lighter, better-balanced meals.

Fish and fowl have become the most requested entrees. In our restaurants, 75 percent of the entrees served consist of fish, shellfish, fowl, and to a lesser extent, young lamb grown by Sonoma farmers.

For a large group, it is wise to decide on a roast or something that can be prepared in advance. For example, it is simpler to arrange Turkey Picatta attractively on a large platter and place the platter in the oven to keep warm than to set up individual plates. To add color, vegetables that have been blanched earlier in the day can be sautéed quickly and placed decoratively around the turkey. Then, instead of flowers, the food becomes your centerpiece as well as the main attraction. Also, food served family-style is always more fun and there is no need for additional help. I even like it in my restaurants.

Many of our dishes are grilled, but practically anything that is grilled can be sautéed, especially in a nonstick pan with very little fat or oil. We marinate the food to be grilled in olive oil first, not only for flavor, but to help prevent sticking. If grilling fish, keep the fish on the one side until it begins to carmelize; if you turn it too soon, the fish will still stick to the grill. For a thinner cut of fish or meat, I sometimes cook it on one side and serve it on a warm plate, uncooked-side down. Remember, most fish or meat is juicier and tastes better when slightly underdone.

Roasted Salmon with Black Pepper and Ginger on Celery Root Puree

Serves 4

INGREDIENTS

4 salmon fillets, about
¾ inch thick, 6 to 7
ounces each
Salt
2 tablespoons (1 ounce)
unsalted butter,
melted
1 ½ tablespoons
crushed black
peppercorns
1 ½ tablespoons
chopped fresh peeled
ginger*

SAUCE
6 tablespoons (3
ounces) unsalted
butter
3 shallots, chopped
2 garlic cloves,
chopped
1 plum tomato, peeled,
seeded, and chopped
2 cups cabernet
sauvignon
1 tablespoon balsamic
vinegar
1 cup Chicken Stock
(see page 41)
Salt
Freshly ground pepper

2 tablespoons olive oil
1 recipe Celery Root
Puree (see page 115)

When I created this, I was looking for a fish entree that would go well with pinot noir, which often has a peppery taste. Salmon, prepared this way, is the ideal dish. I have often served this to a large group, since the salmon can be readied earlier in the day, the slices arranged on large baking trays, and roasted as needed.

1 Season the salmon lightly with salt, brush the top with a little melted butter, and immediately sprinkle evenly with the crushed pepper and chopped ginger. Drizzle the remaining butter over. If you wait too long, the butter will harden and the mixture won't stick. Refrigerate, covered, until needed.

2 Preheat the oven to 500°F.

3 *Prepare the sauce:* In a small sauté pan, melt 2 tablespoons butter until foamy. Over medium heat, sauté the shallots and garlic until the shallots are translucent, 2 to 3 minutes. Stir in the tomato and cook 1 or 2 minutes longer. Pour in the wine and vinegar, turn up the heat a little, and reduce until ½ cup remains. Pour in the chicken stock and reduce by half. Strain into a clean pan. Finish sauce by whisking in the remaining 4 tablespoons butter and season to taste with salt and pepper. Keep warm.

4 Brush some olive oil over a baking tray large enough to hold the salmon slices in one layer and arrange the salmon on the pan. Roast until medium, about 10 minutes. The salmon should be cooked on the outside, but still moist and slightly underdone on the inside.

Presentation: Divide the sauce among 4 warm dinner plates. Spoon equal amounts of celery root puree in the center of each plate and place 1 piece of salmon on top.

EQUIPMENT

Pastry brush
Small sauté pan
Strainer
Whisk
Baking tray

To prepare ahead: The salmon can be prepared as in step 1, salted just before roasting, and refrigerated, covered, until needed. In step 3, strain the sauce into a clean pan and at serving time heat over a low flame and continue with the recipe. The celery root puree also can be prepared earlier in the day. Reheat in a metal bowl or the top of a double boiler set over simmering water, turning the puree with a spoon to heat thoroughly.

*1 ounce sliced blanched almonds can be substituted for the ginger, if desired.

ROASTED RED SNAPPER WITH NEW POTATO CRUST AND RED ONION SAUCE

Serves 3 to 6

INGREDIENTS

¾ pound small new potatoes, about 1 inch in diameter, peeled (If potatoes are too large, shape as necessary.)
About ⅓ cup clarified unsalted butter
Salt
Freshly ground white pepper

SAUCE
2 tablespoons olive oil
1½ cups (about ½ pound) coarsely chopped red onion
2 cups dry red wine
¼ cup port
¼ cup balsamic vinegar

I prefer snapper from the Gulf of Mexico, which has a very delicate texture. This makes a beautiful presentation, especially if the fillets are a little larger. The potatoes are arranged to resemble fish scales.

1 Preheat the oven to 375°F.

2 *Prepare the potatoes:* Using a mandoline or a very sharp knife, cut the potatoes into very thin rounds, as for potato chips. Arrange on a baking sheet in one layer and pour enough melted butter over the potatoes to coat both sides, reserving a little to brush over the fillets. Season with salt and pepper and bake until tender, about 10 minutes. Cool.

3 *Prepare the sauce:* In a 10-inch skillet, heat the olive oil. Over medium-high heat, sauté the onions until glossy, 4 to 5 minutes. Pour in the red wine, port, and vinegar, and season with pepper and thyme. Reduce by one half. Pour in the fish stock and reduce until the sauce begins to thicken. Puree in a blender until smooth and return to the skillet. (You should have

(Continued)
....

½ tablespoon coarse
   black pepper
1 teaspoon chopped
   fresh thyme
½ cup Fish Stock (see
   page 54)
¼ cup heavy cream
2 tablespoons (1 ounce)
   unsalted butter, at
   room temperature

6 red snapper fillets, ½
   inch thick, 3 to 4
   ounces each
Salt
Freshly ground pepper
Chopped fresh thyme
Vegetable or peanut oil
1 small leek, cut into
   julienne

EQUIPMENT

Mandoline or sharp
   knife
Pastry brush
Baking sheets
10-inch skillet
Blender
Strainer
Whisk
Small saucepan

about 1½ cups.) Stir in the cream and cook 1 minute longer. Strain into a clean pan and whisk in the butter. Season to taste with salt and pepper and keep warm.

4 Turn up the oven temperature to 500°F.

5 Brush the fillets with some of the clarified butter and season with salt, pepper, and a touch of thyme. Brush a baking sheet with olive oil and place the fish on it. Arrange the slices of potatoes, one overlapping the other, on each fillet to resemble the scales of a fish. Bake 4 minutes, set the tray under the broiler and, watching carefully, brown the potatoes until golden and crispy, 2 to 3 minutes.

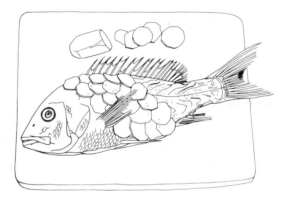

6 Meanwhile, in a small saucepan, heat about one inch of vegetable oil to 350°F. Rinse the leeks in cold water and pat very dry. Carefully drop the leeks into the oil and cook until crispy. Do not brown.

Presentation: Spoon some sauce in the center of each heated plate. Using a wide spatula, place one or two fillets on the sauce and sprinkle with the leeks. Serve immediately.

To prepare ahead: In step 3, puree the sauce. At serving time, reheat over a low flame, and continue with the recipe. In step 5, arrange the potatoes on the fish as directed and refrigerate until ready to bake, salting just before baking.

GRILLED STRIPED BASS ON RED AND WHITE CABBAGE WITH CHINOIS TOMATO SAUCE

Serves 2

INGREDIENTS

2 8-ounce fillets of
   striped bass
1½ tablespoons sesame
   oil
Salt
2 teaspoons peanut oil
5 ounces each red and
   white cabbage, cut
   into 1-inch chunks
1 garlic clove, minced
1⅓ cups Chinois
   Tomato Sauce (see
   page 149)
1 cup Fish Stock (see
   page 54)
Salt
Freshly ground white
   pepper
4 tablespoons (2
   ounces) unsalted
   butter, cut into small
   pieces

Cilantro sprigs

EQUIPMENT

10-inch skillet or wok

Farm-raised freshwater striped bass is readily available. Striped bass from the Atlantic Ocean now has become a game fish.

1 Heat the grill or preheat the broiler.

2 Rub each fillet with sesame oil and season lightly with salt. Set aside.

3 In a 10-inch skillet or wok, heat the peanut oil. Over medium-high heat, sauté the cabbage and garlic for 1 or 2 minutes, coating the cabbage with the oil. Stir in the tomato sauce and fish stock, and cook the cabbage until tender but still chewy, 3 to 4 minutes. Season to taste with salt and pepper. Stir in the butter and keep warm.

4 Meanwhile, grill or broil the fish, about 2½ minutes per side.

Presentation: Spoon the cabbage onto two heated serving plates. Arrange the fish on top and spoon some of the sauce over the fish. Garnish with sprigs of cilantro and serve immediately.

To prepare ahead: In step 2, rub fillet with sesame oil, refrigerating, covered, until needed. Have the remaining ingredients ready and continue the recipe at serving time.

GRILLED HALIBUT WITH TOMATOES
AND SWEET PEPPERS

Serves 4

⅓ cup olive oil

1 medium (6 ounces) onion, minced

4 garlic cloves, minced

Pinch of chili pepper flakes

3 medium (about 1 pound) tomatoes, peeled, seeded, and diced

1 (6 ounces) red bell pepper, cored, seeded, and diced

Pinch of saffron

Pinch of chopped fresh thyme leaves

Pinch of chopped fresh basil leaves plus whole leaves for garnish

½ cup dry white wine

Salt

Freshly ground white pepper

2 pounds fresh Alaskan halibut fillet, cut into 4 portions, 8 ounces each

Grill or sauté pan for fish

Heavy sauté pan

Pastry brush

Though we have halibut in Southern California, the ones we get from Maine, and sometimes from Alaska, are far superior.

1 Heat the grill.*

2 In a heavy sauté pan, heat ¼ cup olive oil. Sauté the onion, garlic, and chili pepper flakes for 3 minutes. Stir in the tomatoes, bell pepper, saffron, thyme, and basil, pour in the wine, and cook over medium heat until the liquid is absorbed, about 30 minutes. Season with salt and pepper to taste. Keep warm.

3 Brush the remaining olive oil over the halibut and season lightly with salt and pepper. Grill until medium, about 2½ minutes each side.

Presentation: Spoon the tomato and bell pepper mixture in the center of 4 heated dinner plates. Place a halibut fillet on top and garnish with the basil leaves.

To prepare ahead: See Note on serving cold.

Note: To serve cold, sauté the fillets until rare. Transfer to the tomato and bell pepper mixture when almost all the liquid is absorbed (step 2) and continue to cook 5 minutes longer. Let cool and serve on a bed of assorted lettuces or with a cucumber salad on the side.

*Halibut can be sautéed in a nonstick pan, 2½ to 3 minutes on each side.

GRILLED SWORDFISH
WITH TOMATILLO VINAIGRETTE

Serves 4

INGREDIENTS

1½ pounds fresh
 swordfish, cut into 4
 6-ounce portions
Salt
2 or 3 basil leaves, cut
 into julienne
2 to 3 tablespoons
 Spicy Cinnamon-
 Chili Paste (see page
 141)
¼ cup olive oil

VINAIGRETTE

¼ pound tomatillos,
 husks removed
6 sprigs cilantro
1 garlic clove
½ teaspoon chopped
 jalapeño pepper
½ cup plus 1
 tablespoon olive oil
2 tablespoons
 champagne vinegar
Salt
Freshly ground pepper

4 basil sprigs

EQUIPMENT

Large dish with sides
Small baking pan
Food processor
Strainer
Small bowl
Whisk

Swordfish is the ideal fish for barbecuing because of its firm, meaty texture. However, you can sear it in a hot skillet or broil it. No matter what the method, the swordfish will be tastier and juicier if cooked medium rare.

1 Place the pieces of fish in a dish large enough to hold them in one layer. Season lightly with salt and sprinkle with the basil leaves. Combine the spicy cinnamon chili paste with the olive oil and mix well. Pour over the fish and turn to coat all sides. Refrigerate for 2 hours, turning once or twice.

2 Preheat the oven to 400°F.

3 *Prepare the vinaigrette:* Arrange the tomatillos, cilantro, garlic, and jalapeño on a small baking pan. Sprinkle with the 1 tablespoon olive oil and bake until tomatillos are tender, 10 to 15 minutes. Scrape into a food processor fitted with the steel blade and puree. Strain through a medium-fine strainer and cool. There should be about ¼ cup.

4 In a small bowl, whisk together the tomatillo puree and vinegar. Slowly whisk in the remaining ½ cup of olive oil and season with salt and pepper to taste. Set aside.

5 Preheat the grill.

6 Remove the swordfish from the marinade and grill 2 minutes on each side for medium rare.

Presentation: Spoon some of the vinaigrette in the center of 4 dinner plates. Set a piece of fish on the vinaigrette and garnish with basil. Serve immediately.

To prepare ahead: Through step 4, salting the fish before grilling.

SEARED TUNA STEAK AU POIVRE

Serves 4

INGREDIENTS

4 tuna steaks, 6 ounces
   each
Salt
¼ cup cracked black
   peppercorns
¼ cup cognac
⅓ cup port
½ cup reduced Brown
   Chicken or Brown
   Veal Stock (see pages
   42, 43)
2 tablespoons unsalted
   butter
2 teaspoons green
   peppercorns, drained

EQUIPMENT

Wax paper or large
   plate
Small and large skillets
Strainer

Since tuna is available year round, this is the choice of many of our customers who don't eat meat. Fresh tuna should have a deep red color.

❶ Season tuna lightly with salt. Pour the peppercorns on a sheet of wax paper or a large plate and press each slice of tuna into the pepper to evenly coat both sides. Refrigerate until needed.

❷ In a small skillet or saucepan, reduce the cognac and port until 2 tablespoons remain. Add the stock and reduce until the sauce thickens. Strain into a clean pan, whisk in the butter, and season to taste. Keep warm.

❸ Heat a skillet large enough to hold the 4 tuna steaks in one layer or preheat a grill. Over high heat, sear the tuna on both sides, 35 to 45 seconds per side. Cut each steak into ½-inch slices.

Presentation: Spoon a little sauce in the center of each of four plates. Arrange one sliced tuna steak on the sauce and garnish with the green peppercorns. Serve immediately.

To prepare ahead: In step 2, add the stock and reduce. When ready to serve, heat the sauce over a low flame and continue with the recipe. Salt the fish when ready to cook.

GRILLED SCALLOPS WITH CHILI-PERSIMMON LOBSTER BUTTER

Serves 6

INGREDIENTS

2 ¼ pounds sea
  scallops
¼ cup plus 1
  tablespoon olive oil
3 tablespoons chopped
  fresh basil
1 medium red onion,
  diced
1 garlic clove, diced
2 small persimmons,
  peeled and minced
2 cups Lobster Stock
  (see page 45) or 1
  cup Chicken Stock
  (see page 41) and 1
  cup Lobster Stock,
  heated
3 tablespoons Spicy
  Chili Paste, without
  cinnamon (see page
  141)
4 tablespoons (2
  ounces) unsalted
  butter
Salt
Freshly ground white
  pepper
Juice of ½ small lemon
Freshly grated nutmeg

EQUIPMENT

12 long skewers
Medium saucepan
Strainer
Whisk

I like the flavor of grilled scallops, but they can be seared quickly in a nonstick pan, without being skewered.

1 Remove the small muscle on the side of each scallop. Using two bamboo skewers, skewer 6 ounces of scallops (about 8 scallops) for each serving. Arrange the skewered scallops on a flat dish and marinate in ¼ cup olive oil and the chopped basil for at least 1 hour, up to 6 hours.

2 Preheat the grill or the broiler.

3 *Prepare the sauce:* In a medium saucepan, heat the remaining 1 tablespoon olive oil. Sauté the onion and garlic until golden, about 10 minutes. Add 1 minced persimmon and the stock and bring to a boil. Stir in the chili paste and cook over medium heat until the sauce thickens. Strain and return to a clean saucepan.

4 Whisk in the butter and the remaining minced persimmon. Season to taste with salt, pepper, lemon juice, and nutmeg. Keep warm.

5 Season the scallops lightly with salt and pepper and arrange on the grill or under the broiler, being careful that the bare ends of the skewers are not directly over or under the flame. Grill 4 minutes on one side, turn and grill 3 minutes on the other side.

Presentation: Spoon some of the sauce on each of 6 plates. Carefully slide the scallops off the skewers and arrange on the sauce. Pass the remaining sauce in a small bowl.

To prepare ahead: Through step 3. At serving time, reheat over a low flame and continue with the recipe.

SHRIMP FRICADELLA WITH DILL AND CAPER SAUCE

Serves 6

....

FRICADELLA
1 tablespoon olive oil
½ cup diced onion
½ cup diced roasted
  red bell pepper
½ cup diced roasted
  yellow bell pepper
½ cup heavy cream
1 pound uncooked
  shrimp, shells
  reserved, coarsely
  chopped
¼ cup chopped fresh
  dill leaves
1 egg, lightly beaten
1 cup packed fresh
  bread crumbs
1½ teaspoons salt
1 teaspoon freshly
  ground white pepper
Pinch of cayenne
  pepper
About 1 cup almond
  meal or fine bread
  crumbs

DILL AND CAPER
SAUCE
1 tablespoon olive oil
4 large shallots, thinly
  sliced
Reserved shrimp shells
3 or 4 sprigs of fresh
  dill
2 cups dry white wine

A Scandinavian shrimp cake, we serve this at Eureka for lunch. An emulsified vinaigrette made with the dill leaves, capers, and mustard can be substituted for the warm sauce.

1 *Prepare the fricadella:* In a medium skillet, heat the olive oil. Over medium heat, sauté the onion and peppers until the onion is translucent, about 10 minutes. Transfer to a medium mixing bowl and cool.

2 In a small saucepan, bring the cream just to a boil and cool slightly. Add to the onion mixture with the remaining ingredients except almond meal and mix well. Form 6 4-inch oval-shaped patties, about 4 ounces each. Bread lightly on all sides in almond meal or fine bread crumbs and refrigerate until needed.

3 *Prepare the dill and caper sauce:* In a medium saucepan, heat the oil. Sauté the shallots, shrimp shells, and dill sprigs for 2 minutes. Pour in the wine and, over high heat, reduce by half. Remove from the heat and whisk in the butter and vinegar. Strain into a clean pan and stir in the dill leaves, capers, and mustard. Season to taste with salt and pepper and keep warm.

4 *Prepare the salad:* In a bowl, combine the salad greens and the fennel. When ready to serve, toss with the oil and vinegar and season with salt and pepper to taste.

5 In 1 or 2 skillets, large enough to hold the fricadella in one layer, heat the 2 or 3 tablespoons olive oil. Over medium heat, sauté the patties for 5 minutes on each side. Toast the bread.

12 tablespoons (6
   ounces) unsalted
   butter, cut into small
   pieces
2 tablespoons balsamic
   vinegar
2 tablespoons chopped
   fresh dill leaves
1 tablespoon drained
   capers
1 tablespoon Dijon
   mustard
Salt
Freshly ground white
   pepper

SALAD
3 cups watercress or
   arugala leaves,
   washed and dried
1 cup thinly sliced
   fennel
¼ cup olive oil
2 tablespoons balsamic
   vinegar
Salt
Freshly ground white
   pepper

2 to 3 tablespoons
   olive oil
6 slices sourdough
   bread

EQUIPMENT

Medium skillet
Medium and large
   bowls
Small and medium
   saucepans
Whisk
Strainer

Presentation: Place 1 slice of bread on each of 6 plates. Arrange some salad on the bread and top with 1 fricadella. Spoon sauce around the bread and drizzle a little over each fricadella. Serve immediately.

To prepare ahead: Through step 3. At serving time, reheat over a low flame and continue with the recipe.

SAUTÉED CHICKEN BREAST WITH WHITE TRUFFLES AND PORT WINE GLAZE

Serves 4

INGREDIENTS

4 ounces goat cheese
½ ounce white truffles
2 whole chicken
   breasts, boned, each
   cut in half
2 tablespoons olive oil
Salt
Freshly ground pepper
½ cup port
½ cup reduced
   Chicken Stock (see
   page 41)
2 tablespoons (1 ounce)
   unsalted butter

EQUIPMENT

Small mixing bowl
Ovenproof sauté pan
Whisk
Mandoline

Sinfully rich mashed potatoes are the perfect companion for the white truffles and should be reserved for special guests and/or special occasions. The treasured white truffle, in season from late October to March, is found mainly in the Piedmont region of Italy. It is prized for its pungent aroma and delicious flavor. The white truffle is very rare, very expensive, and eaten sparingly. A peasant dish becomes noble with a little truffle shaved over it.

1 Preheat the oven to 350°F.

2 In a small bowl, crumble the goat cheese and combine with 1 teaspoon chopped white truffles.

3 Gently slip your fingers under the skin of each chicken breast, lifting it slightly. Divide the cheese-truffle mixture and stuff some under the skin, patting down to distribute it evenly.

4 Rub each breast with a little olive oil and season with salt and pepper to taste. In an ovenproof sauté pan large enough to hold the breasts in one layer, sauté the chicken, skin side down, until golden, about 3 minutes, turn and cook 2 minutes longer. Transfer to the oven for 10 to 12 minutes. Do not overcook.

5 Remove the chicken from the pan and keep warm. Pour out any fat that may remain and deglaze the pan with port. Add the stock and reduce just until the sauce thickens. Whisk in the butter and season with salt and pepper to taste.

Presentation: Place 1 chicken breast on each of 4 heated plates and spoon a little of the sauce over. Using a mandoline, thinly slice the remaining truffle and sprinkle over each chicken breast. Serve immediately. Pass any remaining sauce in a small bowl. Serve with Creamy Mashed Potatoes (see page 117) without the brown onion.

To prepare ahead: Through step 3, refrigerating the chicken until needed.

STUFFED CABBAGE BALLS
Serves 6

INGREDIENTS

1 whole head of cabbage, about 1½ pounds

FILLING
Meat from 2 chicken legs (about 12 ounces)
¼ cup olive oil
1 cup (about ¼ pound) diced onion
½ pound mushrooms, chopped fine
½ pound spinach, stemmed, washed, and dried
2 garlic cloves, minced
1 egg, lightly beaten
2 tablespoons chopped fresh parsley
1 teaspoon salt
Freshly ground white pepper to taste

I prefer using the meat from the chicken legs rather than the breasts for stuffing since the meat requires a longer period of cooking and will not become dry during the process.

❶ Blanch the whole cabbage in water to cover, about 5 minutes. Immediately plunge into cold water. Remove the center core, carefully separate the leaves, and drain on a clean, dry towel. Cut away the hard stem on each leaf and reserve the leaves. (As you peel off the outer leaves, you may have to return the head of cabbage to the boiling water to soften the inner leaves.)

❷ *Prepare the filling:* Coarsely grind the chicken and transfer to a large bowl. Reserve.

❸ In a medium skillet, heat 1 tablespoon olive oil. Over moderate heat, sauté the onion until translucent. Cool. In a clean skillet, heat 2 tablespoons olive oil and sauté the mushrooms until all the liquid evaporates, stirring occasionally. Cool. In a clean skillet, heat the remaining 1 tablespoon olive oil and sauté the spinach until wilted. Drain well, squeezing out all the juice, and chop fine. Cool. Stir the onion, mushrooms, and spinach into the ground chicken. Add the remaining

(Continued)

1 teaspoon chopped
 fresh thyme
½ teaspoon ground
 cumin

SAUCE

3 tablespoons olive oil
1 cup brunoise of
 carrots
1 cup brunoise of
 onions
½ cup brunoise of
 celery
½ pound (about 3)
 Roma tomatoes,
 peeled, seeded, and
 diced
3 garlic cloves, minced
1 cup dry white wine
2 cups Brown Chicken
 or Brown Veal
 Stock, heated (see
 pages 42, 43)
Leaves from 2 sprigs
 fresh thyme
Salt
Freshly ground white
 pepper

Chopped fresh thyme
 or parsley for
 garnish

EQUIPMENT

Pot large enough to
 hold the cabbage
Grinder
Large bowl
Medium skillet
Flameproof, ovenproof
 casserole

ingredients and combine well. To test for taste, sauté a small amount in a little oil and correct seasoning to taste.

④ *Prepare the sauce:* In a flameproof, ovenproof casserole large enough to hold the cabbage balls in one layer, heat the olive oil. Over moderate heat, sauté the carrots, onions, and celery for 5 minutes. Add the tomatoes and garlic and cook 2 or 3 minutes longer. Deglaze with the wine and reduce by half. Pour in the stock, stir in the thyme, and cook 10 minutes longer. Season with salt and pepper to taste.

⑤ Preheat the oven to 400°F.

⑥ *Prepare the cabbage balls:* Spoon about 4 ounces of filling in the center of 1 or 2 cabbage leaves, folding the ends over to completely enclose, forming a ball. Arrange the cabbage balls in the sauce, cover, and bring to a boil. Transfer to the oven and bake 30 minutes. Remove the cabbage balls and keep warm. Set the casserole over high heat and reduce the sauce until slightly thickened. Correct seasoning to taste.

Presentation: Set 1 cabbage ball in the center of each of 6 heated plates. Spoon a little sauce over and garnish with the chopped herbs.

To prepare ahead: In step 6, make the cabbage balls and refrigerate until you are ready to serve.

STIR-FRIED CHICKEN
WITH CASHEWS AND PINE NUTS

Serves 3 or 4

INGREDIENTS

2 tablespoons peanut oil
¾ pound filleted
   chicken, cut into
   1½-inch cubes
Salt
Freshly ground pepper
¼ cup plum wine
1 tablespoon minced
   garlic
2 teaspoons chopped
   peeled ginger root
½ teaspoon crushed
   chili pepper flakes
1¼ cups Chicken
   Stock, heated (see
   page 41)
2 teaspoons Chinois
   Rib Sauce (see page
   136)
1 cup (2 ounces) sliced
   shiitake mushrooms
½ cup each 1-inch
   cubes of yellow and
   red bell pepper
2 green onions, cut
   into 1-inch slices
¼ cup each cashews
   and pine nuts
4 tablespoons (2
   ounces) unsalted
   butter

EQUIPMENT

10-inch skillet or wok

At Chinois, we do not use cornstarch to thicken our sauces. Instead, we prefer stock reductions and the addition of a little butter, which give the sauces a much more delicate and richer consistency.

1 In a 10-inch skillet or a wok, heat the peanut oil until smoking.

2 Season the chicken lightly with salt and pepper and sear, about 1 minute on each side. Deglaze the pan with the plum wine and stir in the garlic, ginger, and chili flakes. Pour in the stock and reduce by half (sauce will begin to thicken). Add the rib sauce, mushrooms, peppers, green onion, and nuts, and cook 1 or 2 minutes longer, stirring occasionally. Stir in the butter and correct seasoning to taste.

Presentation: Spoon the stir-fried chicken onto a large heated serving platter, arranging all the ingredients evenly throughout. Or divide among 3 or 4 heated plates and serve immediately.

To prepare ahead: Have all the ingredients ready and prepare the recipe when ready to serve.

TURKEY PICATTA ON PUMPKIN PUREE

Serves 4 to 6

INGREDIENTS

PUMPKIN PUREE

2 pounds fresh
   pumpkin, cut into
   chunks and seeds
   removed
1 cup water
4 tablespoons (2
   ounces) unsalted
   butter, cut into
   pieces
2 tablespoons dark
   brown sugar
1 teaspoon ground
   allspice
1 teaspoon ground
   cinnamon
1 teaspoon ground
   ginger

TURKEY PICATTA

2 pounds turkey
   breast, cut into 12
   slices, each ⅓ inch
   thick
12 sage leaves
Freshly ground pepper
¼ pound prosciutto (6
   long, thin slices, cut
   in half)
Salt
All-purpose flour
2 tablespoons vegetable
   oil
1 tablespoon chopped
   fresh sage
½ cup port

Many of our customers do not eat veal, so turkey breast is frequently substituted. However, when preparing turkey picatta, you must keep in mind that the picatta should be cooked quickly over high heat so that it is seared on the outside and medium rare on the inside.

1 *Prepare the pumpkin puree:* In a small baking tray, combine the pumpkin chunks with the water. Cover and bake in a preheated 400°F oven until tender, about 1 hour. Drain as necessary. Scoop out the flesh of the chunks of pumpkin, transfer to a bowl, and mash. Stir in the remaining ingredients and mix well.

2 Puree in a food mill and correct seasoning to taste. Keep warm over simmering water, stirring when ready to serve.

3 *Prepare the picatta:* Place 1 sage leaf in the center of each slice of turkey and season with pepper. Top with a slice of prosciutto and press together with the palm of your hand. Season the other side with salt and pepper and dust both sides lightly with flour.

4 Heat a large heavy sauté pan and add the vegetable oil. Sear the turkey scallops, ham-side down, until golden. Turn and sear the other side. As the turkey scallops are cooked, remove from the pan and keep warm. Pour out the oil, add the chopped sage, and deglaze the pan with the port. Add the lemon juice and reduce by half. Whisk in the butter and keep warm.

Presentation: Divide the pumpkin puree and mound in the center of each of 4 warm plates. Surround with 3 scallops and spoon a little sauce over the scallops. Garnish with fried sage leaves.* Serve with Cranberry Catsup (see page 146).

Juice of 1 lemon
2 tablespoons unsalted
  butter

Fried sage leaves for
  garnish

Baking tray
Medium bowl
Food mill
Double boiler or
  stainless steel bowl
  and saucepan
Large sauté pan
Whisk

To prepare ahead: Through step 3, refrigerating the picatta until 15 minutes before you are ready to serve, seasoning with salt at that time. Reheat the pumpkin puree over simmering water, stirring occasionally to heat thoroughly.

*To fry fresh sage leaves, drop in 1 inch of oil until lightly golden, and drain.

GRILLED QUAIL WITH WILD RICE RISOTTO

Serves 4

INGREDIENTS

WILD RICE
RISOTTO
4 tablespoons (2
  ounces) unsalted
  butter
½ cup diced onion
1 cup wild rice, rinsed
  and drained
2 to 3 cups Chicken
  Stock (see page 41)
Salt
Freshly ground pepper
½ cup diced red bell
  pepper
½ cup diced yellow
  bell pepper
1 cup fresh corn
  kernels

I find wild rice, served alone, very dry and not terribly exciting. The addition of cream and Parmesan cheese gives the rice a risottolike consistency; the addition of the diced vegetables, a more colorful and interesting presentation.

1 Preheat the oven to 400°F.

2 *Prepare the risotto:* In an ovenproof 6-cup saucepan or casserole, melt 2 tablespoons butter. Over medium heat, sauté the onion until translucent, about 10 minutes. Stir in the rice and coat well with the butter.

3 In a small saucepan, bring the stock to a boil. Pour 2 cups over the rice and bring back to a boil. Season lightly with salt and pepper, cover the pan and set in the oven. Cook until the rice is tender, 45 to 55 minutes, stirring occasionally, and pouring in additional stock as necessary.

(Continued)

SAUCE
1 large shallot, diced
2 cups Chicken Stock
　(see page 41)
1 cup heavy cream
½ cup grated Parmesan
　cheese
2 tablespoons (1 ounce)
　unsalted butter

4 boned quail, 3
　ounces each, split
　down the back
2 tablespoons olive oil
Salt
Freshly ground pepper

EQUIPMENT

6-cup ovenproof
　casserole
Small and medium
　saucepans
12-inch skillet
Grill
Pastry brush

④ In a 12-inch skillet, melt the remaining 2 tablespoons butter. Sauté the red and yellow peppers 3 or 4 minutes, add the corn kernels, and cook 3 to 4 minutes longer, stirring occasionally. Season lightly with salt and pepper. Scrape into the rice and combine thoroughly. Keep warm.

⑤ Preheat the grill.

⑥ *Prepare the sauce:* In a medium saucepan, reduce the shallot and the stock by half. Pour in the cream and continue to reduce until 1¼ cups remain. Strain and return to a clean pan. Stir in the Parmesan cheese and the 2 tablespoons butter. Pour 1 cup over the rice mixture and combine well. Correct seasoning to taste and keep warm.

⑦ Brush olive oil over the quail and season lightly with salt and pepper. Arrange on the grill, breast side down, and cook 2 minutes. Turn and grill 2 minutes longer. Finish on the breast side, just to crisp.

Presentation: Spoon 1 cup of the risotto in the center of each of 4 heated plates. Set 1 quail, breast-side up, on the risotto and pour a little of the remaining sauce around. Serve immediately.

To prepare ahead: In step 3, cook the rice until almost tender. Step 4 can be completed. In step 6, prepare the sauce. At serving time, pour over the rice and reheat in the oven. Continue with the recipe.

CRISP QUAIL WITH PINEAPPLE AND GREEN ONION

Serves 4

INGREDIENTS

8 quail, about 4 ounces each, cut into quarters

MARINADE

2 tablespoons plum wine or sherry
2 tablespoons chopped fresh, peeled ginger
1 tablespoon finely chopped garlic
1 tablespoon finely chopped green onion
1 teaspoon salt
1 teaspoon freshly ground white pepper

SAUCE

¾ cup plum wine or port
1 tablespoon julienned fresh, peeled ginger
½ cup Brown Stock (Chicken or Veal) (see pages 42, 43)
½ cinnamon stick
1 teaspoon Chili Oil (see page 145)
Salt
Freshly ground white pepper
2 tablespoons (1 ounce) unsalted butter

This is an excellent way to cook quail. The quail will be tender and moist on the inside and crisp on the outside.

1 Place the quail quarters on a plate and toss with the marinade. Let marinate 1 hour, up to 6 hours, refrigerated.

2 *Prepare the sauce:* In a medium skillet, over high heat, combine the wine and ginger and reduce by half. Pour in the stock with the cinnamon stick and cook until the sauce thickens. Add the chili oil and season lightly with salt and pepper. Whisk in the butter and correct seasoning to taste. Keep warm.

3 In a deep, heavy saucepan or a deep-fat fryer, heat about 3 inches of peanut oil to 350°F.

4 Pour the rice flour into a small bowl and make a thick batter using ½ to ¾ cup water. Transfer the quail from the marinade to a clean plate, reserving the marinade. Pour enough of the batter over the quail to coat well, reserving a little batter. Deep fry until golden, 2 to 3 minutes. Do not overcook. Drain on a clean towel and toss in the reserved sauce. Quail is best when still pink on the inside.

5 Coat the green onions with the remaining batter and fry until golden, 1 or 2 minutes. Drain on clean toweling.

(*Continued*)

Peanut oil for deep
    frying

About 1 cup rice flour
6 green onions,
    trimmed and cut in
    half lengthwise
¼ fresh pineapple, cut
    lengthwise, peeled,
    trimmed, and cut
    into 10 thin slices

EQUIPMENT

Medium skillet
Whisk
Deep, heavy saucepan
    or deep-fat fryer
Small bowl

Presentation: Arrange the pineapple slices in a circle around the outer edges of a large ovenproof plate. Warm in the oven. Pile the quail in the center and poke the green onions into the quail at various intervals. Serve immediately.

To prepare ahead: Through step 2, reheating the sauce over a low flame at serving time. The pineapple slices can be arranged on a plate, covered, and then warmed at serving time.

GRILLED SQUAB WITH HUCKLEBERRY SAUCE AND POTATO PARSNIP PANCAKES

Serves 4

Potato Parsnip
  Pancakes (see page
  118)

INGREDIENTS

4 squab, about 1
  pound each
3 tablespoons olive oil

SAUCE
2 cups port
1 cup huckleberries
2 large shallots, sliced
10 to 12 whole black
  peppercorns
1 cup Brown Chicken
  or Brown Veal Stock
  (see pages 42, 43)
6 tablespoons (3
  ounces) unsalted
  butter
Salt
Freshly ground white
  pepper

Potato Parsnip
  Pancakes (see page
  118)

EQUIPMENT

Grill
Medium saucepan
Blender
Strainer
Whisk

Game birds are not sold in markets in this country. Our birds are farm-raised. I think squab is by far the best tasting and closest to a wild bird. If huckleberries are not available, fresh cranberries or currants can be substituted.

1 Split the squab down the back, keeping the breast intact, and remove the rib and backbones. Sprinkle with olive oil and reserve.

2 Preheat the grill.

3 *Prepare the sauce:* In a medium saucepan, reduce the port, ½ cup huckleberries, shallots, and peppercorns until ¼ cup remains. Pour in the stock and continue to reduce just until the sauce thickens. Transfer to a blender and puree. Strain and return to the saucepan. Stir in the remaining ½ cup huckleberries and whisk in the butter. Season to taste with salt and pepper and keep warm. (If sauce thickens too much, thin with a little stock.)

4 Prepare the potato parsnip pancakes.

5 Season the squab lightly with salt and pepper. Grill, skin-side down, about 5 minutes. Turn and grill 5 minutes longer. Finish, skin-side down, just to crisp.

Presentation: Place one potato parsnip pancake in the center of 4 heated plates and top with one squab. Spoon a little sauce over each squab along with some of the whole berries. Pass any remaining sauce in a small bowl.

To prepare ahead: In step 3, strain the sauce and continue with the recipe at serving time.

CHINOIS ROASTED SQUAB ON PAN-FRIED NOODLES WITH SPICY MUSHROOM SAUCE

Serves 2 to 4

INGREDIENTS

4 ounces Chili Pasta
  Dough (see page 186)
2 tablespoons peanut
  oil
2 tablespoons sesame
  oil*

SPICY MUSHROOM
SAUCE
1 tablespoon peanut oil
1 cup shiitake* and
  oyster mushrooms,
  cut into julienne
½ cup dry red wine
¼ cup plum wine
½ cup Brown Stock
  (Chicken, Squab or
  Duck) (see page 42)
1 tablespoon (½
  ounce) unsalted
  butter
Salt
Freshly ground pepper
1 large garlic clove,
  minced
1 green onion, minced
¼ teaspoon minced
  fresh ginger
⅛ teaspoon chili
  pepper flakes,
  chopped very fine

1 1-pound squab
Salt
Freshly ground pepper

There are some dishes at Chinois that people will travel for miles to eat. This is one of them.

① *Prepare the pan-fried noodles:* Roll out the dough as thin as possible and, using a sharp knife or a pasta machine, cut into ¼-inch noodles. Bring a medium pot of water to a boil. Add a pinch of salt and a little olive oil and cook the pasta al dente. Rinse under cold water, drain well, and dry thoroughly.

② In an 8-inch nonstick skillet, over moderate heat, heat 2 tablespoons each of peanut and sesame oils. Spread the noodles evenly over the pan and fry until crisp and golden brown. Turn and brown the other side. The pancake should be crispy on the outside and still slightly soft on the inside. Reserve. (This can be prepared early in the day and reheated at serving time in 1 tablespoon each peanut oil and butter.)

③ Preheat the grill or the oven to 400°F.

④ *Prepare the sauce:* In a 10-inch skillet, heat 1 tablespoon peanut oil. Over medium-high heat, sauté the mushrooms for 2 or 3 minutes. Deglaze the pan with the red and plum wines and reduce to a glaze. Pour in the brown stock and reduce until the sauce thickens. Whisk in the butter and season with salt and pepper to taste. Keep warm. Just before serving, stir in the garlic, green onion, ginger, and chili flakes. Correct seasoning to taste.

⑤ Meanwhile, butterfly the squab and remove all but the leg bones. Season lightly with salt and pepper. Grill, skin-side down, about 5 minutes, turn and grill 5 minutes longer. Finish skin-side down just to crisp. (To sauté, heat 1 tablespoon peanut oil in an ovenproof

1 tablespoon peanut
oil

1 bunch watercress
½ tablespoon rice wine
vinegar**
1 teaspoon sesame oil
Salt
Freshly ground pepper

Pasta machine or
rolling pin
Medium pot
8-inch, 10-inch, and
small skillets
Whisk

skillet. Brown both sides quickly and transfer to the oven. Roast 10 to 12 minutes, or until medium rare.)

6 *Prepare the watercress:* In a small skillet, heat the remaining 1 tablespoon peanut oil. Sauté the watercress for 1 or 2 minutes, just to wilt. Stir in the rice wine vinegar and the remaining 1 teaspoon sesame oil and season with salt and pepper to taste.

7 Separate the breasts, legs, and wings. Cut each breast into 4 slices. Reheat the pancake and cut into quarters.

Presentation: Mound the watercress in the center of a large platter. Arrange the noodles around the salad, points facing in, leaving a little space between each quarter. Place 2 slices of breast on each quarter and alternate the legs and wings around the noodles. Spoon the sauce over the squab and the noodles. Serve immediately.

To prepare ahead: Through step 4, reheating the sauce over a low flame. Or step 5, butterflying the squab and removing the bones.

*Cut the stems from the shiitake mushrooms and use in soups or stocks.
**Ingredients can be purchased in stores that carry oriental products.

Roasted Leg of Baby Lamb with Black Bean Ragout

Serves 4

INGREDIENTS

Trimmed 3-pound leg
  of baby lamb
1 garlic clove, cut into
  thin slivers
1 tablespoon olive oil
3 or 4 sprigs fresh
  thyme plus extra
  sprigs for garnish
¼ teaspoon freshly
  ground white pepper
½ teaspoon salt

Black Bean Ragout (see
  page 116)
Fresh thyme sprigs

EQUIPMENT

Pastry brush
Shallow roasting pan

Baby lamb usually is available in the spring and is very tender. I like lamb medium rare, still pink on the inside. Roasting time will be about 10 minutes longer for those who prefer their meat well done.

1 *Prepare the lamb:* With a sharp knife, make 4 thin slits, spaced evenly, in the lamb and insert the slivers of garlic into the slits. Brush the olive oil over the leg and season with the thyme and pepper. Place in a dish and refrigerate, covered, overnight.

2 Preheat the oven to 450°F.

3 Season the lamb with salt and set in a shallow roasting pan. Roast 40 minutes for medium rare.

Presentation: Cut the lamb into thin slices. Spoon a portion of the black bean ragout in the middle of each of 4 heated plates. Arrange slices of lamb on the ragout and garnish with a sprig of thyme. Serve immediately.

To prepare ahead: Through step 1. The ragout can be prepared ahead and reheated over a low flame when needed.

BRAISED MOROCCAN LAMB

Serves 4 to 6

INGREDIENTS

1 boned and trimmed lamb shoulder, about 1 ¾ pounds
2 teaspoons ground cumin
Freshly ground pepper
½ teaspoon chopped fresh thyme
Salt
4 tablespoons olive oil
½ pound (1 large) onion, coarsely chopped
1 large carrot, peeled and coarsely chopped
1 celery stalk, coarsely chopped
2 garlic cloves, sliced
1 teaspoon chopped fresh rosemary
1 cup dry red wine
2 cups Brown Chicken, Brown Veal or Lamb Stock (see pages 42, 43)
6 ounces tomatoes, ends removed and coarsely chopped
5 ½ ounces blanched whole almonds, lightly toasted*
4 ounces whole dried pitted prunes
4 ounces whole dried apricots

This recipe was given to me by a Moroccan friend and it has become the main course for our Passover dinner every year. If you prefer veal shanks, you can replace the lamb with the shanks.

1 Preheat the oven to 450°F.

2 Lay the lamb out, skin-side down, and sprinkle with 1 teaspoon each cumin and pepper and thyme. Roll and tie well with butcher's string. Season the outside lightly with salt and pepper.

3 Heat 2 tablespoons of the oil in an ovenproof casserole slightly larger than the lamb. Brown the lamb on all sides, then pour out the oil.

4 Add the remaining 2 tablespoons oil to the casserole, stir in the onion, carrot, celery, and garlic and, over medium-high heat, cook until the onion has colored slightly, 4 to 5 minutes. Sprinkle with the remaining 1 teaspoon of cumin and the rosemary, deglaze the pan with the red wine, and bring to a boil. Pour in the stock, add the tomatoes, season with ½ teaspoon each of salt and pepper, cover, and transfer to the oven. Braise until almost tender, about 1 hour.

5 Remove the meat and keep warm. With a slotted spoon, separate the vegetables from the sauce and puree in a blender. Scrape back into the sauce and reduce just until the sauce thickens slightly. Strain into a clean casserole and season with salt and pepper to taste. Place the meat in the sauce, surround with the almonds, prunes, and apricots and return to the oven for about 15 minutes longer, until the lamb is very tender and the dried fruit is soft. (If the sauce thickens too much, thin with a little stock.)

(Continued)

Butcher's string
2 flameproof,
   ovenproof casseroles
Slotted spoon
Blender
Strainer

Presentation: Cut the lamb into thin slices and arrange on heated plates. Spoon some sauce over, placing the prunes and apricots on and around the meat. Serve immediately. Pass any remaining sauce in a small bowl.

To prepare ahead: In step 5, strain the sauce into a clean casserole. At serving time, return the meat to the pan along with the prunes and apricots and continue with the recipe.

*To toast almonds, spread on a baking tray and bake in a preheated 350°F oven until lightly browned, about 20 minutes.

ROASTED LAMB BALLS ON CREAMY MASHED POTATOES WITH BROWN ONIONS

Makes 20 lamb balls, to serve 4 or 6

INGREDIENTS

1 or 2 tablespoons plus
   1 teaspoon olive oil
½ cup diced onion
1 pound coarsely
   ground lamb
1 egg, lightly beaten
¾ cup fresh bread
   crumbs
3 tablespoons chopped
   cilantro
1 tablespoon minced
   garlic
2 teaspoons salt
2 teaspoons freshly
   ground white pepper
1 teaspoon paprika
1 teaspoon ground
   cumin
1 teaspoon chopped
   fresh rosemary
1 teaspoon Chili Oil
   (see page 145)

A slightly different version of the usual meatball. Since I am from Austria, I serve them with potatoes rather than spaghetti.

1 In a small skillet, heat 1 teaspoon olive oil. Over medium heat, sauté the onion just until wilted. Cool.

2 Preheat oven to 450°F.

3 In a medium mixing bowl, combine the ground lamb with the sautéed onions, the egg, bread crumbs, cilantro, garlic, salt, pepper, paprika, cumin, rosemary, and chili oil. Mix well. Form 20 balls, each about 1½ inches in diameter.

4 In 1 or 2 ovenproof skillets large enough to hold the lamb balls in one layer, heat the 1 tablespoon of olive oil (if using 2 skillets, you will need the remaining tablespoon of oil). Brown the lamb balls on all sides,* then transfer to the oven and roast for 10 minutes. The balls should be firm on the outside and tender on the inside.

1 recipe Creamy
  Mashed Potatoes
  with Brown Onions
  (see page 117)
1 recipe Black Olive
  Cabernet Sauce (see
  page 135)
Sprigs of Italian parsley
  for garnish

Small skillet
Medium mixing bowl
1 or 2 large ovenproof
  skillets

Presentation: Spoon some of the mashed potato down the center of each of 5 or 6 warmed plates. Arrange 3 or 4 lamb balls on top and spoon the sauce over. Sprinkle with the brown onions and garnish with sprigs of Italian parsley.

To prepare ahead: Through step 3, refrigerating covered, until needed. The mashed potatoes can be kept warm over simmering water, the onion rings sliced. The sauce can be prepared earlier in the day and reheated over a low flame.

*At this point, the lamb balls can be put on skewers and grilled, if desired.

MEAT LOAF ON VEGETABLE PUREE WITH MUSHROOM SAUCE

Serves 8

MEAT LOAF
1 pound (about 4 large)
  Japanese eggplants
5 to 6 tablespoons
  olive oil
1 tablespoon salt
½ teaspoon freshly
  ground white pepper
2 shallots, minced
½ pound mushrooms,
  minced
½ cup heavy cream
2 pounds medium
  ground lamb, veal,
  or pork, or a
  combination
2 eggs, lightly beaten
2 tablespoons minced
  garlic

We don't serve this in any of my restaurants, but I prepare it at home for my friends during the cooler months of the year. The recipe may look complicated, but even a novice in the kitchen will have excellent results and win rave reviews.

1 Preheat the oven to 450°F. Oil a 9 × 4½ × 2½-inch loaf pan.

2 *Prepare the meat loaf:* Trim the ends and cut a thin slice, lengthwise, from both sides of each eggplant. Cut into lengthwise slices, each about ¼ inch thick. In a large skillet, heat 2 tablespoons of the oil, and over medium high heat, lightly brown the eggplant slices on both sides, adding more oil as necessary. As the slices brown, remove to a baking pan. When all the slices have been browned, place in the oven and cook until tender, about 5 minutes. Drain on paper towels, cool, and season lightly with salt and pepper. Lower the oven temperature to 400°F.

(Continued)

2 teaspoons ground
   cumin
1 teaspoon chopped
   fresh thyme

Vegetable Puree (see
   page 111)

MUSHROOM
SAUCE
2 tablespoons olive oil
½ pound mushrooms,
   thinly sliced
½ cup port
1 cup Brown Veal
   Stock (see page 43)
6 tablespoons (3
   ounces) unsalted
   butter
Salt
Freshly ground pepper

EQUIPMENT

9 × 4½ × 2½-inch loaf
   pan
Large and smaller
   skillets
Large bowl
Baking pan with sides
Aluminum foil
Medium saucepan
Whisk

3 In a smaller skillet, heat the remaining 2 tablespoons oil. Sauté the shallots until blond, add the mushrooms, season lightly with salt and pepper, and cook over medium-high heat for 3 or 4 minutes. Pour in the cream and cook until all the cream is absorbed, stirring occasionally. Cool.

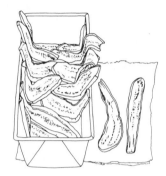

4 Using the best slices of eggplant, line the bottom and the long sides of the prepared loaf pan. Chop the remaining eggplant. In a large bowl, combine the chopped eggplant and the mushrooms with the ground meat. Stir in the eggs, garlic, cumin to taste, thyme, and the remaining salt and pepper and mix well. Fill the loaf pan with the meat mixture, patting down to level, and fold over the ends of the eggplant as necessary. Place the loaf pan in a larger baking pan and fill the larger pan with boiling water halfway up the sides of the loaf pan. Cover with aluminum foil and bake 1 hour 10 minutes, removing the foil after 35 minutes.

5 Meanwhile, prepare the vegetable puree.

6 *Prepare the mushroom sauce:* In a saucepan, heat the olive oil. Over medium high heat, sauté the mushrooms, 3 to 4 minutes. Pour in the port and reduce by half. Add the stock and reduce just until the sauce thickens slightly. Whisk in the butter and season with salt and pepper to taste. Keep warm.

7 Remove the meat loaf from the oven and let rest for 10 minutes. Carefully pour the juices out of the pan, then invert onto a cutting board. Cut into 8 slices.

Presentation: Spoon a little vegetable puree in the center of each of 8 heated dinner plates. Arrange 1 slice of meat loaf on the puree and spoon some of the sauce, with the mushrooms, over the meat. Serve immediately, passing the remaining sauce in a small bowl.

To prepare ahead: In step 4, fill the loaf pan and refrigerate, covered. Thirty minutes before baking, remove from the refrigerator. Have your vegetables for the puree ready. While the meat loaf is baking, prepare the puree and the sauce and keep warm. Continue with the recipe.

Note: If Japanese eggplants are not available, you can use American eggplants, trimming as necessary.

MANDARIN NOODLES WITH SAUTÉED TENDERLOIN AND VEGETABLES

Serves 4 to 6

INGREDIENTS

1 tablespoon peanut oil
3 tablespoons (1½ ounces) unsalted butter
6 ounces tenderloin steak, cut into thin strips
½ cup (2 ounces) julienned mixed vegetables, such as carrots, asparagus
1 ounce enoki mushrooms
Salt
Freshly ground pepper
⅓ cup plum wine
½ teaspoon ground cinnamon

If you buy a whole tenderloin, reserve the center cut for grilling or roasting and use the ends for this dish.

❶ In a large skillet or wok, heat the oil and 1 tablespoon butter. Over high heat, add the tenderloin strips and sear lightly on all sides. Add the vegetables and enoki mushrooms and cook just until the meat is pink, stirring occasionally. Season with salt and pepper to taste, transfer to a warm plate and reserve.

❷ Deglaze the pan with the plum wine, add the cinnamon and reduce by half. Add the veal stock and continue to reduce until slightly thickened. Whisk in the remaining 2 tablespoons of butter. Add the cooked noodles, the reserved meat and vegetables, stir in the lime juice, and just heat through. Correct seasoning to taste.

(Continued)

⅔ cup Brown Veal
    Stock (see page 43)
2 cups (4 ounces)
    cooked herb
    fettuccine (using
    Herb Pasta Dough,
    page 185)
Juice of ½ lime
1½ cups washed,
    trimmed, and
    thoroughly dried
    spinach leaves (if
    large, cut in half)
8 to 10 endive leaves
2 tablespoons chopped
    green onion
Togarashi, optional*

EQUIPMENT

Wok or large skillet
Whisk

Presentation: Pile the spinach in the center of a large serving platter and surround with the endive leaves. Spoon the steak, noodles, and sauce on the spinach and garnish with the chopped scallions. Sprinkle lightly with togarashi, if desired, and serve immediately.

To prepare ahead: Have all your ingredients ready and prepare the recipe at serving time.

*Togarashi is an oriental seasoning that can be purchased in most markets that carry oriental products.

QUESADILLA EUREKA

Serves 2

INGREDIENTS

ANCHO CHILE
PASTE
2 ounces dried ancho
    chiles
½ cup garlic cloves
½ cup olive oil
½ cup cilantro leaves
3 large (3 ounces) green
    onions, coarsely
    chopped
1 tablespoon balsamic
    vinegar

I love homemade tortillas, but do not like the commercial ones. So I decided to replace the tortillas with potato slices and I think the end result is even tastier.

① *Prepare the ancho chile paste:* Wash the ancho chiles and soften in warm water to cover. Cut in half, stem, and seed. In a blender, combine the chiles with the remaining ingredients and puree.

② Spread some of the paste over both sides of the steak and let marinate, refrigerated, at least 6 hours.

③ *Prepare the salsa:* In a small bowl, combine all the

1 tablespoon honey
Juice of 1 lime

1 8-ounce New York
  steak

SALSA
1 medium tomato,
  peeled, seeded, and
  chopped
½ jalapeño pepper,
  cored, seeded, and
  chopped
2 tablespoons chopped
  onion
2 tablespoons chopped
  cilantro leaves
1 tablespoon olive oil
Salt
Freshly ground pepper

SOUR CREAM
CILANTRO SAUCE
3 to 4 tablespoons sour
  cream
½ bunch cilantro,
  leaves only
Juice of ½ lime
Salt
Freshly ground white
  pepper

QUESADILLA
¼ pound baking
  potato, peeled and
  cut into very thin
  rounds
¼ cup clarified butter
Salt
2 ounces shredded
  mozzarella cheese
1 ounce fresh goat
  cheese

ingredients and season with salt and pepper to taste. Refrigerate, covered, until needed.

4 *Prepare the sauce:* In a blender, combine 3 tablespoons sour cream, the cilantro, and lime juice, and blend until smooth. Pour into a small bowl and season with salt and pepper to taste. Refrigerate, covered, until needed. The sauce should thicken slightly as it sits; if not, stir in the remaining tablespoon of sour cream.

5 Preheat the oven to 450°F.

6 *Prepare the quesadilla:* Place the potato slices in a medium bowl, pour the clarified butter over, and toss to coat the slices. Season lightly with salt. Arrange half the potatoes, flower fashion, in an 8-inch ovenproof skillet. Cook over medium heat until the ends begin to brown and the potatoes stick together. (This will keep the cheeses from running through.) Sprinkle with the cheeses and cover with the remaining potatoes, arranged the same way as the bottom layer. Set in the oven for 10 minutes, carefully flip the potatoes with a wide spatula and brown on a medium-high flame. Return to the oven for 5 minutes longer. Cut into 4 quarters and keep warm.

7 Grill or pan fry the steak to desired degree of doneness. Cut into 6 or 8 slices.

(Continued)

1 cup mixed salad
  greens
Sprigs of cilantro for
  garnish

EQUIPMENT

Blender
2 small bowls
Medium bowl
8-inch ovenproof
  skillet
Grill or pan large
  enough to hold the
  steak

Presentation: Spread a layer of greens down the center of each of two plates and top with the salsa. Arrange 3 or 4 slices of steak on the salsa and spoon some of the sour cream cilantro sauce over the steak. Place 2 quarters of the quesadilla on either side and garnish the plate with sprigs of cilantro. Serve immediately.

To prepare ahead: Through step 4.

PORK LOIN WITH THAI SAUCE AND PAPAYA SALAD

Serves 4

INGREDIENTS

THAI PASTE
4 ounces (¾ cup)
  unsalted raw cashews
1 ounce peeled fresh
  ginger
½ cup plum wine
¼ cup peanut oil
½ cup (3 large) sliced
  green onions
½ cup chopped
  cilantro leaves
6 garlic cloves
1 chile pepper,
  jalapeño or red
  serrano, cored,
  seeded, and coarsely
  chopped
1½ tablespoons
  turmeric

Many people like the taste of pork, but are under the impression that pork is fatty. The way pigs are raised today, pork, especially the loin, is quite lean and relatively inexpensive.

① *Prepare the Thai paste:* Preheat the oven to 400°F. Spread the cashews on a baking tray and roast until golden brown, turning as needed, about 10 minutes. Cool.

② In a small pan, cook the ginger in the plum wine until the wine evaporates. With a mortar and pestle or in a blender, puree all the Thai paste ingredients. Reserve.

③ *Prepare the salad:* In a medium bowl, combine the papaya, onion, cilantro, and jalapeño. In a small bowl, whisk together the lime juice, vinegar, and honey. At serving time, toss with the salad and season with salt and pepper to taste.

1 tablespoon honey
1 tablespoon sesame oil
1 tablespoon balsamic
  vinegar
1 tablespoon cumin
1 teaspoon freshly
  ground white pepper
½ teaspoon coarse salt

SALAD
1 or 2 papayas or
  mangoes (12 ounces),
  peeled, seeded, and
  diced
½ red onion (about
  2½ ounces), diced
¼ cup cilantro leaves
¼ jalapeño pepper,
  cored, seeded, and
  chopped fine
Juice of 2 limes
1 tablespoon balsamic
  vinegar
1 teaspoon honey
Salt
Freshly ground white
  pepper
4 radicchio leaves

1½ pounds pork loin,
  cut into 4 6-ounce
  medallions
Salt
Freshly ground pepper
1 tablespoon peanut oil
½ cup port
1 cup Brown Veal
  Stock (see page 43)
Lime juice

④ Raise the oven temperature to 450°F. Season the pork medallions with salt and pepper and flatten slightly with a cleaver or a heavy plate. In an ovenproof skillet, heat the peanut oil. Over high heat, brown both sides of the medallions. Transfer to the oven and roast until medium rare, about 15 minutes. Remove the medallions to a plate and keep warm.

⑤ Pour the grease from the skillet and deglaze the pan with port. Pour in the stock and cook over high heat until the sauce thickens slightly. Whisk in ¼ cup of the Thai paste and season to taste with salt, pepper, and lime juice. Keep warm.

Presentation: Cut each medallion into slices. Pour a little sauce in the center of four warmed plates and arrange slices of pork on one side of the sauce. Mound a little salad in each radicchio leaf, set alongside the slices of pork, and garnish with a few cilantro leaves. Serve immediately.

To prepare ahead: In step 3, combine the salad ingredients and refrigerate, covered. Continue with the recipe at serving time.

EQUIPMENT
Baking tray
Small saucepan
Blender or mortar and
  pestle
Medium and small
  bowls
Whisk
Ovenproof skillet

BILLY WILDER'S CALVES' LIVER

Serves 4

POTATO PUREE

1½ pounds (about 2
  large) baking
  potatoes, peeled and
  quartered
⅔ cup heavy cream
4 tablespoons (2
  ounces) unsalted
  butter
2 tablespoons chopped
  fresh parsley
Salt
Freshly ground white
  pepper
Freshly grated nutmeg

1½ pounds (about 2
  large) onions
Flour
Peanut oil for deep
  frying

1½ pounds calves'
  liver, cut into
  ¼-inch thick slices
All-purpose flour
Salt
Freshly ground pepper
⅓ cup peanut oil
¼ cup balsamic
  vinegar
⅓ cup reduced Brown
  Veal Stock (see page
  43)
3 tablespoons chopped
  fresh parsley

Billy Wilder is a legend as a filmmaker. He makes fine movies and loves fine food. This is one of his favorite dishes at Spago.

① *Prepare the potato puree:* In a medium saucepan, place the potatoes with lightly salted water to cover. Bring to a boil, lower heat, and cook until tender, about 25 minutes. Puree in a food mill, return to a clean pan, and keep warm.

② Heat the cream and stir into the potatoes. In a small skillet, over moderate heat, melt the butter and cook until the butter is brown and has a nutty aroma. Pour into the potatoes, add the parsley, and mix well. Season with salt, pepper, and nutmeg to taste and keep warm over simmering water.

③ Meanwhile, cut each onion into thin round slices. Separate into rings and dust lightly with flour. In a deep-fat fryer or a deep, heavy saucepan, heat about 3 inches of oil to 350°F. Gently drop the rings, a few at a time, into the oil and cook until golden brown. Remove with a slotted spoon and drain on paper towels or a clean cloth towel.

④ Dust the pieces of liver lightly with flour and season with salt and pepper to taste. In one or two large skillets, heat the oil. Over medium-high heat, brown the liver on both sides, keeping the inside pink. This should take 1 or 2 minutes per side. Transfer to a warm plate. Pour out the oil and deglaze the pan with the balsamic vinegar and the stock. Strain into a clean pan and stir in the parsley, lemon juice, and butter. Season with salt and pepper to taste.

Juice of ½ medium
lemon
2 tablespoons (1 ounce)
unsalted butter

EQUIPMENT

Medium saucepan
Food mill
Small saucepan
Small skillet
Deep-fat fryer or deep
saucepan
Large skillet(s)
Strainer

Presentation: Divide the potatoes equally in the center of each of 4 heated plates. Arrange 2 or 3 slices of liver on the potatoes and spoon the sauce over. Surround with the fried onion rings and serve immediately.

To prepare ahead: Through step 2, stirring the potato puree occasionally to make sure it is heated through. In step 3, cut the onion rings into rounds and continue with the recipe when you are ready to serve.

GRILLED CALVES' LIVER WITH PANCETTA SAUCE

Serves 4

INGREDIENTS

2 pounds calves' liver,
trimmed of
membranes and
nerves
Olive oil
Salt
Freshly ground pepper

PANCETTA SAUCE
2 ounces pancetta,
diced
1 shallot, minced
1 garlic clove, minced
2 tablespoons balsamic
vinegar
¼ cup dry red wine
¼ cup tomato
concasse

It is important to buy fresh liver. When liver has been frozen, the texture becomes mushy when cooked. Have your butcher remove the skin and veins.

1 Cut liver into ¼-inch thick slices. There should be 2 or 3 slices per serving. Arrange in a glass or ceramic dish and drizzle with olive oil. Refrigerate until needed.

2 Preheat grill.

3 *Prepare the pancetta sauce:* In a small skillet or saucepan, cook the pancetta over moderate heat until crisp (no oil is necessary, since pancetta has enough fat on it), about 5 or 6 minutes. Drain off the fat, add the shallot and garlic, and sauté 2 to 3 minutes. Pour in the vinegar and wine and reduce by half. Strain and return to a clean pan. Stir in the tomato concasse, butter, and thyme, season to taste with salt and pepper, and keep warm.

(Continued)

4 tablespoons (2
    ounces) unsalted
    butter
Leaves of 2 sprigs fresh
    thyme plus 4 whole
    sprigs
Salt
Freshly ground pepper

Glass or ceramic dish
Grill
Small skillet
Strainer

④ Season the liver lightly with salt and pepper. Grill to desired degree of doneness, 2½ to 3 minutes per side for medium rare.

Presentation: Spoon a little sauce on each of 4 heated plates. Arrange 2 or 3 slices of liver on a plate and spoon some of the remaining sauce over. Garnish with 1 sprig of fresh thyme. Serve immediately.

To prepare ahead: In step 3, strain into a clean pan. At serving time, reheat over a low flame and continue with the recipe.

GRILLED VEAL TONGUE ON WARM WHITE BEAN SALAD WITH BASIL VINAIGRETTE

Serves 6

INGREDIENTS

2 veal tongues, about
    1¼ pounds each
3 to 4 cups Chicken
    Stock (see page 41)
½ medium (4 ounces)
    onion, cut into large
    dice
2 medium (3 to 4
    ounces) carrots, cut
    into large dice
1 celery stalk, cut into
    large dice
2 bay leaves
1 tablespoon whole
    peppercorns
1 large sprig of fresh
    thyme

Postrio serves this with a thick slice of grilled onion.* It is an inexpensive, well-balanced meal.

① *Prepare the tongue:* Place the tongues in a large, wide stainless steel saucepan or roasting pan and pour in enough stock and/or water to cover. Add the onion, carrot, celery, bay leaves, whole peppercorns, and the sprig of thyme. Bring the stock to a boil, lower the flame, and simmer until the tongues are tender, 1 to 1½ hours. Remove the tongues, plunge into cold water for a few seconds, drain, and carefully remove the outer layer of skin. Return to the stock and let cool. (This can be done the day before and refrigerated until needed.)

② *Prepare the beans:* Place the beans in a medium bowl and pour in enough cold water to cover by 2 or 3 inches. Let soak overnight. Drain. Transfer the beans to

Olive oil
Salt
Freshly ground pepper

BEAN SALAD
2 cups small white
   beans, rinsed
6 to 7 cups Chicken
   Stock (see page 41)
   or half stock and
   half water, heated
1 tablespoon salt
Freshly ground white
   pepper
3 tablespoons olive oil
1 tablespoon minced
   garlic
¼ cup (2 or 3 large
   sprigs) fresh basil
   leaves, cut into
   julienne
⅓ cup champagne
   vinegar
½ cup tomato
   concasse
3 cups assorted greens,
   cut into bite-size
   pieces

BASIL VINAIGRETTE
½ cup (5 or 6 large
   sprigs) fresh basil
   leaves, chopped
¼ cup champagne
   vinegar
2 tablespoons grated
   Parmesan cheese
½ cup olive oil
Salt
Freshly ground pepper

a 6-cup saucepan and cover with 5 cups of stock/water. Season with the salt and a few grinds of pepper and bring to a boil. Lower the heat and simmer until the beans are tender, about 2 hours, stirring often to prevent scorching, adding the remaining cup of liquid as necessary. Drain.

3 *Meanwhile, prepare the vinaigrette:* In a blender, combine the basil, vinegar, and Parmesan cheese until the basil is pureed. With the motor running, pour the oil through the opening and blend until smooth. Season with salt and pepper to taste, pour into a small bowl, and set aside. Whisk before using.

4 Preheat the grill.

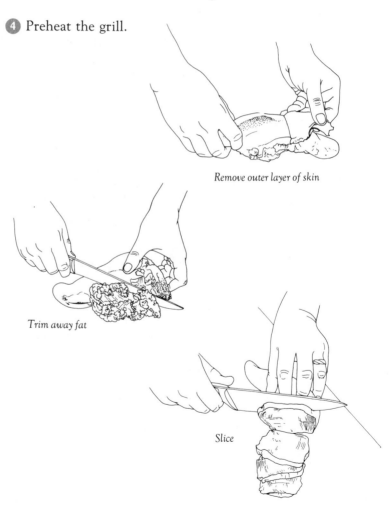

Remove outer layer of skin

Trim away fat

Slice

(Continued)

Large saucepan or
   roasting pan
Medium bowl
6-cup saucepan
Blender
Whisk
Grill
Large skillet

5 Remove the tongue from the stock and scrape away the gelatinous layer that clings. Trim away the fat and gristle and cut each tongue, across the grain, into slices about ¾ inch thick. Coat the slices with olive oil and season with salt and pepper to taste.

6 When ready to serve, finish the bean salad: In a large skillet, heat the olive oil. Sweat the garlic, add the basil and the beans, and stir over a low flame. Pour in the vinegar, and when the beans are heated through, stir in the concasse. Correct seasoning to taste and keep warm.

Presentation: Mound some greens in the center of each of 6 large plates. Divide the warm beans and spoon over the greens. Grill the slices of tongue on both sides to heat through and arrange 2 or 3 slices on each serving of beans. Pour a little vinaigrette around the salad and serve immediately.

To prepare ahead: Through step 3.

*To prepare the onion, trim 2 large onions and cut each crosswise into 3 thick slices. Coat lightly with olive oil and season with salt and pepper to taste. Grill until brown on both sides. Serve with the tongue salad.

VEAL MEDALLIONS ON APPLE COMPOTE WITH BLACK PEPPER CIDER SAUCE

Serves 4

INGREDIENTS

SAUCE

1 cup Brown Veal
  Stock (see page 43)
2 tablespoons apple
  cider jelly
½ cup heavy cream
1 tablespoon unsalted
  butter
1 tablespoon crushed
  black peppercorns or
  to taste

APPLE COMPOTE

2 pounds large pippin
  or Granny Smith
  apples
1 tablespoon unsalted
  butter
2 teaspoons apple cider
  jelly
¼ cup dry white wine
½ cup heavy cream
Salt
Freshly ground pepper
Pinch of freshly ground
  nutmeg

If you buy thick slices of veal medallions, you can cook them medium rare for juicier, tastier meat. In cooking school, students are taught to use white pepper on white meat. I definitely prefer coarsely ground black pepper because it has much more flavor.

1 *Prepare the sauce:* In a 10-inch skillet, combine the veal stock and jelly. Over medium-high heat, reduce until ½ cup remains, being careful that the sides of the pan don't burn because of the sugar in the jelly. Pour in the cream and reduce just until the sauce thickens. Whisk in the butter and the peppercorns and keep warm. If the sauce thickens too much, thin with a little stock.

2 *Prepare the compote:* Peel, core, and quarter the apples. Cut into thin slices. In a 12-inch skillet, melt the butter. Sauté the apples, first over high heat, then over lower heat, until soft. Add the jelly and the wine and stir until the jelly melts. Pour in the cream and stir until the apples are coated. Season with salt, pepper, and nutmeg to taste. Keep warm.

3 *Prepare the medallions:* Lightly dust the medallions with flour and season with salt and pepper to taste. Heat 1 or 2 heavy skillets and add the vegetable oil and butter (if using 2 skillets you may need a little more oil and butter). Sauté the medallions until golden, about 3 or 4 minutes each side.

(Continued)

1 ½ pounds veal loin,
  cut into 8 3-ounce
  medallions
1 or 2 tablespoons
  all-purpose flour
Salt
Freshly ground pepper
1 tablespoon vegetable
  oil
1 tablespoon (½
  ounce) unsalted
  butter

EQUIPMENT

10-inch, 12-inch, and 1
  or 2 large skillets
Whisk

Presentation: Divide the compote and place in the center of 4 heated plates. Arrange 2 medallions on the compote and spoon a little sauce over. Serve immediately.

To prepare ahead: Through step 2. At serving time, reheat the sauce and the compote over a low flame.

BRAISED VEAL SHANKS WITH RED WINE SAUCE

Serves 8

INGREDIENTS

2 cups assorted dried
  fruits (prunes,
  apricots, figs)
1 bottle port (about
  3 ½ cups)
8 veal shanks, about 12
  ounces each, cut 1 ½
  inches thick
½ cup all-purpose
  flour
Salt
Freshly ground white
  pepper
¼ cup olive oil
½ cup brunoise of
  onion

I favor braising for the cuts of meat that usually take a longer time to cook. Braising keeps the meat moist and results in a delicious sauce without the use of cream or butter. This dish can be made the day before, cooled, and reheated as needed.

1 In a small bowl, marinate the dried fruit, with enough port to cover, overnight.

2 Dust the shanks with flour. (The simplest way is to pour the flour into a bag and, one by one, place the shanks in the bag, coat with the flour, and shake off the excess.) Season lightly with salt and pepper.

3 Preheat the oven to 400°F.

½ cup brunoise of
carrot

½ cup brunoise of
celery

1 cup blanched whole
almonds

1 bottle dry red wine
(about 3½ cups)

2 to 4 cups Brown
Veal Stock (see page
43)

1 recipe Couscous (see
page 127)

Small bowl
Large ovenproof
roasting pan with
cover
Tongs to remove
shanks

4 In a large ovenproof roasting pan, heat the olive oil.
Brown the shanks on all sides. Do not crowd the pan,
browning in batches if necessary. Add the vegetables,
almonds, dried fruit, and the marinating liquid. Pour in
the remaining port and the red wine and bring to a
boil. Turn the flame to medium and reduce the sauce
by half. (The length of time required depends upon the
size of the pan.)

5 Pour in enough veal stock to cover the shanks and
bring to a boil. Cover the pan, transfer to the oven,
and cook until the shanks are tender, 35 to 45 minutes.
Remove the shanks and keep warm. Reduce the sauce
just until it thickens. Correct seasoning to taste and
return the shanks to the pan.

Presentation: Mound the couscous in the center of
each of 8 heated plates. Top with one veal shank and
spoon the sauce over, including some almonds and
fruit. Serve immediately. Have small forks on hand to
scoop out the marrow from the bones.

To prepare ahead: Through step 5, reheating over a
low flame when ready to serve. If the sauce thickens
too much, thin with a little more stock.

Eureka Venison (Lamb, Beef, Duck, or Chicken) and Black Bean Chili

Serves 10 to 12

¾ cup vegetable oil

2½ pounds boned and trimmed venison, lamb, beef, duck, or dark meat chicken, coarsely ground or diced

6 dried pasilla chiles (2 to 3 ounces), cored and seeded

2 pounds (3 to 4 large) onions, diced, plus 1 medium onion

3 bay leaves

1 small head garlic, peeled and minced

2 tablespoons crushed black peppercorns

2 tablespoons ground cumin

2 tablespoons paprika

3½ cups Chicken Stock, heated (see page 41)

2 pounds tomatoes, peeled, seeded, and coarsely chopped

3 bottles (12 ounces each) Eureka beer*

2 jalapeño peppers, cored, seeded, and chopped fine

2 serrano chiles, cored, seeded, and chopped fine

We created this dish for the opening of Eureka Brewery. It should be served with a full-bodied beer.

1 Heat a large skillet. Pour in ½ cup oil and, over medium heat, sauté the meat or chicken until the liquid evaporates, 10 to 15 minutes, turning the meat to cook on all sides.

2 Meanwhile, in a large pot, heat the remaining ¼ cup oil. Over medium heat, sauté the pasilla chiles for about 2 minutes. Remove the chiles and reserve. In the same pot, sauté the 2 pounds diced onions until they color slightly, about 10 minutes. Add the bay leaves, garlic, peppercorns, cumin, and paprika, and stir through.

3 Cook the reserved pasilla chilies in 2 cups of chicken stock until very tender. Transfer to a blender or a food processor and puree. Pour into the pot with the sautéed onions and cook until most of the liquid is absorbed. Add the tomatoes, the meat (venison, lamb or beef, *but not the chicken*), pour in the beer, and cook over medium heat about 2 hours, stirring occasionally. If using chicken, add for the last *30 minutes* of cooking. Stir in the jalapeño and serrano peppers, oregano, thyme, lemon zest and juice, and combine well. (If more liquid is needed, add the liquid from the cooked beans, as in step 4.)

4 While the chili is cooking, drain the beans, reserving the liquid, and place in a saucepan with the onion, carrot, and celery stalk. Pour in the remaining 1½ cups stock and the water and cook over

1 bunch fresh oregano,
  leaves chopped fine
1 bunch fresh thyme,
  leaves chopped fine
Zest of 2 medium
  lemons, chopped fine
Juice of 2 medium
  lemons
½ pound black beans,
  soaked overnight in
  water to cover by 2
  inches
½ medium carrot
½ medium celery stalk
1½ cups water
1 bunch cilantro, leaves
  chopped fine
¼ cup molasses
Salt

EQUIPMENT

Large skillet
Large pot
Blender or food
  processor
2 medium saucepans
Strainer

medium-high heat until tender, about 2 hours, adding water if necessary. Remove the onion, carrot, and celery, and drain, reserving the liquid to use as needed for the chili.

5 Add the drained beans and the cilantro to the chili pot and stir in the molasses. Correct the seasoning, adding salt to taste. Remove the bay leaves.

Presentation: Serve the chili in bowls, topped with bits of queso fresco or jalapeño jack cheese. Pass a stack of warm flour tortillas and bowls of chopped onions, chopped jicama, and sour cream. (Or you can line each bowl with one warm tortilla and spoon the chili onto the tortilla.) Serve immediately.

To prepare ahead: Through step 5, reheating on a low flame at serving time.

*If Eureka beer is unavailable, any dark beer may be substituted.

VEGETABLES

Vegetable Puree

Vegetable Chips

Stir-fried Vegetables

Sautéed Baby Vegetables

Celery Root Puree

Black Bean Ragout

Creamy Mashed Potatoes with Brown Onions

Potato Parsnip Pancakes

Crisp Potato Galette

Sweet Potato Crisp

Gratin of Sweet Potatoes

Ratatouille

Eggplant Compote

Pickled Eggplant

Fried Spinach Leaves

Couscous

One of the most comforting foods of my childhood was a bowl of creamy mashed potatoes brought directly from the pot to the table by my mother. After years of cooking and sampling all kinds of dishes, potatoes are still my favorite. Today, my recipes are a bit more exotic—a smooth potato puree whipped light with butter and cream, topped with brown onions or perhaps shavings of fresh white truffle, a crisp potato galette, potatoes combined with parsnips for pancakes, combined with celery root and pureed, and sweet potatoes that defy description.

Many people think of vegetable puree as decoration on nouvelle cuisine plates, usually thin and made from asparagus or green beans. I prefer a more starchy puree, especially in cold weather. In winter, when our appetites are heartier, a zesty sauce and a warm puree are a wonderful accompaniment to any meat, fish, or fowl.

To make the puree, always use a food mill or a potato masher; a blender or food processor will give your puree a gluey consistency. I love to whip milk or cream and butter into the pureed vegetables to lighten the texture. However, these days, I am trying to watch my cholesterol and use extra-virgin olive oil and chicken stock instead.

In California we are particularly fortunate; many vegetables are available year round. I like to use young vegetables; they are the sweetest and most tender and require very little cooking. But whatever the vegetable, buy the freshest available and ones that will add color to your main dish.

VEGETABLE PUREE

Serves 8

3 tablespoons olive oil
1 pound onions, cut into chunks
1 pound baking potatoes, peeled and cut into chunks
1 pound broccoli florets
About 2 cups Chicken or Vegetable Stock, heated (see pages 41, 46)
3 garlic cloves, sliced
1 teaspoon chopped fresh thyme
Salt
Freshly ground white pepper
1 cup heavy cream

Large saucepan
Food mill

Potatoes are the base of this vegetable puree. Broccoli can be replaced with peas, carrots, cauliflower, or green beans. Garlic or leeks can be used instead of onions.

① In a large saucepan, heat the olive oil. Over high heat, sauté the onions until glossy, 2 to 3 minutes. Add the potatoes, broccoli, and chicken stock or water to cover. Stir in the garlic, thyme, salt, and pepper to taste and cook until tender, 25 to 30 minutes. Pour in the cream and continue to cook until the sauce is absorbed, 15 to 20 minutes. Puree through a food mill, return to a clean saucepan, and correct seasoning to taste. Keep warm.

To prepare ahead: Through step 1, reheating in a stainless steel bowl or the top of a double boiler set over simmering water.

VEGETABLE CHIPS

Serves 4

INGREDIENTS

1 pound parsnips,
    peeled and trimmed
1 pound carrots, peeled
    and trimmed
1 pound beets, peeled
    and trimmed
½ pound baking
    potato, scrubbed
    clean, but unpeeled
½ pound onion
Peanut oil for deep
    frying
About ½ cup
    all-purpose flour
Salt
Freshly ground pepper

EQUIPMENT

Mandoline or very
    sharp knife
Deep-fat fryer or deep,
    heavy saucepan
Deep-fat thermometer
Slotted spoon

Here again, you can be creative with your choice of vegetables—yams or sweet potatoes, sliced into thin rounds, or julienned leeks, as well as the ones I have chosen below.

1 Cut the parsnips and carrots into 3- to 4-inch lengths. Using a mandoline or a very sharp knife, cut each piece into very thin *lengthwise* slices and set aside.

2 Cut the beets, potato, and onion into very thin round slices. Place the beets and potatoes in separate bowls of cold water to cover. Dry thoroughly before dropping into the hot oil.

3 In a deep-fat fryer or a deep, heavy saucepan, heat about 3 inches of oil to 325 to 350°F. (It's best to use a thermometer for the exact temperature.) Starting with the parsnips, drop a few at a time into the hot oil. Cook until lightly browned, turning to brown both sides, 1 to 2 minutes. Remove with a slotted spoon and drain on a clean towel. Repeat with the carrots, beets, and potatoes. Season lightly with salt and pepper.

4 Place the flour in a large dish. Dredge the onions in the flour, shaking off the excess flour. Fry and drain as above, a few at a time. Season lightly with salt and pepper.

5 Serve warm or at room temperature, a few of each vegetable for each serving.

To prepare ahead: Through step 5, serving at room temperature.

STIR-FRIED VEGETABLES

Serves 2 to 4

INGREDIENTS

1 tablespoon peanut oil
¼ pound Chinese
  snow peas, cut into
  1-inch chunks
2 ounces oyster
  mushrooms, whole
  or cut in half,
  depending upon size
2 ounces shiitake
  mushrooms, whole
  or cut in half, stems
  removed (stems can
  be added to stocks
  for flavor)
2 ounces each red and
  yellow bell pepper
  strips, cut into
  1-inch chunks
½ large Japanese
  eggplant, cut into 6
  or 7 slices
¼ medium bok choy,
  cut into 1-inch
  chunks
5 or 6 broccoli florets
5 young asparagus, cut
  into 1½- to 2-inch
  lengths
⅓ cup Chicken Stock,
  heated (see page 41)
1 tablespoon soy sauce
Salt
Freshly ground pepper

EQUIPMENT

Wok or large skillet

The combination of the oil, stock, and soy sauce produces a glaze for the vegetables. When cooked, the vegetables should be shiny and crispy with no stock remaining in the pan.

1 In a wok or large skillet, heat the oil. Over high heat, stir fry all the vegetables, coating them with the oil. Pour in the stock and the soy sauce and stir until al dente, about 2 minutes longer. Season with salt and pepper to taste, keeping in mind that the soy sauce is salty. Serve immediately.

To prepare ahead: Have all the ingredients cleaned and cut, and cook when ready to serve.

SAUTÉED BABY VEGETABLES

Serves 4

2 tablespoons (1 ounce)
unsalted butter
12 to 15 sugar snap
peas
8 baby carrots, peeled
and trimmed
8 baby yellow squash,
trimmed
1 red bell pepper,
cored, seeded, and
cut into ¼-inch
strips
3 tablespoons Chicken
Stock, heated (see
page 41)
Salt
Freshly ground pepper

10-inch skillet
Slotted spoon

Most vegetables are at their best when they are young. Baby vegetables have the most intense flavor. You can use any combination of vegetables as long as they are fresh and provide a variety of color. Cooking time will vary with size, but cooking them quickly will keep the flavor intact and most of the vitamins will be retained.

1 In a 10-inch skillet, heat the butter until foamy. Over medium heat, sauté the vegetables for 1 or 2 minutes, to coat with the butter. Pour in the stock and season lightly with salt and pepper. Cook for 3 or 4 minutes longer, just until the vegetables are tender but still crispy. Correct seasoning to taste.

2 Remove the vegetables with a slotted spoon and serve with entree of your choice.

To prepare ahead: Have the vegetables cleaned and trimmed. When ready to serve, continue with the recipe.

CELERY ROOT PUREE

Makes about 2 ½ cups

INGREDIENTS

1 celery root (about
   1 ½ pounds), peeled,
   trimmed, and cut
   into 1-inch cubes
1 or 2 small baking
   potatoes (about 4
   ounces), peeled and
   cut into 1-inch cubes
1 teaspoon salt
½ cup heavy cream
2 tablespoons (1 ounce)
   unsalted butter
Freshly ground white
   pepper

EQUIPMENT

Medium saucepan
Strainer
Food mill

To puree the vegetables, use a food mill or sieve. Do not use a food processor or blender.

1 Place the celery root and potato in a medium saucepan and cover with cold water. Season with salt and cook until soft, 15 to 20 minutes. Drain the water and return the celery and potato to the pan. Pour in the cream and simmmer over medium heat, stirring occasionally to prevent sticking, until thickened and most of the cream is absorbed, about 10 minutes.

2 Remove from the heat, stir in the butter, and season with salt and pepper to taste. Puree in a food mill, return to the pan, and keep warm over simmering water. Use as needed.

To prepare ahead: Through step 2, keeping warm over simmering water, stirring occasionally to heat thoroughly.

BLACK BEAN RAGOUT

Serves 4 to 6

2 cups (about ¾ pound) black beans, picked over and rinsed

3 tablespoons olive oil

1 medium (6 ounces) onion, minced

1 garlic clove, minced

Leaves from 3 to 4 sprigs fresh thyme

7 to 8 cups Chicken Stock (see page 41), water, or half stock and half water, heated

1 tablespoon salt

Freshly ground pepper

½ cup tomato concasse

8 large fresh basil leaves, chopped

EQUIPMENT

Large bowl

Strainer

Small skillet

2 ½-quart saucepan

Blender

Pinto, cannellini, or kidney beans can be substituted for the black beans. Dry beans should be soaked overnight, but fresh fava beans, cranberry beans, or flageolets require no soaking and cook very quickly.

1 In a large bowl, place the beans with enough cold water to cover by 2 or 3 inches and let soak overnight. Drain.

2 In a small skillet, heat 1 tablespoon olive oil. Over medium heat, sauté the onion, garlic, and thyme until the onion is translucent, about 5 minutes. Scrape into a 2½-quart saucepan, add the beans, and stir through. Pour in 6 cups of the stock and/or water, season with salt and pepper, and bring to a boil. Lower the heat and simmer until the beans are tender, about 2 hours, stirring often to prevent scorching, adding the remaining liquid as necessary. When the beans are cooked, most of the liquid will have been absorbed.

3 Remove 1 cup of the beans and puree in a blender. Return to the pan, add the tomato concasse, the basil, and the remaining 2 tablespoons of oil and stir through. Correct seasoning to taste and keep warm. Use as needed.

To prepare ahead: Through step 3, the beans can be kept warm or reheated over a low flame.

CREAMY MASHED POTATOES
WITH BROWN ONIONS

Serves 5 or 6

INGREDIENTS

2 ½ pounds baking
   potatoes, peeled and
   cut into chunks
Salt
8 tablespoons (4
   ounces) unsalted
   butter, cut into small
   pieces, at room
   temperature
½ cup heavy cream,
   brought to a boil
Freshly ground white
   pepper
Freshly grated nutmeg
Vegetable oil
½ pound onions, cut
   into thinly sliced
   rings
All-purpose flour

EQUIPMENT

Saucepan large enough
   to hold the potatoes
Strainer
Food mill
Deep-fat fryer or heavy
   saucepan
Stainless steel bowl
Slotted spoon

*If I were to choose my favorite topping for mashed potatoes,
it would be shaved white truffles. But the fried onions, or, if
desired, leeks, are delicious too, adding flavor and texture to
the potatoes.*

1 In a saucepan, cook the potatoes in lightly salted
water to cover, until tender. Drain well.

2 Mash the potatoes through a food mill into a
stainless steel bowl. Stir in the butter and warm cream
and combine thoroughly. Season to taste with salt,
pepper, and nutmeg. Set over simmering water to keep
warm.

3 Meanwhile, in a deep-fat fryer or a deep, heavy
saucepan, heat about 3 inches of oil. Dust the onion
rings with flour and carefully drop into the heated oil.
Cook until golden. Remove with a slotted spoon and
drain on a clean towel. Season lightly with salt.

Presentation: Spoon some of the mashed potatoes onto
5 or 6 warmed plates and top with a few of the
browned onions. Serve immediately.

To prepare ahead: Through step 2, keeping the
potatoes warm over simmering water.

Potato Parsnip Pancakes

Makes 8 pancakes

INGREDIENTS

1 pound baking
  potatoes, peeled
1 pound parsnips,
  peeled
1 teaspoon salt
½ teaspoon freshly
  ground white pepper
2 egg whites
About 2 tablespoons
  unsalted butter,
  melted

EQUIPMENT

8 4-inch nonstick tart
  pans or rings,
  optional
Grater
Medium mixing bowl
Nonstick baking tray

Parsnips have a high sugar content and browning them gives them a caramelized flavor. I recommend using nonstick pans for the best results.

1 Preheat the oven to 375°F.

2 Grate the potatoes and parsnips into a medium bowl and season with salt and pepper. Stir in the egg whites and mix well.

3 Brush 8 4-inch nonstick tart pans or rings with melted butter. Using ½-cup portions, spread the mixture into the prepared pans and brush the tops with melted butter. (For easier handling, place the pans on a baking tray.)

4 Bake 45 minutes, turning after about 25 minutes, to brown and crisp both sides of the pancakes. (Invert the pancakes onto the tray and then return to the pan with a spatula.) Drain on paper towels and serve immediately.

Note: These pancakes also can be made directly on a baking tray. Brush a nonstick baking tray with melted butter and form about ⅓ cup of the mixture into patties. Bake as above, turning with a spatula.

To prepare ahead: In step 4, bake the pancakes about 30 minutes and continue with the recipe at serving time.

CRISP POTATO GALETTE

Serves 4 to 6

INGREDIENTS

1 ½ pounds baking
   potatoes, peeled
2 teaspoons chopped
   fresh thyme
½ teaspoon salt
¼ teaspoon freshly
   ground white pepper
½ cup olive oil

EQUIPMENT

Mandoline
Medium bowl
10-inch non-Teflon
   skillet

The potato galette is served for breakfast at Postrio, but there's no reason why it can't be served at any meal since it goes well with many dishes—grilled chicken, steak, etc.

1 With a mandoline, cut the potatoes into julienne. In a medium bowl, combine the potatoes, thyme, salt, and pepper.

2 In a *non-*Teflon 10-inch skillet, heat the oil to the smoking point. Carefully spread the potatoes into the pan and, over medium heat, cook until you can see them browning around the edges and the galette pulls away from the sides of the skillet. (If the heat is too high, the potatoes won't cook in the middle; if too low, the potatoes will stick to the pan.)

3 When the underside is golden brown and the potatoes hold together, it's time to flip the galette. Using a wide spatula, turn the galette. (If you find this difficult, slide out onto a large plate, browned-side down. Place the skillet over the top and flip back into the skillet, browned-side up.) Cook until golden brown on the second side.

Presentation: Place the potato galette on a heated plate a little larger than the galette. Cut into 4 or 6 wedges and serve immediately. Or you can cut the galette into wedges and serve one slice on each plate with eggs, sausages, chicken, or meat.

To prepare ahead: Through step 3, keeping warm in a low oven. Place the finished galette on a rack set on a baking tray so that some of the oil drips off.

SWEET POTATO CRISP

Serves 10

INGREDIENTS

2 tablespoons unsalted
   butter
½ pound Granny
   Smith apples, peeled,
   cored, quartered,
   and cut into ¼-inch
   slices
1 ¼ pounds sweet
   potatoes or yams,
   peeled and cut into
   thinly sliced rounds,
   about ⅛ inch thick
½ teaspoon salt
½ teaspoon cinnamon
¼ teaspoon freshly
   ground white pepper
½ cup melted unsalted
   butter

EQUIPMENT

10 3-inch tart pans
10-inch skillet
Medium bowl
Baking tray

These next two recipes, combining sweet potatoes and apples, are a natural choice for your holiday dinner, like Thanksgiving or Christmas. At Spago, we like to serve these with squab, venison, or wild turkey.

1 Preheat the oven to 350°F. Butter 10 3-inch nonstick tart pans.

2 In a 10-inch skillet, melt the 2 tablespoons butter. Over medium-high heat, sauté the apples until lightly caramelized, 6 to 8 minutes.

3 Place the sweet potatoes in a medium bowl and season with salt, cinnamon, and pepper. Pour ¼ cup melted butter over and mix well. In each tart pan, arrange a layer of potatoes in a circle, one slice overlapping the other. Divide the apples equally, place on top, and cover with the remaining potatoes, again in a circle, one slice overlapping the other. Pour a little of the remaining ¼ cup melted butter into each pan. For easier handling, set the pans on a baking tray and bake until the potatoes are tender, lightly browned, and crispy, 30 to 35 minutes. Invert the pans of potatoes onto the baking tray and if the underside has not browned, return to the oven for about 5 minutes longer. Serve immediately.

Note: These can be arranged directly on a baking tray if tart pans are not available.

To prepare ahead: In step 3, bake the crisps for about 20 minutes, finishing the baking at serving time.

GRATIN OF SWEET POTATOES

Serves 6

INGREDIENTS

4 tablespoons (2
  ounces) unsalted
  butter
1 pound Granny Smith
  apples, peeled,
  cored, quartered,
  and cut into ¼-inch
  slices
1½ pounds sweet
  potatoes or yams,
  peeled and cut into
  thinly sliced rounds
½ teaspoon salt
½ teaspoon cinnamon
¼ teaspoon freshly
  ground white pepper
Freshly grated nutmeg
1¼ cups heavy cream,
  half and half, or milk
½ cup fresh bread
  crumbs

EQUIPMENT

10-inch skillet
Medium bowl
10-inch gratin dish
Aluminum foil

1. Preheat the oven to 375°F.

2. In a 10-inch skillet, melt 2 tablespoons butter. Over medium-high heat, sauté the apples until slightly caramelized, 6 to 8 minutes.

3. Place the potatoes in a medium bowl and season with salt, cinnamon, pepper, and nutmeg. Pour over the cream and mix well.

4. Butter a 10-inch gratin dish and layer with half the potatoes, one overlapping the other. Cover with the apples and arrange the remaining potatoes on top. Cover the dish with aluminum foil and bake for 1 hour, or until the potatoes are tender. Remove from the oven.

5. Turn the oven to 500°F. Sprinkle the bread crumbs over the potatoes and dot with the remaining 2 tablespoons of butter. Return to the oven to brown, watching carefully to prevent burning. Serve immediately.

To prepare ahead: Through step 4, baking for 30 minutes and continuing with the recipe at serving time.

RATATOUILLE

Serves 4 to 6

½ cup olive oil
1 pound onions, cut
  into 1-inch cubes
1 pound Japanese
  eggplant, trimmed
  and cut into 1-inch
  cubes
1 pound yellow bell
  peppers, cored,
  seeded, and cut into
  1-inch cubes
1 pound plum
  tomatoes, trimmed,
  seeded, and cut into
  1-inch cubes
½ pound zucchini,
  trimmed and cut into
  1-inch cubes
2 garlic cloves, minced
Leaves of 1 large sprig
  of fresh thyme
1 teaspoon salt
½ teaspoon white
  pepper
2 tablespoons sherry
  wine vinegar

4 to 6 basil leaves, cut
  into julienne
3 green onions, white
  part only, cut into
  thin slices

Large skillet
Large mixing bowl

Ratatouille can be used in many different ways. It can be served hot as a vegetable, cold as a salad or appetizer with the addition of olive oil and a good vinegar, or it can be placed under grilled fish or chicken, eliminating the use of a sauce or other vegetable.

1 In a large skillet or saucepan, heat ¼ cup olive oil. Sauté the onion over medium heat until transparent, about 5 minutes. Stir in the remaining vegetables, the garlic, thyme, salt, and pepper. Lower the heat, and cook, covered, for 30 minutes, stirring occasionally to prevent sticking.

2 Transfer to a large bowl and cool to room temperature. Toss with the vinegar, the remaining ¼ cup olive oil, and correct seasoning to taste.

Presentation: When ready to serve, toss the vegetables and transfer to a serving bowl. Sprinkle with the julienne basil and the green onion.

To prepare ahead: Through step 1. Ratatouille should be served at room temperature.

EGGPLANT COMPOTE

Makes about 2 cups

INGREDIENTS

1 pound (about 6 large)
Japanese eggplants
2 tablespoons sesame
oil
1 teaspoon Chinois
Mix (see page 142)
1 tablespoon peanut oil
1 cup (½ large) diced
red onion
½ cup (½ medium)
diced red bell pepper
½ cup (½ medium)
diced yellow bell
pepper
2 tablespoons (¼
small) diced green
bell pepper
½ bunch cilantro,
leaves only, to make
¼ cup
¼ teaspoon salt
Freshly ground pepper

EQUIPMENT

Baking tray
Medium mixing bowl
Wok

At Chinois, Eggplant Compote is served with grilled veal chops, but this complements grilled lamb or chicken as well.

1 Peel and trim the eggplants. Cut in half lengthwise, and arrange on a baking tray. Spoon the sesame oil over the eggplants and season with the Chinois mix. Let marinate for 1 hour.

2 Preheat the oven to 375°F.

3 Bake the eggplants until tender, 35 to 40 minutes. Cool, dice, and transfer to a medium mixing bowl.

4 In a wok, heat the peanut oil. Over medium-high heat, sauté the onion and the red, yellow, and green bell peppers until al dente, about 5 minutes. Cool. Add to the eggplants with the cilantro and season with salt and pepper to taste. Serve at room temperature.

To prepare ahead: Through step 4.

PICKLED EGGPLANT

Each makes about 3 cups

MARINADES

ITALIAN-STYLE

½ cup champagne
  vinegar
½ cup water
3 garlic cloves, crushed
  slightly
1 teaspoon salt
½ teaspoon chili
  pepper flakes
5 sprigs fresh thyme
5 or 6 sprigs fresh basil

THAI-STYLE

½ cup water
¼ cup champagne
  vinegar
¼ cup sushi vinegar*
1 serrano chile,
  quartered, with seeds
½ medium (3 ounces)
  red onion, cut into
  julienne
3 garlic cloves, crushed
  slightly
Juice of 1 lime
½ ounce fresh ginger,
  peeled and cut into
  julienne
1½ tablespoons fish
  sauce*
1 tablespoon black soy
  sauce*
½ teaspoon salt

This can be used as a garnish for sandwiches, but can also be added to salads.

1 For each sauce, combine all the marinade ingredients, except the fresh herbs, in a medium saucepan or skillet and bring to a boil. Boil for 2 or 3 minutes.

2 Meanwhile, peel and trim the eggplant. Cut into thick lengthwise slices, and then cut each slice in half crosswise. Cut into batonnets, about ⅛ inch thick, and place in a mixing bowl.

3 Pour the marinade of your choice over the eggplant, add the fresh herbs, and let marinate for 15 to 20 minutes, tossing every 5 minutes. Refrigerate, covered. When ready to serve, remove the sprigs of herbs.

To prepare ahead: Through step 3, the eggplant can be kept for one week.

*Can be purchased in markets that carry oriental foods.
**To toast, pour the cumin into a small skillet and sauté for a few minutes to bring out the flavor. Watch carefully to prevent burning.

½ teaspoon chili
   pepper flakes
¼ bunch cilantro
5 or 6 sprigs fresh basil
3 sprigs fresh mint

MIDDLE-EASTERN-
STYLE
½ cup champagne
   vinegar
½ cup water
3 garlic cloves, crushed
   slightly
2 teaspoons toasted
   ground cumin**
1 teaspoon salt
½ teaspoon chili
   pepper flakes
Zest of 1 medium
   lemon
½ bunch fresh oregano

About ¾ pound (1
   large) eggplant for
   each marinade

EQUIPMENT

Medium saucepan
Mixing bowl

FRIED SPINACH LEAVES

Wok or deep, heavy
   saucepan
Deep-fat thermometer
Slotted spoon

As a single leaf garnish, you can substitute the Japanese oba leaf, which you can purchase in markets that carry Japanese products.

1 In a wok or a deep, heavy saucepan, heat about 3 inches of peanut oil to 375°F. Clean the spinach leaves well, trim and dry thoroughly. Fry until crisp and translucent, about 2 minutes. Remove with a slotted spoon and drain on clean toweling. Season with salt to taste and serve immediately.

To prepare ahead: Have the spinach cleaned and ready. At serving time, heat the oil and continue with the recipe.

Note: The procedure is the same for small or large quantities. However, if cooking a large amount of spinach, fry in batches and keep warm in a low oven.

COUSCOUS

Serves 8

....

INGREDIENTS

2 tablespoons olive oil
1 tablespoon (½ ounce) unsalted butter
1 cup fine mirepoix (see page 245)
1 tablespoon (4 or 5 cloves) minced garlic
3 cups couscous (the quick kind)
3 cups Chicken Stock, heated (see page 41)
¼ cup chopped fresh mint
Salt
Freshly ground white pepper

EQUIPMENT

Large saucepan or wok

Couscous can be served hot or cold. Hot, with braised meat or fowl and sauce spooned over. Or by adding olive oil, vinegar, and finely chopped fresh herbs, it becomes a delicious salad. Seasoning with cumin, saffron, or turmeric will give this dish a distinctive Middle Eastern flavor.

1 In a large saucepan or a wok, heat the olive oil and butter. Sweat the mirepoix and the garlic for 2 or 3 minutes. Add the couscous and coat well. Pour in the stock and cook for 2 minutes, stirring occasionally. Stir in the mint and mix thoroughly. Season with salt and pepper to taste and keep warm.

To prepare ahead: Through step 1, about 1 hour before serving, keeping warm until needed.

DRESSINGS, SAUCES, AND CONDIMENTS

Spago House Salad Dressing

Chinois Vinaigrette

Tomato-Basil Sauce

Black Pepper Sauce

Black Olive Cabernet Sauce

Chinois Rib Sauce

Cucumber Sauce

Tangerine Sauce

Chinese Mustard

Herb Mustard

Spicy Cinnamon-Chili Paste

Chinois Mix

Spiced Cranberry Relish

Spicy Fruit Chutney

Chili Oil

Cranberry Catsup

Tomato Catsup

Roasted Garlic

Chinois Tomato Sauce

Postrio Fresh Tomato-Vegetable Juice

Strawberry Jam

In the old times a chef's ability was always measured by how well he made his sauces. And as the old Brillat Savarin said, one is born a rotisseur but becomes a saucier. But these days, sauces are used much more as an enhancement for dishes and less as a cover-up! Because of modern transportation and refrigeration, fish, meat, and vegetables can be sent thousands of miles in hours to preserve the freshness; so that when it comes to the actual cooking, there is no need to overwhelm a dish with sauces—instead they can accent and elevate your creations. Dressings should always be well seasoned; sauces should be perfectly reduced just to the right point and maybe finished with a touch of butter. For a vinaigrette, use only the best vinegars and oils; for the diet-conscious, butter can be replaced by adding enough vegetables (carrots, celery and onion) to your reduction, which, when cooked and pureed finely in a blender, will give your sauce a nice consistency as well as a complex flavor.

SPAGO HOUSE SALAD DRESSING

Makes 1 ¼ cups

INGREDIENTS

2 large shallots, minced
  (1 heaping
  tablespoon)
1 tablespoon Dijon
  mustard
2 tablespoons zinfandel
  vinegar
2 tablespoons sherry
  wine vinegar
½ cup olive oil
½ cup vegetable oil
Salt
Freshly ground white
  pepper

EQUIPMENT

Small bowl
Whisk

The foundation of any good vinaigrette is its ingredients. Use only the best. I prefer the extra-virgin olive oils from Italy, the hazelnut and walnut oils from France. I like aged balsamic vinegar, or a good sherry wine or red wine vinegar. To get the best red wine vinegar, combine 3 cups red wine vinegar with 1 cup zinfandel or any other strong red wine. Only freshly ground pepper will be good enough. Dijon or dry powdered mustard, finely minced shallots, and/or fresh herbs give additional body and flavor to your vinaigrette.

1 In a small bowl, whisk together the shallots and the mustard. Whisk in the vinegars and then the olive and vegetable oil. Season with salt and pepper to taste. Transfer to a covered container and refrigerate until needed.

To prepare ahead: Through step 1, the dressing will keep, refrigerated, up to 1 week. If necessary, whisk before using.

CHINOIS VINAIGRETTE

Makes about ¾ cup

INGREDIENTS

¼ cup plus 2
   tablespoons rice
   wine vinegar
¼ cup peanut oil
¼ cup soy sauce
2 tablespoons sesame
   oil
Juice of 1 medium
   lemon
Salt
Freshly ground pepper

EQUIPMENT

Small bowl
Whisk

At Chinois, we combine rice wine vinegar, peanut oil, soy sauce, and sesame oil to give the vinaigrette a distinctive oriental flavor.

1 In a small bowl whisk together all the ingredients, seasoning with salt and pepper to taste. Use as needed.

To prepare ahead: Through step 1, refrigerating, covered, until needed.

TOMATO-BASIL SAUCE

Makes about 2 cups

INGREDIENTS

2 tablespoons olive oil
1 small onion, minced
2 garlic cloves, minced
1 pound plum
  tomatoes, cored,
  seeded, and diced
1 cup Chicken Stock,
  heated (see page 41)
6 to 8 fresh basil leaves
6 tablespoons (3
  ounces) unsalted
  butter, cut into small
  pieces
Salt
Freshly ground pepper

EQUIPMENT

Medium and small
  saucepans
Strainer
Whisk

This sauce goes well with grilled or roasted fish or chicken.

1 In a medium saucepan, heat the olive oil. Sauté the onion over medium-high heat just until wilted, 4 to 5 minutes. Add the garlic and cook 1 minute longer. Stir in the tomatoes, cook 2 or 3 minutes, and pour in the chicken stock. Reduce until the sauce thickens, 15 to 20 minutes. Strain into a clean saucepan.

2 Cut the basil leaves into julienne and add to the sauce. Whisk in the butter, piece by piece, and season to taste with salt and pepper. Keep warm.

To prepare ahead: Through step 2. Cool and refrigerate, covered, until needed. Reheat on a low flame.

BLACK PEPPER SAUCE

Makes 1 cup

INGREDIENTS

2 tablespoons minced
   shallots
½ cup port
1 cup dry red wine
1 cup Brown Veal
   Stock (see page 43)
6 tablespoons (3
   ounces) unsalted
   butter, at room
   temperature, cut into
   small pieces
2 teaspoons cracked
   black pepper
Salt

EQUIPMENT

Two small saucepans
Strainer
Whisk

Always buy whole black peppercorns and grind or crack them as needed for maximum flavor. This sauce goes well with sautéed veal medallions, steak, or squab.

1 In a small saucepan, combine the shallots, port, and red wine. Over medium-high heat, reduce until ½ cup remains. Pour in the stock and continue to reduce until 1 cup remains. Strain into a clean pan.

2 Slowly whisk in the butter, stir in the pepper, and season to taste with salt. Keep warm over simmering water. Use as needed.

To prepare ahead: In step 1, reduce to 1 cup. When ready to serve, reheat over a low flame and continue with the recipe.

Black Olive Cabernet Sauce

Makes about 1 ¼ cups

INGREDIENTS

2 cups cabernet
   sauvignon
½ cup chopped onion
1 tablespoon chopped
   garlic
1 teaspoon chopped
   fresh thyme
1 cup Brown Chicken
   or Veal Stock, plus
   additional as
   necessary (see pages
   42, 43)
½ teaspoon honey
6 tablespoons (3
   ounces) unsalted
   butter, cut into small
   pieces
½ cup niçoise olives,
   pitted* and coarsely
   chopped
Salt
Freshly ground pepper

EQUIPMENT

Two small saucepans
Whisk
Strainer
Rolling pin, optional

I recommend using the small black niçoise olives for this sauce. The sauce will add to the flavor of lamb, steak, chicken, or veal.

① In a small saucepan, combine the wine, onion, garlic, and thyme. Over high heat, reduce by one half. Pour in the stock and continue to reduce until ⅔ cup remains.

② Remove from the heat. Stir in the honey and slowly whisk in the butter. Strain into a clean pan and add the chopped olives. Season to taste with salt and pepper and keep warm. (If the sauce thickens too much, add a little stock.) Use as needed.

To prepare ahead: Through step 2, keeping warm over simmering water. Or reheat over a low flame.

*To make it easier to pit the olives, roll a rolling pin over the olives, then pit them.

CHINOIS RIB SAUCE

Makes about 1⅓ cups

INGREDIENTS

1¼ cups rice wine
 vinegar*
1 cup honey
¾ cup soy sauce
¾ cup mirin*
2 green onions,
 chopped
1 teaspoon minced
 garlic
1 teaspoon chopped
 fresh ginger
¾ teaspoon crushed
 dried chili pepper

EQUIPMENT

4-cup saucepan
Strainer

Not only do we serve this sauce with our spareribs at Chinois, but we stir a little into many of our dishes for additional flavor and color.

1 In a 4-cup enamel or stainless steel saucepan, combine all the ingredients and cook, over medium-high heat, until syrupy, 50 to 60 minutes. Strain into a clean container and cool.

2 Refrigerate, covered, and use as needed.

To prepare ahead: Through step 2, the sauce will keep up to 2 weeks.

*Rice wine vinegar and mirin can be purchased in markets that carry Japanese products.

CUCUMBER SAUCE

Makes about 2 cups

INGREDIENTS

1 Japanese cucumber,
  about 12 ounces
⅓ to ½ cup rice wine
  vinegar
Salt
Freshly ground white
  pepper
2 egg yolks
¼ cup light sesame oil
¼ cup vegetable oil

EQUIPMENT

Melon baller
Blender
Medium bowl
Whisk

I like to serve this with spicy shrimp or scallops. This cool and refreshing sauce is a nice contrast to the pungency of the fish.

1 Cut the cucumber in half lengthwise, scoop out the center containing the seeds, and discard, leaving the entire outer shell. (A melon baller makes scooping out the seeds easy.) Cut the shell into chunks and place in a blender with ⅓ cup vinegar. Puree until smooth and season with salt and pepper to taste. Set aside.

2 In a medium bowl, whisk together the egg yolks and the sesame and vegetable oils. Gradually whisk in enough cucumber puree to give the sauce a nice green color and the consistency of lightly whipped cream. Correct seasoning to taste, adding the remaining vinegar if necessary. Use as needed.

To prepare ahead: Through step 2, refrigerating, covered.

TANGERINE SAUCE

Makes about 2 cups

2 cups fresh tangerine
  juice*
4 shallots, chopped
1 bunch cilantro, leaves
  only
2 teaspoons chopped
  fresh ginger
Juice of 2 limes
1 egg yolk
2 tablespoons sushi
  vinegar**
1 teaspoon soy sauce
1 cup peanut oil

Small saucepan
Blender

This goes well with cold fish, fish salad, barbecued chicken, or duck salad.

❶ In a small saucepan, combine the tangerine juice, chopped shallots, cilantro leaves, and 1 teaspoon chopped ginger. Cook until syrupy and reduced by about ¾.

❷ Scrape the contents of the saucepan into a blender, add the lime juice, egg yolk, sushi vinegar, soy sauce, and the remaining 1 teaspoon chopped ginger and blend until well combined.

❸ With the motor running, gradually pour the peanut oil into the blender until smooth. Pour into a jar and refrigerate, covered, until needed.

To prepare ahead: Through step 3, the sauce will keep, refrigerated, for up to 1 week.

*Orange juice can be substituted for the tangerine juice.
**Can be purchased in markets that carry oriental products.

CHINESE MUSTARD

Makes about 2 cups

INGREDIENTS

1 cup (1 bunch) packed
   cilantro, leaves only
2 jalapeño peppers,
   with seeds, cut into
   chunks
3 garlic cloves
2½ inches (about 2
   ounces) ginger root,
   peeled and cut into
   chunks
½ cup vegetable oil
1 cup Dijon mustard
1 tablespoon honey

EQUIPMENT

Blender
Small bowl
Whisk

You can experiment making your own flavored mustards by varying the fresh herbs and spices to your taste.

1 In a blender, puree the cilantro, jalapeños, garlic, ginger, and oil until smooth. Scrape into a small bowl.

2 Whisk in the mustard and the honey. Refrigerate, covered, until needed.

To prepare ahead: Through step 2, the mustard will keep 2 or 3 months.

HERB MUSTARD

Makes about 1 ¾ cups

INGREDIENTS

¼ cup chopped parsley
(leaves from about
½ bunch parsley)
2 tablespoons chopped
fresh chives
2 tablespoons chopped
fresh thyme leaves
1 cup whole-grain
mustard
½ cup Dijon mustard

EQUIPMENT

Small bowl
Whisk

1 In a small bowl, combine the parsley, chives, thyme, and whole-grain mustard and mix well. Whisk in the Dijon mustard until smooth. Refrigerate, covered, until needed.

To prepare ahead: Through step 1, the mustard will keep 2 or 3 months.

Spicy Cinnamon-Chili Paste

Makes about 1 ½ cups

1 pound (2 or 3) red
   bell peppers, cored,
   cut in half, and
   seeded
2 jalapeño peppers,
   cored
1 bunch cilantro
12 garlic cloves
1 tablespoon ground
   cinnamon
1 tablespoon coriander
About ½ teaspoon salt

EQUIPMENT

Heavy aluminum foil
Baking tray
Food processor or
   blender

I use this paste to perk up marinades or sauces.

① Preheat the oven to 500°F.

② Place all of the ingredients, *except the salt*, in a large piece of heavy aluminum foil. Wrap securely and airtight, place on a baking tray, and bake 45 minutes, until the peppers are tender.

③ Unwrap the package, being careful that the steam does not burn you, and puree the ingredients in a food processor or blender. Season with salt to taste and cool.

④ Use as needed.

To prepare ahead: Through step 3, the paste, tightly covered, can be refrigerated for up to 1 month and frozen for up to 3 months.

Note: 1 or 2 tablespoons in tomato sauce will perk up the sauce. Combined with olive oil, it makes a pungent marinade for fish.

CHINOIS MIX

Makes about 1 cup

INGREDIENTS

5 ounces ginger, peeled and cut into 1-inch chunks
4 ounces peeled garlic (about 15 large cloves)
Stems of 2 green onions, minced
2 teaspoons Chinese pepper flakes*

EQUIPMENT

Blender

If you like spicy, well-seasoned food, you can sprinkle this mixture on almost any seafood or poultry before cooking. Or you can combine the mix with a sauce or lemon butter just before serving.

1 In a blender, chop the ginger and garlic. Scrape onto a board and continue to chop until fine, adding the green onions and the pepper flakes, and combining well.

2 Transfer to a covered jar and refrigerate until needed.

To prepare ahead: Through step 2, the mix will keep, refrigerated, for up to 1 week.

Note: This can be used to flavor chicken or fish as well as vegetables.

*Can be purchased in markets that carry oriental products.

SPICED CRANBERRY RELISH

Serves 6 to 8

INGREDIENTS

Peel and juice of 1
medium orange
Peel and juice of ½
medium lemon
3 cups port
1 package (12 ounces)
fresh cranberries,
washed
½ medium red onion,
diced
1 ounce fresh ginger,
peeled and cut into
julienne
3 tablespoons dark
brown sugar
1 teaspoon salt
1 teaspoon white
pepper
½ teaspoon ground
cinnamon
2 tablespoons Grand
Marnier

EQUIPMENT

Small saucepan
Medium saucepan

My version of the traditional cranberry sauce. It goes especially well with the conventional roasted turkey and also with quail, pheasant, duck, or game.

1 Cut the orange and lemon peels into julienne. In a small saucepan, heat the juices and ½ cup port. Over medium-high heat, cook the peels until tender, about 10 minutes. Reserve.

2 In a medium saucepan, combine the cranberries, onion, 2 cups port, ginger, brown sugar, salt, pepper, and cinnamon. Over medium-high heat, cook until the relish thickens, 15 to 20 minutes, stirring occasionally. Stir in the remaining ½ cup port, the Grand Marnier, and the reserved orange and lemon peel mixture. Cool. Transfer to a serving bowl and refrigerate, covered, until needed.

To prepare ahead: Through step 2, the relish will keep up to 1 week.

Note: You may want to garnish your turkey with julienned orange and lemon peel. If so, increase the number of oranges to 2 and use 1 whole lemon. Remove the extra peel before adding to the relish.

SPICY FRUIT CHUTNEY

Makes about 4 cups

INGREDIENTS

1 teaspoon olive oil
½ medium (about 4 ounces) red bell pepper, cored, seeded, and cut into brunoise
1 jalapeño pepper, cored, seeded, and cut into brunoise
½ large (about 6 ounces) red onion, cut into brunoise
¼ cup plus 2 teaspoons brown sugar, packed
1 tablespoon fresh ginger, peeled and cut into brunoise
1 large garlic clove, cut into brunoise
½ cup currants
¼ teaspoon dry mustard

I like to keep this handy in my refrigerator to serve with grilled foods. The longer it stands, the more intense the flavor becomes.

1 In a large stainless steel or enamel saucepan, heat the olive oil. Stir in the red pepper, jalapeño, onion, 2 teaspoons brown sugar, ginger, and garlic and, over medium heat, simmer, stirring occasionally, until the vegetables are wilted, 6 to 8 minutes.

2 Stir in the currants, the remaining ¼ cup brown sugar, mustard, cayenne, turmeric, salt, and vinegar and continue to cook 10 minutes longer. Add the apples, cook 2 minutes, then the peaches, and last of all, the pears. Cook until the fruit is tender (the firmer fruit is added first). Correct seasoning to taste and cool. Transfer to one or two containers and refrigerate, covered, until needed. Serve with grilled or roasted meat or chicken.

To prepare ahead: Through step 2, the chutney will keep for up to 3 weeks, refrigerated.

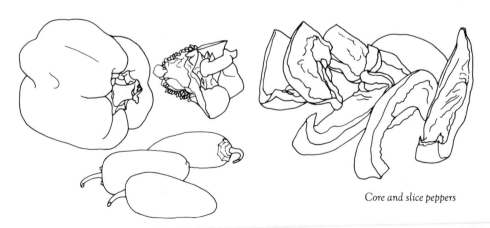

Core and slice peppers

¼ teaspoon cayenne
   pepper
¼ teaspoon turmeric
¼ teaspoon salt
¾ cup champagne
   vinegar
1 pound (2 medium)
   apples, peeled,
   seeded, and cut into
   brunoise
1 pound (2 to 3)
   peaches, blanched,
   peeled, pitted, and
   cut into brunoise
½ pound (1 large)
   pears, peeled, cored,
   and cut into
   brunoise

EQUIPMENT

Large saucepan
Large wooden spoon

Julienne

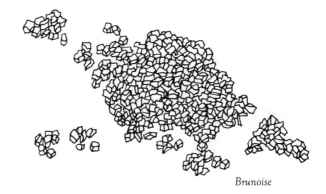

Brunoise

CHILI OIL

Makes 1 cup

INGREDIENTS

1 cup peanut or olive
   oil
¼ cup dried chili
   pepper flakes

EQUIPMENT

Small saucepan

❶ In a small saucepan, heat the oil. Stir in the chili pepper flakes and remove from the heat. Cool. Store in a covered jar and use as needed.

To prepare ahead: Through step 1.

CRANBERRY CATSUP

Makes about 1 ½ cups

1 pound fresh
   cranberries, rinsed
½ small (2 ounces)
   onion, diced
¼ cup plus 1
   tablespoon packed
   brown sugar
½ cup cider vinegar
Peel of 1 medium
   orange, chopped fine
1 large garlic clove
1 ½ teaspoons salt
1 teaspoon pickling
   spice

Medium saucepan
Wooden spoon
Food mill

This catsup is thick and tart. I serve it with chicken or turkey picatta, squab, or venison. Since fresh cranberries can be frozen, this can be made all year round.

1 In a medium stainless steel or enamel saucepan, combine all the ingredients. Cook over a low flame, stirring often, until thick and almost smooth, 25 to 30 minutes. There is very little liquid used so you must be careful of scorching.

2 Strain through a food mill. Cool and refrigerate in a covered container until needed.

To prepare ahead: Through step 2, catsup will keep up to 3 weeks.

Tomato Catsup

Makes about 2 cups

2 pounds ripe (about 5 or 6 medium) tomatoes, rinsed and diced

2 large garlic cloves, smashed

½ small (4 ounces) onion, diced

¼ large (1 ounce) red bell pepper, diced

½ cup plus 2 tablespoons light corn syrup

½ cup plus 2 tablespoons cider vinegar

1 tablespoon salt

2 teaspoons pickling spices

¼ cup tomato paste

EQUIPMENT

Medium saucepan
Wooden spoon
Food mill

At Postrio, we make our own catsup, to the delight of our customers. The length of time it takes for the catsup to thicken depends upon the water content of the tomatoes. So be patient—it really is worth the wait. Try this only when you can get flavorful, vine-ripened tomatoes.

1 In a medium stainless steel or enamel saucepan, over a low flame, cook the tomatoes and garlic until the sauce begins to bubble. Add the onion and red pepper and cook 1 or 2 minutes. Stir in the corn syrup, vinegar, salt, and pickling spices and continue to simmer over the low flame until the sauce reduces and thickens, about 1½ hours, stirring occasionally. (The sauce will reduce by about one half.) Do not rush. Cook over a low flame to prevent scorching.

2 Strain through a food mill and stir in the tomato paste. Correct seasoning to taste, cool, and refrigerate in a covered container until needed. The catsup will thicken slightly as it cools, but it is not the consistency of store-bought catsup.

To prepare ahead: Through step 2, the catsup will keep up to three weeks.

ROASTED GARLIC

Makes about 1 cup

5 to 6 ounces peeled
  garlic cloves
2 tablespoons Chili Oil
  (see page 145)

Heavy ovenproof pan

*Roasted garlic can be tossed in salads, scattered throughout
your pasta, or sprinkled over cooked fish or chicken. Watch
the garlic as it browns—when too brown, it takes on a bitter
taste.*

1 Preheat oven to 500°F.

2 Cut each garlic clove into thick slices. Spoon 1
tablespoon chili oil into a heavy ovenproof pan and
arrange the cloves in a single layer. Drizzle with the
remaining 1 tablespoon oil. Roast about 20 minutes,
stirring occasionally, until lightly browned and crispy.
Use as needed.

To prepare ahead: Through step 2.

CHINOIS TOMATO SAUCE

Makes about 4 cups

INGREDIENTS

2 ½ pounds plum
   tomatoes, cut into
   chunks
1 jalapeño pepper,
   cored and seeded
½ bunch cilantro
½ large red bell
   pepper, cored,
   seeded, and cut into
   chunks
4 or 5 garlic cloves
½ cup minced (4 or 5
   large) shallots
Salt

EQUIPMENT

Blender
Medium mesh strainer
Large bowl

We use this at Chinois. Adding a little olive oil, salt, and pepper will give you a salsa that can be used for seviche or sautéed fish salads.

① In a blender, puree the tomatoes, jalapeño, cilantro, red pepper, and garlic. (This may have to be done in two batches.) Strain through a medium mesh strainer, pressing down to extract all the sauce, into a large bowl and stir in the minced shallots. Refrigerate, covered, until needed, up to one week.

To prepare ahead: Through step 1, the sauce can be frozen in small quantities. Defrost, refrigerated, overnight.

POSTRIO FRESH TOMATO-VEGETABLE JUICE

Makes about 1 quart

3 pounds very ripe
    tomatoes
1 small (about 2
    ounces) parsnip
1 medium (about 2
    ounces) carrot
1 stalk (about 2
    ounces) celery
2 peeled (about 1
    ounce) shallots
12 sprigs Italian parsley
2 tablespoons tomato
    paste
¾ teaspoon sugar
½ teaspoon freshly
    ground pepper
½ teaspoon salt

Blender
Fine strainer
Medium bowl

*Our homemade version of V-8 juice. I love it as a mix for
Bloody Marys.*

1 Wash all the vegetables and coarsely chop into
1-inch cubes.

2 Combine the chopped vegetables with all the
remaining ingredients and puree in a blender until
completely smooth. (You will have to do this in two
batches.) Strain into a bowl through a fine strainer,
pressing down to squeeze out all the juices.

3 Correct seasoning to taste and refrigerate in a
covered container until needed.

To prepare ahead: Through step 3 will keep up to 1
week.

STRAWBERRY JAM

Makes 2 cups

INGREDIENTS

2 boxes (about 1½
    pounds) strawberries,
    trimmed
1 vanilla bean
Pinch of salt
¾ cup sugar

EQUIPMENT

Medium saucepan
Wooden spoon

Once you sample your own homemade jam, it will be difficult to buy jarred jams.

1 Rinse the berries, cut in half if desired, and place in a medium enamel or stainless steel saucepan. Split the vanilla bean down the center and scrape into the pan along with the salt. Over a medium flame, cook until reduced by half, about 20 minutes, stirring occasionally and skimming any foam that settles on top. (The berries give off their own juice.) Stir in the sugar and cook until 2 cups remain (as the jam cools, it thickens slightly). Or if you like a thicker jam, reduce a little more, watching carefully to prevent scorching. Transfer to a clean jar and cool. Refrigerate, covered, until needed.

To prepare ahead: Through step 1, the jam will keep, refrigerated, for up to 1 month.

BREAKFASTS, BRUNCHES, AND BREADS

Postrio Pancake Batter

Sourdough Starter for Waffles

Sourdough Waffles

Fritter Batter

Holiday Pancakes with Smoked Fish

Granola

Smoked Salmon Hash Topped with Guacamole

Poached Egg on Sausage Patty with Spicy Salsa

Breakfast Steak with Red Bell Pepper Relish

Corned Beef Hash

Olive-French Bread

Spago 6-Grain Country Bread

Black Pepper Scones

Buttermilk Biscuits

Walking into a home filled with the warm smells of coffee brewing, sausage patties sizzling in the pan, and waffles baking makes one feel instantly comfortable. For many people, breakfast is the most important meal of the day, and often the only hot one eaten. It would be difficult to dash out of the house with nothing more than a doughnut under the belt if there was a tempting bowl of granola or a stack of hot pancakes waiting on the table.

For me, brunch is a pleasurable way to entertain on any given Saturday, Sunday, or holiday. Served late morning into early afternoon, it combines breakfast and lunch and is a leisurely experience, casual and easy. Since my kitchen at home is warm and inviting, not filled with trendy electrical appliances, I find my friends like to congregate in the kitchen.

Usually, I prepare a few dishes, set them out on the buffet and allow people to help themselves. If I'm making pancakes and/or waffles, I have the batter ready, the griddle and waffle iron heating, and spoon the batter out on demand. Sometimes I fold berries into the batter, other times I fill my nicest bowl with an assortment of warm poached fruit.

And to make the brunch even more festive, I like to serve chilled champagne poured over fresh orange juice or peach juice.

POSTRIO PANCAKE BATTER

Makes 12 3½-inch pancakes

INGREDIENTS

2 eggs, separated
½ cup sour cream
½ cup nonfat milk
½ cup (4 ounces)
    unsalted butter,
    melted
½ cup pastry flour
½ cup all-purpose
    flour
1 tablespoon sugar
½ teaspoon baking
    powder
½ teaspoon salt

EQUIPMENT

1 small bowl, 2 larger
    bowls
Whisk
Griddle
¼-cup measure

At 4:00 A.M. every morning, the kitchen at Postrio sets up for breakfast that begins at 7:00 A.M. The batter is made fresh every day; the pancakes are thick and tender.

1 In a small bowl, whisk together the egg yolks, sour cream, milk, and melted butter.

2 In a larger bowl, sift together the pastry and all-purpose flours, sugar, baking powder, and salt. Make a well in the center, pour the egg-yolk mixture into the well, and whisk just enough to incorporate into the dry ingredients.

3 In a clean bowl, with a clean whisk, whip the egg whites until shiny and firm, but not dry. Stir a little into the batter, then fold in the remaining whites.

4 Heat the griddle and butter lightly. Over medium heat, using a ¼-cup measure, pour the batter onto the griddle. When each pancake is golden brown on one side, turn with a wide spatula and brown the other side. As the pancakes are cooked, transfer to a tray lined with a clean towel and keep warm in a low oven.

Presentation: Arrange 3 or 4 pancakes on a warm plate. Serve with warmed pure maple syrup or Fruit Syrup (see Note below). Garnish with a few slices of seasonal fruit and serve immediately.

To prepare ahead: Through step 3, placing the bowl in an ice-water bath. You can prepare the batter 1 or 2 hours before you want to make the pancakes. Whisk when ready to serve.

Note: To make fruit syrup, combine 1 part fruit (blueberries, sliced strawberries, or any other berry, sliced peaches, or plums) with 3 parts maple syrup and a little grated orange rind. The fruit can be pureed, if desired. Serve warm.

SOURDOUGH STARTER FOR WAFFLES

Makes about 4 cups

INGREDIENTS

3 cups all-purpose flour
2 cups nonfat milk
1 cup plain yogurt
1 small potato, peeled
  and finely grated

EQUIPMENT

Medium bowl

Sourdough starter can be kept going indefinitely if "fed" properly. When you take out 1 ½ or 2 cups of the starter, replace with 1 ½ or 2 cups of flour and 1 ½ or 2 cups of milk. This should be done at least every two weeks and the starter kept refrigerated in a covered container. However, if not "fed" properly, the starter may acquire a pinkish color and should be discarded and a new starter developed.

1 In a medium bowl, combine all the ingredients until smooth. Cover with a clean towel and set in a warm place, until the batter begins to bubble and has a somewhat pleasant sour smell, about 24 hours.

2 Place in a covered container and refrigerate for at least 3 days before using.

SOURDOUGH WAFFLES

Makes 5 8-inch waffles

INGREDIENTS

1 ½ cups Sourdough
  Starter (see page 156)
½ cup nonfat milk
8 tablespoons (4
  ounces) unsalted
  butter, melted
1 egg
1 cup all-purpose flour
2 tablespoons sugar
1 ½ teaspoons baking
  powder
¼ teaspoon salt

EQUIPMENT

2 bowls, small and
  large
Sifter
Waffle iron
4-ounce ladle

1 In a large bowl, combine the starter, milk, melted butter, and egg.

2 In a small bowl, sift together the flour, sugar, baking powder, and salt. Add to the starter mixture and stir until well combined. Let proof, covered, in a warm spot until bubbles begin to form, about ½ hour.

3 Heat the waffle iron. Using a 4-ounce ladle, ladle the batter into the waffle iron and bake until golden brown. Repeat with the remaining batter. Serve immediately.

Presentation: Place one 8-inch waffle on each of 5 heated plates. Serve warm with warm maple syrup or fruit syrup (see Note page 155). Garnish with fresh fruit, such as sliced oranges, peaches, berries. Serve immediately.

To prepare ahead: Through step 2, the batter can be made the night before, refrigerated, covered, then brought to room temperature and proofed when needed.

FRITTER BATTER

Makes about 2 cups

INGREDIENTS

1 cup all-purpose flour
1 tablespoon baking
    powder
Salt
Freshly ground white
    pepper
¼ teaspoon ground
    cinnamon
Freshly grated nutmeg
1 egg
1 cup buttermilk

EQUIPMENT

Medium and small
    bowls
Sifter
Whisk
Slotted spoon

This is enough batter for 1 pound of apples and 1 pound of bananas. The bananas should not be too ripe for best results.

1 In a medium bowl, sift together the flour, baking powder, a dash of salt and pepper, cinnamon, and the nutmeg to taste.

2 In a small bowl, whisk together the egg and the buttermilk. Whisk into the flour mixture until smooth. Let rest for 30 minutes. Use as needed.*

To prepare ahead: Through step 2.

Presentation: Arrange one or two bunches of batonnets and/or a few chunks of bananas on a plate. Dust with sifted powdered sugar and serve immediately. You can serve with fruit syrup (see Note page 155) or Strawberry Jam (see page 151).

Note: The apple batonnets, dusted with sugar, go well with squab.

*At Postrio, the apples (red or golden delicious) are peeled, cored, and cut into batonnets. Bunches of batonnets are dropped into the batter, coated well, then carefully placed in hot peanut or vegetable oil until golden. They are removed with a slotted spoon to drain on a clean towel. (See any recipe for deep frying.)
   Cut the bananas into 3-inch diagonal chunks, dip the chunks into the batter and fry as above. Drain the fruit on a clean towel.

HOLIDAY PANCAKES WITH SMOKED FISH

Serves 8 to 10

PANCAKE BATTER

2 cups all-purpose flour
1 teaspoon baking
    powder
3 eggs, separated
1½ cups buttermilk
6 tablespoons (3
    ounces) unsalted
    butter, melted
5 tablespoons vegetable
    oil
1 cup diced onions
2 heaping tablespoons
    chopped fresh dill
1½ teaspoons salt
1½ teaspoons white
    pepper

About 1 cup sour
    cream
2 tablespoons chopped
    fresh dill
Salt
Freshly ground white
    pepper
4 to 5 ounces smoked
    salmon, whitefish, or
    sturgeon, cut into
    paper-thin slices
Fresh lemon juice
8 to 10 dill sprigs for
    garnish

This pancake is not to be served with syrup or fresh berries, but goes well with smoked fish, caviar, or salmon roe.

1 *Prepare the pancake batter:* In a small bowl, sift together the flour and baking powder. Reserve.

2 In a separate bowl, whisk together the egg yolks, buttermilk, and 3 tablespoons melted butter. Reserve.

3 In a medium skillet, heat 2 tablespoons of the oil. Over medium-high heat, sauté the onions until golden, 6 to 8 minutes. Transfer to a large bowl, cool slightly, and stir in the dill. Stir in the flour mixture, salt, and then the egg yolk mixture.

4 Using a wire whisk or an electric mixer, whisk the egg whites until shiny and firm but not dry. Stir a little into the batter, then fold in the remaining whites.

5 In a small bowl, whisk together the sour cream and dill and season with salt and pepper to taste. Refrigerate until needed.*

6 In a small bowl, combine the remaining 3 tablespoons melted butter with the remaining 3 tablespoons oil. Heat a 10-inch nonstick skillet or griddle and brush with some of the butter mixture. For each pancake, pour ½ cup of batter onto the griddle and, over a medium flame, cook until brown on one side. Turn and brown the other side, brushing the skillet or griddle with the butter mixture as necessary. (This makes a pancake approximately 6 inches in diameter.) As the pancakes are cooked, transfer to a tray lined with a clean towel and keep warm in a low oven while preparing the remaining pancakes.

(Continued)

2 or 3 small bowls and
   a large bowl
Sifter
Whisk or electric
   mixer
Medium skillet
Pastry brush
10-inch nonstick skillet
   or griddle

Presentation: Place one pancake on each of 8 or 10 heated plates. Spread some of the sour cream mixture over the pancake and arrange a slice of smoked fish on the cream. Squeeze a little lemon juice over the fish and garnish with a sprig of dill. Serve immediately.

To prepare ahead: Through step 4, keeping the batter chilled in a bowl of ice water.

Note: You can also make smaller pancakes, using 2 tablespoons of batter, making 2½-inch pancakes. You can cut the smoked fish into smaller pieces or chop and stir into the cream as above.

*Salmon can be chopped, stirred into the sour cream, and spread over the pancake as above.

GRANOLA

Makes 2½ pounds, about 10 cups

1 pound rolled oats
   (*not* the quick oats)
¼ pound sliced (about
   1 cup) blanched
   almonds
¼ pound raw whole
   (about ¾ cup)
   cashews
½ cup brown sugar or
   ⅓ cup honey
1 tablespoon chopped
   orange zest
1 teaspoon ground
   cinnamon
½ teaspoon freshly
   grated nutmeg

Granola generally is eaten for breakfast with milk, but I like to eat it in the afternoon as a snack with a cup of tea.

❶ Preheat the oven to 325°F. *Lightly* butter two baking pans, each 12 × 17 inches. (The granola fits this size pan perfectly.)

❷ In an electric mixer, fitted with a paddle and on the lowest speed, combine the oats, almonds, cashews, sugar, orange zest, cinnamon, and nutmeg. Mix for 1 minute.

❸ Meanwhile, in a small saucepan, melt the butter with the maple syrup. Pour into the oat mixture and mix just until absorbed. Scrape into one of the prepared pans, spread and pat down evenly over the entire pan, making a layer about ½ inch thick.

½ pound (2 sticks)
 unsalted butter, cut
 into pieces
⅓ cup pure maple
 syrup
1 cup unsweetened
 shredded coconut,
 toasted*
¼ pound (about 1 cup)
 coarsely chopped
 dried fruit of your
 choice, such as dates,
 raisins, apricots,
 cherries, etc.

EQUIPMENT

Electric mixer with
 paddle
2 baking trays, 12 × 17
 inches
Small saucepan
Large bowl

④ Bake 45 to 55 minutes, inverting halfway through. To invert, remove the pan from the oven, lay the second pan over to fit exactly and turn. Scrape off any particles that stick to the first pan and pat back down on the layer of granola. (You don't want to break up the granola until it is cool.) Return to the oven and continue baking until the granola is golden brown and sticks together.

⑤ Remove from the oven and cool completely. Break into chunks in a large bowl and stir in the toasted coconut and dried fruits, distributing them as evenly as you can through the granola. Transfer to a well-sealed container and use as needed.

To prepare ahead: Through step 5 will keep up to 1 week.

*Unsweetened coconut can be purchased in health food stores.
 To toast the coconut, spread in an ovenproof pan and place in the oven while the granola is baking, watching carefully to prevent burning. It should take about 10 minutes.

SMOKED SALMON HASH TOPPED WITH GUACAMOLE

Serves 4

INGREDIENTS

3 tablespoons olive oil plus additional as necessary
¾ cup diced red onion
1 cup diced red bell pepper
1½ cups peeled and diced red rose potatoes
Salt
Freshly ground white pepper
½ pound smoked salmon, coarsely chopped
1 tablespoon minced fresh dill
4 eggs

GUACAMOLE
½ medium ripe avocado or 1 small avocado
½ small jalapeño pepper, seeded and minced
¼ teaspoon chopped cilantro
Juice of half a lemon
Salt
Freshly ground white pepper

If desired, smoked ham or leftover roast beef may be substituted for the smoked salmon.

1 In a small skillet, heat 1 tablespoon oil. Over medium heat, sauté the onion and red bell pepper until tender, 3 to 4 minutes. Transfer to a medium bowl.

2 In a small nonstick skillet, heat 1 tablespoon oil. Over medium heat, sauté the potatoes until tender, covering the pan, about 5 minutes. Potatoes will be lightly browned. Season with salt and pepper to taste and add to the onions and peppers. Cool. Stir in the salmon and the dill and correct seasoning to taste. Whisk the eggs and add to the bowl. Mix well.

3 *Meanwhile, prepare the guacamole:* Scoop out the inside of the avocado into a small bowl and mash well. Stir in the remaining ingredients, season with salt and pepper to taste, and set aside.

4 In a small nonstick skillet, heat the remaining tablespoon of oil. Using ½-cup portions, pour the smoked salmon mixture into the skillet and cook until browned on one side, about 2 minutes. Turn and brown the other side, using more oil as necessary. Transfer to a heated platter and keep warm. Repeat with remaining egg mixture.

5 Toss the lettuce with a little vinaigrette.

2 cups thinly sliced
romaine lettuce
2 to 3 tablespoons
Chinois Vinaigrette
(see page 132)
Cilantro leaves for
garnish

EQUIPMENT

Small skillet
Small nonstick skillet
Small and medium
bowls
½-cup ladle or
measuring cup

Presentation: Divide the lettuce and arrange in the center of each of 4 plates. Place two smoked salmon cakes on the lettuce and top with some guacamole. Garnish with cilantro and serve immediately.

To prepare ahead: In step 2, prepare the potatoes, onion, and peppers, and combine with the salmon and dill. Have the guacamole ingredients ready to be combined and continue with the recipe at serving time.

POACHED EGG ON SAUSAGE PATTY WITH SPICY SALSA

Serves 4

INGREDIENTS

1½ pounds bulk
sausage meat (See
Note below)
2 tablespoons chopped
fresh herbs, such as
chives, parsley, and
thyme leaves
3 garlic cloves, minced

If poaching eggs seems too complicated, you can fry the eggs, sunny-side up, and keep warm.

1 Combine the sausage meat with the fresh herbs and garlic, and mix well. Form 4 6-ounce patties and refrigerate until needed.

2 *Prepare the salsa:* In a medium bowl, combine the tomatoes, onion, jalapeño, and ¼ cup chopped cilantro with the lime juice and olive oil. Season with salt and pepper to taste. Set aside.

(Continued)

SPICY SALSA

2 medium (about 10
  ounces) tomatoes,
  seeded and diced
½ medium red onion,
  diced
1 jalapeño pepper,
  cored, seeded, and
  diced
¼ cup chopped
  cilantro plus 8 sprigs
  for garnish
Juice of 2 medium
  limes
1 tablespoon olive oil
Salt
Freshly ground pepper

CILANTRO CREAM

4 tablespoons sour
  cream
2 tablespoons heavy
  cream
1 tablespoon chopped
  cilantro

2 tablespoons white
  wine vinegar
4 eggs
2 teaspoons olive oil

EQUIPMENT

Medium and small
  bowl
Wide saucepan
Ovenproof skillet
Slotted spoon

3 *Prepare the cilantro cream:* In a small bowl, stir together the sour cream, heavy cream, and 1 tablespoon chopped cilantro, and season with salt and pepper to taste. Refrigerate, covered, until needed.

4 Preheat the oven to 400°F.

5 In an ovenproof skillet large enough to hold the four patties in one layer, heat 2 teaspoons olive oil. Sear both sides of the patties and then transfer to the oven. Bake 10 minutes. Drain on clean toweling.

6 *Meanwhile, poach the eggs**: In a wide saucepan, bring to a boil 1 quart of water. Add the vinegar and reduce the heat, bringing the water down to a simmer. Break the eggs, one at a time, into a small saucer or cup and slide carefully into the simmering water. Cook 3 to 4 minutes. The yolks should still be soft and the whites firm to the touch. With a slotted spoon, remove the eggs to a plate lined with a towel and keep warm.

Presentation: Place 1 sausage patty in the center of each of 4 warmed plates. Carefully drop one poached egg on each patty and top with a dollop of the cilantro cream. Surround with the salsa and garnish with sprigs of cilantro. Serve immediately.

To prepare ahead: Through step 3.

Note: If you can't find bulk sausage meat, remove the meat from the casing of link sausages.

*To prepare poached eggs in advance, see page 166.

BREAKFAST STEAK WITH RED BELL PEPPER RELISH

Serves 3 to 4

INGREDIENTS

1 medium (4 ounces)
  onion, minced
1 red bell pepper (4
  ounces), cored,
  seeded, and diced
tablespoons chopped
  fresh herbs, such as
  chives, parsley, and
  tarragon, plus a few
  sprigs for garnish
2 tablespoons red wine
  vinegar
¼ cup plus 1 teaspoon
  olive oil
Salt
Freshly ground pepper
1 medium (about 5
  ounces) potato,
  peeled and cut into
  ½-inch cubes
1 12-ounce New York
  steak
6 eggs
3 tablespoons (1 ½
  ounces) unsalted
  butter

EQUIPMENT

Small bowl
Nonstick medium pan
Small skillet
Pastry brush
Sauté pan or grill
Medium bowl
10-inch skillet

*This is an elegant version of the traditional roast beef hash.
If you omit the eggs, this can be served for supper, the
onion, peppers, and potatoes accompanying the steak.*

1 *Prepare the relish:* In a small bowl, combine ¼ of the
minced onion, ¼ of the diced red pepper, the chopped
herbs, vinegar, and 2 tablespoons olive oil. Season with
salt and pepper to taste and set aside.

2 In a nonstick pan, heat 1 tablespoon olive oil. Sauté
the potatoes over medium heat until browned and
tender, 10 to 12 minutes. Keep warm.

3 In a small skillet, heat 1 tablespoon olive oil. Sauté
the remaining onion and pepper over medium-high heat
until the pepper is tender but still crisp, 4 to 5 minutes.
Keep warm.

4 Season the steak with salt and pepper and brush
with the remaining 1 teaspoon of olive oil. Cook over
high heat in a sauté pan or on a preheated grill to
desired degree of doneness.

5 In a medium bowl, whisk the eggs with a little salt
and pepper. Stir in the cooked onion, peppers, and
potatoes. Over moderate heat, melt the butter in a
10-inch skillet. Pour in the potato-egg mixture and
scramble. Do not overcook. Correct seasoning to taste.

Presentation: Cut the steak into thin slices and fan the
slices around the edge of a warmed serving plate.
Arrange the scrambled eggs in the center and garnish
with the herb sprigs. Spoon the relish over the meat.

To prepare ahead: Through step 1. Have all the
remaining ingredients ready and continue with the
recipe at serving time.

CORNED BEEF HASH

Serves 6

INGREDIENTS

6 tablespoons (3 ounces) unsalted butter

About 1½ pounds red or white rose potatoes, peeled, to make 4 cups diced potatoes

⅔ cup diced (½ large) red or yellow bell pepper

⅔ cup diced (½ medium) red onion

⅔ cup diced (1 medium) white part of leek

4 to 5 pounds cooked, trimmed corned beef,* diced to make 5 or 6 cups

1 tablespoon plus 1 teaspoon chopped fresh herbs (thyme, chives, basil)

Freshly ground pepper

Salt

1 or 2 poached eggs per person

Though my parents were rather poor, one of my childhood favorites was corned beef hash. You had to look hard to find the meat, but since we raised chickens, eggs were in abundance. We children always had at least two eggs with the hash; my father would have six—and he still has no problem with his cholesterol.

1 In 1 or 2 skillets or a large wok, melt the butter. Over medium heat, sauté the potatoes, bell pepper, onion, and leek for about 5 minutes. Add the corned beef, and herbs and season lightly with pepper. Sauté until the potatoes are tender and lightly browned, stirring occasionally. (This hash does not come out pancake-style.)

2 *Prepare the poached eggs:* If you have egg poaching cups, place in a large saucepan with simmering water to cover and poach for 3 to 4 minutes. If not, bring a large skillet filled with water, ¾ up the sides, to a boil, then reduce to a simmer. Stir in the vinegar. Break each egg into a small ramekin or cup and slide into the simmering water. Poach 3 to 4 minutes. Have a second skillet of simmering water ready and with a slotted spoon, transfer each egg to the second skillet for 1 or 2 seconds to clear the vinegar taste. Again, with a slotted spoon, remove the eggs to a clean towel to remove excess moisture. Repeat with the remaining eggs as necessary. (See To Prepare Ahead below.)

2 tablespoons white
wine vinegar
Tomato Catsup,
optional (see page
147)
Chopped chives for
garnish

1 or 2 skillets or large
wok
Egg poachers, optional,
or ramekins or cups
Large saucepan or
skillet for eggs
Slotted spoon

Presentation: Divide the hash and mound in the center of 6 warmed plates. Top with 1 or 2 eggs and serve with tomato catsup on the side, if desired. Garnish with chopped chives and serve immediately.

To prepare ahead: Have all the ingredients for the hash diced, and when ready to serve, continue with the recipe. The eggs also can be poached ahead of time. Poach earlier in the day, remove with a slotted spoon, carefully place in a bowl of chilled water, and refrigerate uncovered until needed. Reheat for 3 or 4 seconds in simmering water and remove as above.

*To make corned beef, place the cured brisket (see below) in a large, wide, heavy roasting pan and pour in enough chicken stock or half chicken stock and half water to cover by about 2 inches (6 to 7 cups). Add 2 bay leaves, 1 whole leek, chopped, 1 celery stalk, chopped, and a few peppercorns. Bring to a boil, lower the heat and simmer until tender, 4 to 5 hours, adding boiling water or stock as necessary to keep the corned beef covered. Turn the meat a few times during this process to ensure even cooking. Slice across the grain.

To cure the beef, prepare a brine solution. For each 2½ quarts of cold water, stir in 1 cup of salt, 2 to 3 tablespoons pickling spice, 1 onion, sliced, and 4 or 5 garlic cloves. Place the meat in a glass or enamel vessel large enough to hold the beef with at least enough water to cover by at least two inches. (Do not use a metal container since the salt will react chemically with the metal.) Cover the meat with the prepared brine solution. To keep the meat completely submerged, top with a heavy plate or a sterilized container filled with water. Cover the entire vessel and keep in a cool spot (the lowest shelf of your refrigerator) for about 2 weeks, turning the meat every few days. Rinse the meat before cooking.

Dark crusty breads have always been an important part of the Austrian diet. The smell of hearty grain bread cooling in my mother's kitchen is a trademark of my childhood. During my years in France, I grew to love pale and sourdough breads, as well. Bread is an integral part of most European cuisines . . . slathered with homemade preserves at breakfast; following a fork through a spicy Morrocan lamb stew; paired with delicate cheeses or savory meats for an evening snack.

When I came to America, ethnic bakeries and restaurants were the most common sources of good bread. Many Americans seemed satisfied with the spongy white loaves found on supermarket shelves and the dry, flavorless rolls waiting on the tables of many restaurants.

We started experimenting with different kinds of bread a few years ago at Spago, since we could not find the breads we wanted at any of the commercial bakeries. We developed our own recipes and now have consistently good breads which we bake daily. Postrio and Eureka bake their own breads as well, all a little different, all delicious.

For the home baker, it is more practical to find a day that can be spent in the kitchen. Bread making is not difficult, but it can be time-consuming. After the bread has been baked and cooled, it can be cut into slices and frozen. When I was growing up, there was no freezer in our home. My mother used to sprinkle the stale bread with water and then heat it in the oven. It tasted pretty good that way, too.

OLIVE-FRENCH BREAD

Makes 2 loaves, about 21 ounces each

INGREDIENTS

5 cups plus 2
  teaspoons bread
  flour
2 cups cold water
1 ½ packages fresh
  yeast, crumbled, or
  active dry yeast
4 ounces niçoise olives,
  pitted and sliced*
2 teaspoons salt

EQUIPMENT

Electric mixer with
  dough hook
Baking tray
Single-edge razor,
  optional
Baking stone
Rolling pin, optional
Plant mister

*To make it easier to pit olives,
roll a rolling pin over the olives,
then pit.

Timing is very important. Run the mixer exactly as specified. The olives give the bread a Mediterranean flavor.

1 Insert the dough hook into an electric mixer and on 1 or low speed, combine 5 cups flour and the water for 4 minutes. Sprinkle the yeast over the dough, turn the speed to 2, and mix 4 minutes longer. (Dough will pull cleanly away from the bowl.)

2 Toss the olives with the 2 teaspoons flour, add to the dough with the salt and mix 2 minutes longer. Remove the bowl from the mixer, cover with a clean tea towel, and let rest for 15 minutes.

3 Turn the dough out on a heavily floured surface, lightly knead into a ball, and let rest, covered, for 45 minutes.

4 Punch out the air, cut the dough in half, about 21 ounces each half, and fold as for Spago 6-Grain Bread (see page 170) or shape into two baguettes. Place the loaves on one or two baking trays, sprinkle with flour, cover with the towel, and let rest for 45 minutes.

5 Preheat the oven to 400°F.

6 With a single-edge razor blade or a very sharp knife, make a slash down the center of each loaf. Carefully slide the breads onto a baking stone and bake 10 minutes. Spray with water (a spray can or bottle used for misting plants works well) and continue baking until the bread is well browned, about 1 hour 10 minutes longer. (Baking at 400°F will give you a crustier bread, but you can bake the bread at 425°F for 1 hour 10 minutes.) Cool on a rack.

To prepare ahead: Through step 6.

Spago 6-Grain Country Bread

Makes 3 loaves, about 1½ pounds each

INGREDIENTS

6 cups 6-grain mix*
1½ cups all-purpose
   flour
3¼ cups water at 58°F
1 package (¼ ounce)
   active dry yeast

EQUIPMENT

Electric mixer with
   dough hook
Linen tea towel
Single-edge razor blade
Baking stone
Plant mister

An oven thermometer is very important for bread baking since oven temperature is not always accurate. This is good freshly baked, but I like it even more the next day, toasted and spread with butter and a good marmalade.

❶ Insert the dough hook into an electric mixer and on 1 or low speed, combine the grain mix and the flour. Pour in the water, sprinkle in the yeast, and raise the speed to 2. Let the machine run 15 to 20 minutes, scraping the dough from the dough hook as necessary. When the dough is ready, the temperature of the dough should be between 78°F and 80°F and the dough will pull cleanly away from the sides of the bowl, but will still be sticky.

❷ To remove the dough from the bowl easily, sprinkle a little flour over and around the dough and with floured hands, turn out onto a heavily floured board. You must work quickly because the dough is sticky. Pat down into a rectangle about ¼ inch thick. Gently fold the 4 sides toward the center, like an envelope, and invert, folded sides down. Sprinkle a little flour on top and cover with a linen tea towel (not terry cloth) and let rest for 70 minutes. (The timing is very important.)

❸ Cut the dough into 3 pieces, each about 24 ounces. Flatten each piece into an 8-inch square, fold in half, and press down on the seam. Turn, seam-side up, and press down on the long seam to flatten. Fold one long end toward the center and then fold the other end over, folding the dough into thirds. Fold the dough in half, from top to bottom, press down on the seam, and gently roll into an 8-inch long loaf. Cover with the lightly floured tea towel and let rise 1½ to 2 hours. Repeat with the two remaining pieces of dough.

4 Preheat the oven to 400°F.

5 With a single-edge razor blade or a very sharp knife, make 5 diagonal slashes across the top of each loaf. Carefully slide the breads onto a baking stone and bake 10 minutes. Spray with a little water (a mister for plants can be used) and continue baking about 1 hour longer, or until the breads are richly browned.

6 Cool on a rack and slice.

To prepare ahead: Through step 6. If wrapped well and refrigerated, the bread will keep 2 to 3 days. This is wonderful toasted.

Flatten into an 8-inch square

Fold in half and press down on seam

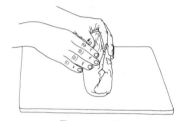

Turn seam-side up

Fold one long end toward center

Fold the other long end toward center

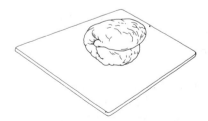

Fold dough in half from top to bottom

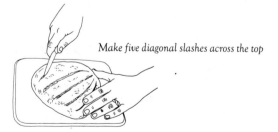

Make five diagonal slashes across the top

*Can be purchased from American Spoon Food (see list of resources).

BLACK PEPPER SCONES

Makes 18 scones

INGREDIENTS

4 cups plus 1
    tablespoon
    all-purpose flour
½ cup sugar
2½ teaspoons baking
    powder
½ teaspoon salt
13 tablespoons (6½
    ounces) unsalted
    butter, cut into small
    pieces
1½ tablespoons
    medium grind black
    pepper
2½ teaspoons finely
    chopped lemon peel
1½ cups heavy cream
    plus additional for
    brushing

EQUIPMENT

Large mixing bowl
Pastry blender or two
    knives
Rolling pin
1 or 2 baking trays
Pastry brush
Parchment paper

*The scones can be cut out with
a 2½ inch cookie cutter if
desired. Roll out the dough,
cut, and place on a baking tray.
Reroll the dough and continue
cutting out circles. Proceed as in
step 5.

I love the flavor of fresh black pepper in bread or scones. However, 1 cup of dried blueberries, sour cherries, or raisins can be used, eliminating the pepper.

1 Into a large bowl, sift together the flour, sugar, baking powder, and salt. Using two knives or a pastry blender, cut in the butter until the mixture resembles coarse meal. Gently stir in the pepper and the lemon peel. Add the 1½ cups cream all at once and mix until the dough just comes together.

2 Turn out onto a lightly floured surface and knead the dough into a ball. For a flakier consistency, do not knead the dough into a smooth ball. If smooth, the scone will be more cakelike. Wrap in plastic wrap and refrigerate for at least 30 minutes, up to overnight.

3 Cut the dough into 3 equal pieces, each about 14 ounces. Working with one piece at a time, keeping the other two pieces covered, roll out to a circle, 6 inches in diameter and ½ inch thick.* Cut the circle into 6 wedges and arrange the wedges on one or two baking trays lined with parchment paper. Repeat with the remaining dough. Refrigerate until needed.

4 Preheat the oven to 350°F.

5 When ready to serve, lightly brush the scones with cream and bake until golden, about 35 minutes.

Presentation: Serve warm with butter and/or jam.

To prepare ahead: Through step 3, refrigerating until needed. The finished scones can be refrigerated, covered, for up to 3 days and reheated when ready to serve.

BUTTERMILK BISCUITS

Makes 20 to 22 biscuits

INGREDIENTS

2 ¾ cups all-purpose
  flour
1 ½ tablespoons sugar
1 tablespoon plus 1
  teaspoon baking
  powder
¾ tablespoon salt
¼ teaspoon baking
  soda
10 tablespoons (5
  ounces) chilled
  unsalted butter, cut
  into small pieces
¼ cup minced onion
1 tablespoon chopped
  fresh or 2 teaspoons
  dried thyme
1 cup buttermilk
1 or 2 tablespoons
  milk or cream
¼ cup grated Parmesan
  cheese, optional

EQUIPMENT

Food processor
Rolling pin
2-inch cookie cutter
1 or 2 baking trays
Parchment paper
Pastry brush

To this basic recipe you may want to add some finely chopped jalapeño or toasted sesame seeds. Plumped raisins can also be added, eliminating the Parmesan cheese and minced onion.

1 In a food processor fitted with the steel blade, combine the flour, sugar, baking powder, salt, and baking soda. Add the butter, onion, and thyme, and process until the mixture resembles fine meal. With the machine running, pour the buttermilk through the feed tube, just until the dough comes together.

2 Turn out onto a well-floured work surface and knead lightly into a round ball. Roll out the dough to about 1-inch thickness, and with a 2-inch cookie cutter, cut out as many biscuits as you can. Knead the dough together and reroll to a 1-inch thickness and again cut out as many biscuits as you can. Repeat this procedure until you have used all the dough, giving you 20 to 22 biscuits. Arrange the biscuits, as cut, on one or two parchment-lined baking trays. Refrigerate for at least 1 hour, up to 24 hours.

3 Preheat the oven to 350°F.

4 Brush the top of each biscuit with milk or cream and sprinkle with the Parmesan cheese, if desired. Bake 25 to 35 minutes, until lightly golden. Serve warm.

To prepare ahead: Through step 2, refrigerating the biscuits until serving time. The biscuits are most delicious when served right from the oven, cooling on the table.

PIZZAS, PASTA, AND RISOTTO

Pizza Dough

Topping for Spicy Chicken Pizza

Topping for Mexican Pizza

Topping for Vegetarian Pizza

Topping for Spicy Scallop Pizza

Regular Pasta Dough

Herb Pasta Dough

Chili Pasta Dough

Angel Hair Pasta with Wild Mushrooms

Fettuccine with Roasted Red Peppers

Chicken Lasagna

Three-Cheese Ravioli

Pasta Rounds with Spinach-Ricotta Mousse

Smoked Salmon Ravioli with Lime-Dill Butter Sauce

Duck Ravioli with Red Pepper Sauce

Wild Mushroom Risotto

François' Seafood Risotto with Crisp Ginger

During my years at L'Oustau de Baumaniere in Provence, my treasured days off always included wine and pizza at nearby Chez Gu. As I sat relaxing with my friends, I dreamed of opening a restaurant in America with a pizzeria right next door. How disappointed I was when I came to Los Angeles and discovered that pizzas were prisoners of fast-food restaurants.

Now on the menus of many fine restaurants, pizza has achieved a new status and has become one of America's most popular foods. At Spago we have many customers who would never start a meal without one of their favorite pizzas: spicy chicken, Mexican, or whatever the special of the day might be.

Pizza is one of the most sociable foods, easily prepared at home, and goes well with anything from champagne to beer. Use your imagination when creating your pizzas, but always start with fresh ingredients.

A very hot oven will produce a crust crispy on the outside and chewy inside. Using a pizza stone somewhat duplicates the effect of a brick oven and allows the pizza to cook evenly.

For centuries, pasta has been a staple in the diet of people all over the world. Today you can find it on reducing diets and diets to gain weight; the health conscious swear by it, and even my two-year-old son, Cameron, knows the difference between homemade and store-bought noodles. Pasta comes in assorted shapes and sizes and can be combined with a host of ingredients—vegetables, fish, meat, or fowl. The sauce can be simple or rich, spicy or plain. All our restaurants feature different kinds of pasta. At Spago, we serve it with an Italian influence; at Chinois we make pan-fried Chinese noodles to go with the main dish; at our newest venture, Eureka, we season the pastas with Latin-American spices.

Pasta should be cooked in a large amount of boiling water that has been splashed with a little olive oil, with salt added just before the pasta is dropped into the pot.

Risotto, a recent addition to our menu, has received overwhelming approval. To make risotto, arborio rice, a round, short-grain rice, is used. Arborio rice is found in most markets that sell fine foods. It is not difficult to prepare, but needs to be watched carefully in order to produce the proper consistency.

Whether for pizza, pasta, or risotto, a good olive oil is absolutely essential. It is worth the additional money you may have to spend to get a good quality oil. I recommend a flavorful extra-virgin olive oil from Italy.

PIZZA DOUGH

Makes 4 7- or 8-inch pizzas, 6 ounces each

INGREDIENTS

1 package active dry or
   fresh yeast
1 teaspoon honey or
   sugar
¾ cup warm water
   (105° to 115°F)
2¾ cups all-purpose
   flour
1 teaspoon salt
2 tablespoons olive oil
   (or Chili and Garlic
   Oil; see page 179),
   plus additional for
   brushing
Topping of your choice
   (See pages 180–183)

EQUIPMENT

Small bowl
Mixer with dough
   hook
Pastry brush
Small rolling pin
Pizza stone
Pizza cutter

Pizza dough is a simple yeast dough. Around Napoli, the people used to make pizzas out of leftover bread dough, the toppings tomatoes, fresh herbs, and sometimes buffalo mozzarella from the water buffalo grazing nearby. I add honey to the dough, which gives the crust a nice golden color when cooked.

1 In a small bowl, dissolve the yeast and honey in ¼ cup of the warm water.

2 In a mixer fitted with a dough hook, combine the flour and the salt. Pour in 2 tablespoons of the oil and when absorbed, scrape in the dissolved yeast. Add the remaining ½ cup of water and knead on low speed about 5 minutes.

3 Turn out onto a board and knead 2 or 3 minutes longer. Dough should be smooth and firm. Let rise in a warm spot, covered with a damp towel, about 30 minutes. (Dough will stretch when lightly pulled.)

4 Divide the dough into 4 balls, about 6 ounces each. Work each ball by pulling down the sides and tucking under the bottom of the ball. Repeat 4 or 5 times. Then on a smooth unfloured surface, roll the ball under the palm of your hand until the dough is smooth and firm, about 1 minute. Cover with a damp towel and let rest 15 to 20 minutes. At this point, the balls can be loosely covered with plastic wrap and refrigerated for 1 to 2 days.

5 Preheat the oven to 525°F. Place a pizza stone in the oven.

6 To prepare each pizza, place a ball of dough on a lightly floured surface. Press down on the center, spreading the dough, or roll into a 7- or 8-inch circle, with the outer border a little thicker than the inner circle. Brush lightly with oil and arrange the topping of your choice only over the inner circle.

7 Arrange the pizza on the baking stone and bake 15 to 20 minutes, or until the pizzas are nicely browned. Transfer to a firm surface and cut into slices with a pizza cutter. Serve immediately.

To prepare ahead: Through step 4. Or through step 7, baking 8 or 9 minutes, until the cheese melts and the pizza dough is lightly golden brown. (At this point, the pizza can be cooled, wrapped well and frozen. When needed, remove from the freezer, unwrap, and bake in a preheated oven until brown.) At serving time, return to the oven and continue with the recipe.

CHILI AND GARLIC OIL

INGREDIENTS

1 whole head (about 2 ½ ounces) garlic, peeled, cloves, separated
2 cups olive oil
1 tablespoon chili flakes

EQUIPMENT

Small saucepan

1 In a small saucepan, combine the cloves of garlic and olive and bring to a boil. Turn down the heat and simmer until garlic turns golden brown, 10 to 15 minutes.

2 Let cool and then add the chili flakes. Let sit for at least 2 hours before using.

To prepare ahead: Through step 2, oil will last 2 to 3 weeks.

Topping for Spicy Chicken Pizza

Makes 4 7- or 8-inch pizzas

The following pizza toppings are four of the most popular pizzas served at Spago. I have listed the amounts used at the restaurant. Arrange the toppings in the order listed. However, you may want to try your own variations—and come up with some interesting combinations.

The following pizza toppings are four of the most popular pizzas served at Spago. I have listed the amounts used at the restaurant. Arrange the toppings in the order listed. However, you may want to try your own variations—and come up with some interesting combinations.

INGREDIENTS

3 cups (about 1 pound skinned and boned) cubed chicken

MARINADE
½ cup plus 1 tablespoon olive oil
3½ tablespoons lime juice
2 teaspoons chopped jalapeño pepper
Pinch of chopped cilantro
Salt

TOPPING
3 cups grated mozzarella cheese
2 cups grated fontina cheese
1 pound (about 6) plum tomatoes, ends removed, cut into thin slices
½ cup cubed eggplant, sautéed or grilled
½ cup grilled onion, chopped
Chopped chives
4 teaspoons grated Parmesan cheese
3 cups sautéed marinated chicken

EQUIPMENT

Medium bowl
8- or 10-inch skillet

1 Arrange the cubed chicken in a medium bowl and toss with the marinade ingredients, using ½ cup olive oil. Season lightly with salt. Let marinate for about 1 hour, refrigerated.

2 In a skillet large enough to hold the chicken in one layer, heat the remaining 1 tablespoon oil. Sauté the chicken just to brown on all sides.

3 Preheat oven to 525°F and prepare the pizza as directed on pages 178–79 in steps 6 and 7 for Pizza Dough.

To prepare ahead: Through step 2. Or see Pizza Dough.

TOPPING FOR MEXICAN PIZZA*

Makes 4 7- or 8-inch pizzas

INGREDIENTS

3 cups grated
   mozzarella cheese
2 cups fontina cheese
6 (about 1 pound)
   plum tomatoes, ends
   removed and cut
   into thin slices
1 cup whole cilantro
   leaves
Sliced roasted jalapeño
   peppers (see above)
2 cups (8 ounces) sliced
   roasted or sautéed
   red bell pepper
½ cup sliced Roasted
   Garlic (see page 148)
4 teaspoons grated
   Parmesan cheese

2 cups (about 6 ounces)
   sliced Maui or
   Vidalia onion
Pinches of chopped
   cilantro

① Roast 6 or 8 (3 or 4 ounces) whole jalapeño peppers, then core, seed, and cut into thin slices. Taste should determine how much to use.

② Preheat oven to 525°F and prepare the pizza as directed on pages 178–79 in steps 6 and 7 for Pizza Dough.

③ When the pizzas are baked, remove from the oven and sprinkle with the onion and chopped cilantro.

*The ingredients are listed in the order we arrange them at Spago.

Topping for Vegetarian Pizza

Makes 4 7- or 8-inch pizzas

INGREDIENTS

3 cups grated
   mozzarella cheese
2 cups grated fontina
   cheese
2 cups (about ½
   pound) sliced fresh
   artichoke hearts,
   cooked
2 cups (about 5 ounces)
   sliced eggplant,
   grilled or sautéed
4 teaspoons grated
   Parmesan cheese
¼ cup grated
   mozzarella cheese
1 teaspoon chopped
   fresh oregano

1 Sauté the eggplant and mushrooms separately, each in 1 tablespoon olive oil. Use more oil if necessary.

2 Arrange ingredients on the pizza dough in the order listed at left. See Pizza Dough recipe on pages 178–179, steps 6 and 7.

Note: The vegetables listed are the ones we usually use. You can substitute vegetables of your choice as desired.

Topping for Spicy Scallop Pizza

Makes four 7- or 8-inch pizzas

MARINADE
2 ounces (about 2
    small) jalapeño
    peppers
3 garlic cloves,
    chopped
1 tablespoon plus 1
    teaspoon chopped
    fresh thyme
Salt
Freshly ground white
    pepper

2 cups (scant 1 pound)
    trimmed scallops,
    cut in half,
    horizontally

3 cups grated
    mozzarella cheese
2 cups grated fontina
    cheese
¾ pound (about 4)
    Roma tomatoes,
    ends removed and
    cut into thin slices
1 cup (about 4 ounces)
    sliced cooked
    artichoke hearts
1⅓ cups (about 4
    ounces) thinly sliced
    red onion
1½ cups coarsely
    chopped cilantro
Scallops (see step 1)
4 teaspoons grated
    Parmesan cheese

1 In a medium bowl, combine the marinade ingredients. Add the scallops and toss to coat well. Season lightly with salt and pepper and refrigerate until needed.

2 When ready to bake, brush the pizza dough with Chili and Garlic Oil (see page 179) and arrange the ingredients as listed, reserving a little of the cilantro to sprinkle on top of the scallops.

3 Bake in preheated 525 degree oven as described in step 7 for Pizza Dough (see page 179).

To prepare ahead: Through step 1. Do not freeze.

Medium bowl
Pastry brush

REGULAR PASTA DOUGH

Makes 1 ½ pounds

INGREDIENTS

1 ½ cups semolina
  flour
1 ½ cups all-purpose
  flour
2 teaspoons salt
4 large eggs
2 to 3 tablespoons
  olive oil

EQUIPMENT

Food processor
Pasta machine or
  rolling pin

Fresh pasta is made in many parts of the world. Where I grew up, the pasta is made with wheat flour and since wheat flour is very soft, the noodles are not cooked al dente, so that they can absorb some of the sauce. We also don't make spaghetti, linguini, or fettuccine. These pastas come primarily from Italy, where semolina flour is commonly used. At our restaurants, we use half semolina and half all-purpose flour, resulting in a more manageable dough.

1 In a food processor fitted with the steel blade, combine the flours, salt, eggs, and 2 tablespoons of olive oil, adding the third tablespoon if needed. Process until the dough holds together when pinched. Turn out on a lightly floured work surface and knead by hand, forming a smooth ball. Wrap in plastic wrap and let rest at room temperature for 30 minutes.

2 Cut the dough into 4 equal pieces and roll out 1 piece at a time, keeping the remaining dough wrapped until needed. Cut as desired.

To prepare ahead: Through step 1, the dough can be refrigerated, but brought back to room temperature before cutting. In step 2, dough can be cut, placed on semolina-dusted trays, and refrigerated, covered, until serving time. At this point, the noodles can also be frozen and cooked directly from the freezer.

HERB PASTA DOUGH

Makes 1 ½ pounds

INGREDIENTS

½ cup water
1 tablespoon chopped
   fresh thyme leaves
1 tablespoon chopped
   fresh rosemary leaves
1 tablespoon chopped
   fresh sage leaves
1 ½ cups semolina
   flour
1 ½ cups all-purpose
   flour
3 large eggs
1 to 2 tablespoons
   olive oil
1 teaspoon salt

EQUIPMENT

Small saucepan
Food processor
Pasta machine or
   rolling pin

If the pasta dough is flavorful, any simple sauce can be added.

1 *Prepare the herb tea:* In a very small saucepan, bring the water to a boil. Add the herbs and bring back to a boil. Lower the heat and reduce to ¼ cup. Remove the pan from the heat, cover, and let steep for 15 minutes.

2 In a food processor fitted with the steel blade, place the semolina and all-purpose flours, the eggs, 1 tablespoon olive oil, salt, and the herb tea. Process until the dough holds together when pinched, adding the remaining tablespoon of olive oil if necessary. Turn out onto a lightly floured work surface and knead by hand, forming a smooth ball. Wrap in plastic wrap and let rest at room temperature for 2 hours.

3 Cut the dough into 4 pieces and roll out 1 piece at a time, keeping the remaining dough covered until needed. Cut as desired.

To prepare ahead: Through step 2, the dough can be refrigerated, but brought back to room temperature before cutting. In step 3, the dough can be cut, placed on semolina-dusted trays and refrigerated, covered, until serving time. At this point, the noodles can also be frozen and cooked directly from the freezer.

CHILI PASTA DOUGH

Makes 1 ½ pounds

INGREDIENTS

1 ½ cups all-purpose
  flour
1 ½ cups semolina
  flour
1 teaspoon salt
4 large eggs
2 to 3 tablespoons
  Chili Oil (see page
  145)

EQUIPMENT

Food processor
Pasta machine or
  rolling pin

1 In a food processor fitted with the steel blade, combine the flours, salt, eggs, and 2 tablespoons of oil, adding the third if needed. Process just until the dough holds together when pinched. Turn out onto a very lightly floured surface and knead into a ball. Wrap in plastic wrap and let rest at room temperature at least 30 minutes.

2 When ready to roll out the dough, cut into 4 pieces and roll and cut as desired, keeping the unused dough covered to prevent drying out.

To prepare ahead: Through step 1. At this point, the dough can also be wrapped and refrigerated overnight and brought back to room temperature until needed. Then continue with recipe. Through step 2, see Regular Pasta Dough (page 184).

ANGEL HAIR PASTA WITH WILD MUSHROOMS

Serves 4

SAUCE

9 ounces wild
  mushrooms (morels,
  shiitake, chanterelles,
  porcini, black
  trumpet, etc.)
1 tablespoon olive oil
3 tablespoons (1 ½
  ounces) unsalted
  butter
2 shallots, minced
1 teaspoon finely
  minced garlic
1 cup Chicken Stock,
  White or Brown (see
  pages 41, 42)
1 teaspoon chopped
  thyme

1 pound fresh angel
  hair pasta
2 cups trimmed arugula
  (about 2 ounces)
3 tablespoons grated
  Parmesan cheese plus
  additional as needed
Salt
Freshly ground pepper

EQUIPMENT

Large skillet
Large pot
Colander or strainer

There was a time when wild mushrooms were scarce. Mostly, they came in cans or were dried. Today, most good markets carry a variety of wild mushrooms as well as cultivated ones like shiitake or oyster mushrooms, which are also quite flavorful.

1 Bring a large pot of water to a boil. Add a little salt and olive oil.

2 *Prepare the sauce:* Depending upon the size, cut each mushroom into 2 or 3 pieces—you don't want them too small. In a large skillet, heat the oil and 1 tablespoon butter. Over medium-high heat, stir in the shallots, garlic, and the mushrooms, and cook 3 to 4 minutes. Deglaze the pan with the chicken stock, sprinkle with thyme, and reduce by half.

3 Cook the angel hair in the pot of boiling water until al dente, about 1 minute.* Drain.

4 To the skillet, add the arugula and the remaining 2 tablespoons butter. Stir in the pasta and the 3 tablespoons grated cheese and toss to combine well. Heat thoroughly. Correct seasoning with freshly ground pepper and salt.

Presentation: Divide the pasta and mushrooms evenly and mound in the center of 4 heated plates. Sprinkle lightly with Parmesan cheese and serve immediately.

To prepare ahead: In step 2, reduce the sauce slightly and continue with the recipe at serving time.

*Fresh angel hair pasta cooks very quickly so it is important that it is not overcooked. Store-bought pasta will take a little longer to cook. Follow package directions.

FETTUCCINE WITH ROASTED RED PEPPERS

Serves 2

INGREDIENTS

3 tablespoons olive oil
¼ cup chopped onion
2 tablespoons minced garlic
2 large red bell peppers (about 1 pound), roasted, peeled, cored, seeded, and cut into ¼-inch strips
Pinch of chili pepper flakes
Salt
Freshly ground pepper
⅔ cup Chicken Stock (see page 41)
½ pound Regular Pasta Dough (see page 184), cut into fettuccine noodles
1 teaspoon chopped fresh thyme
½ teaspoon sherry wine vinegar
Chopped cilantro for garnish

EQUIPMENT

Medium skillet
Blender
Large pot
Colander or strainer

Adding grilled shrimp, sautéed scallops, or barbecued chicken, cut into thin slices, will convert this simple pasta into an impressive main dish.

1 In a medium skillet, heat 2 tablespoons olive oil until smoking. Sauté the onions and garlic until translucent, 2 to 3 minutes. Stir in the roasted peppers and chili flakes and cook 3 to 4 minutes longer. Season with salt and pepper to taste. Remove about ¼ of the mixture and reserve.

2 Pour the chicken stock into the pan and bring to a boil. Transfer the ingredients to a blender and puree until smooth. Return to the pan and keep warm.

3 Meanwhile, bring to a boil a large pot of water with the remaining 1 tablespoon olive oil. Add a little salt and cook the noodles until al dente. Drain and stir into the sauce. Stir in the chopped thyme, vinegar, and reserved roasted pepper mixture. Correct seasoning to taste.

Presentation: Arrange the pasta in the middle of 2 heated plates, spooning the sauce over. Garnish with the chopped cilantro and serve immediately.

To prepare ahead: Through step 2, reheating, over a low flame, when ready to serve and then continuing with the recipe.

CHICKEN LASAGNA

Makes 6 4-inch lasagnas or 1 9-inch lasagna*

TOMATO SAUCE
3 tablespoons olive oil
½ medium onion,
  diced
5 garlic cloves, minced
2 pounds (about 6
  medium) tomatoes,
  peeled, seeded, and
  diced
1 teaspoon diced
  jalapeño pepper,
  optional
Leaves from 3 sprigs
  fresh thyme
1 tablespoon chopped
  fresh basil leaves
Salt
Freshly ground pepper

¾ pound (½ recipe)
  Regular Pasta Dough
  (see page 184)
Semolina flour

1 pound spinach
  leaves, stemmed and
  cleaned
2 tablespoons olive oil
1 garlic clove, minced
Salt
Freshly ground pepper
2 cups bite-size pieces
  cooked chicken,
  turkey, or leftover
  roast, like veal or
  pork

When prepared in individual tart rings this is a very elegant presentation. Only when I serve it family-style do I make it in a large pan.

1 *Prepare the tomato sauce:* In a large sauté pan, heat the oil. Over medium-high heat, sauté the onion and garlic until translucent, about 5 minutes. Stir in the tomatoes, jalapeño, thyme, and basil, lower the heat, and cook until the sauce thickens, about 15 minutes. Season with salt and pepper to taste and set aside. You should have about 2 cups of sauce.

2 Prepare the pasta and cut into 3 pieces, 4 ounces each. Sprinkle the work surface with semolina flour. Using a pasta machine, a rolling pin, or a combination of both, roll out one piece of dough as thin as possible and large enough to cut out 8 4-inch circles. Using a 4-inch flan ring as a guide, cut out 8 circles of dough with the point of a small sharp knife. (Scraps can be folded and reworked as necessary.) Repeat with the remaining pieces of dough, and as the circles of dough are cut out, transfer to a cookie sheet lightly dusted with semolina flour. Bring to a boil a large pot of water with a little olive oil. Salt the water and cook the pasta circles until al dente, about 1 minute. Remove, rinse under cold water, and set on a dry towel until ready to assemble the lasagna.

3 *Prepare the filling:* Blanch the spinach and drain thoroughly. Chop coarsely. In a small skillet, heat 2 tablespoons of olive oil. Add the garlic and sauté the spinach just until coated with the oil and garlic. Season with salt and pepper and set aside.

(Continued)

3 tablespoons grated
  Parmesan cheese
4 ounces mascarpone
  or cream cheese
6 ounces grated
  mozzarella cheese

½ cup Chicken Stock
  (see page 41)

EQUIPMENT

Large sauté pan
Pasta machine and/or
  rolling pin
6 4-inch flan rings
Cookie sheet or baking
  tray
Large pot
Small skillet
Small bowl

4 In a small bowl, combine the chicken with 3 tablespoons of the tomato sauce and 1 tablespoon grated Parmesan cheese. Season generously with black pepper and salt to taste.

5 Oil a baking tray and the inside of six 4-inch flan rings and arrange the rings on the tray. Preheat the oven to 400°F.

6 To assemble each lasagna, press a pasta circle into one of the rings. Spread some of the mascarpone evenly over the circle and cover with a layer of the chopped spinach. Top with a second circle and spread with a layer of the chicken mixture. Top with a third circle, spoon a little tomato sauce (1½ or 2 tablespoons) over, and cover with a final circle of pasta. Sprinkle with mozzarella and a little Parmesan cheese. Repeat with the remaining rings, pasta, mascarpone, spinach, chicken, sauce, mozzarella, and Parmesan cheeses. (At this point, the lasagnas can be refrigerated, removing from the refrigerator thirty minutes before you are ready to bake them.)

7 Bake 20 to 25 minutes, or until the cheese has melted and the lasagna is nicely browned.

8 Pour the ½ cup chicken stock into the reserved sauce and heat, stirring to combine. Correct seasoning to taste.

Presentation: Spoon a little of the tomato sauce in the center of 6 warm dinner plates. Place each lasagna on the sauce and remove the rings, using a small knife as necessary to cut around the dough. Serve immediately.

To prepare ahead: Through step 6.

*To make one 9-inch lasagna, cut the pasta dough into 4 pieces, 3 ounces each. Roll out each piece as thin as possible and large enough to cut out a 9-inch circle. Using a 9-inch flan ring as a guide, cut out a 9-inch circle and repeat with the remaining dough. Cook the circles 4 to 5 minutes and proceed as above, layering with a pasta circle, mascarpone, spinach, a second pasta circle, the chicken mixture, the third circle, 1 cup of tomato sauce, the final circle, and the mozzarella and Parmesan cheeses. Bake 30 to 35 minutes. Serve as above.

THREE-CHEESE RAVIOLI

Makes 20 to 22 ravioli

INGREDIENTS

4 ounces goat cheese
2 ounces blue cheese
2 ounces grated
Parmesan cheese*
1 small baked potato,
pulp removed from
the shell and mashed
2 eggs
2 tablespoons chopped
fresh chervil plus
sprigs for garnish
2 tablespoons chopped
fresh chives
Salt
Freshly ground white
pepper
½ recipe (¾ pound)
Regular Pasta Dough
(see page 184)
Semolina flour
1 egg, lightly beaten,
for egg wash
Olive oil

SAUCE
1 cup Chicken Stock
(see page 41)
Freshly ground white
pepper
8 tablespoons (4
ounces) unsalted
butter, at room
temperature
3 tablespoons grated
Parmesan cheese*

My mother used to make her own farmer cheese for her cheese ravioli. Then she would add baked potato, chervil, black pepper, and salt, and form rather large dumpling-style ravioli. Using goat, blue, and Parmesan cheeses gives the filling a more intense flavor.

1 *Prepare the filling:* In a small bowl, combine the goat cheese, blue cheese, grated Parmesan cheese, mashed potato, and eggs. Mix well. Stir in 2 tablespoons of the chopped chervil and the chives, and season to taste with salt and pepper. Refrigerate until needed.

2 Cut the pasta dough in half and work with one half at a time, keeping the other half covered. Lightly dust the work surface with semolina flour. With a machine or by hand, roll out one piece of dough approximately 30 inches long and 5 inches wide. Brush the bottom half of the dough with egg wash and using a heaping teaspoon of filling, spoon out 10 to 11 mounds, about 2½ inches apart. Cover the mounds with the unegg-washed half of the dough and press the dough down around each mound. With a round cookie cutter (about 4-inch), cut the ravioli into half-moon shapes. Dust a tray with semolina and arrange the ravioli on the tray. Repeat with the second half of the dough and the remaining egg wash and filling. Refrigerate, covered, until needed.

(Continued)

1 tablespoon chopped
  fresh chervil
1 teaspoon chopped
  fresh sage
1 teaspoon chopped
  fresh marjoram

EQUIPMENT

Small mixing bowl
Pasta machine and/or
  rolling pin
4-inch round cookie
  cutter
Tray or large platter
Large pot
Medium saucepan
Whisk
Slotted spoon

3 At serving time, while you make the sauce, bring a large pot of water to a boil with a little olive oil.

4 *Prepare the sauce:* In a medium saucepan, bring the chicken stock to a boil with freshly ground pepper. Whisk in the butter and cook until slightly thickened. Keep warm. Just before adding the ravioli, stir in the Parmesan cheese.

5 Add a little salt to the boiling water and cook the ravioli for 5 minutes. Remove with a slotted spoon and drain on a clean towel.

6 Stir the chervil, sage, and marjoram into the sauce and season to taste with salt and pepper. Add the ravioli and let simmer for 1 or 2 minutes to heat through.

Presentation: Divide the ravioli among 4 heated bowls. Spoon the sauce over and garnish with a small sprig of chervil. Serve immediately.

To prepare ahead: Through step 2.

*There are many kinds of Parmesan cheese available, but nothing compares with reggiano, which is aged for at least eighteen months. For the most flavor, buy a solid piece of cheese and grate as needed.

Pasta Rounds with Spinach-Ricotta Mousse

Makes 10 4-inch rounds

1 pound ricotta cheese
½ pound mascarpone cheese
1 bunch (about ½ pound) spinach, stemmed and washed
2 tablespoons (1 ounce) unsalted butter
¼ cup pine nuts
¾ pound mozzarella cheese, diced
1 ounce dry aged goat cheese, grated
1 egg, lightly beaten
1 teaspoon salt

Since the rounds can be prepared in advance, they can be made earlier in the day and baked just before serving.

❶ *Prepare the filling:* In a food processor fitted with the steel blade, puree the ricotta, mascarpone, and half the spinach. Transfer to a medium mixing bowl.

❷ In a small skillet or saucepan, melt 1 tablespoon of the butter. Sauté the remaining spinach just until wilted, 2 to 3 minutes, coarsely chop, and cool.

❸ In a small skillet, toast the pine nuts over medium heat, stirring constantly, about 2 minutes. Cool and fold into the cheese mixture with the cooled spinach, mozzarella, goat cheese, egg, salt, and pepper. Correct seasoning to taste and set aside.

(Continued)

1 teaspoon freshly
  ground white pepper
¾ recipe (18 ounces)
  Regular Pasta Dough
  (see page 184) or
  Herb Pasta Dough
  (see page 185)
Semolina flour
⅓ cup grated Parmesan
  cheese

3 cups Tomato-Basil
  Sauce (see page 133)

EQUIPMENT

Food processor
Small skillet
Large mixing bowl
Pasta machine and/or
  rolling pin
Pastry brush
10 4-inch tart pans
Baking tray

④ Cut the pasta dough into 4 pieces. On a surface dusted lightly with semolina flour, with a machine or by hand, roll out the first piece to a rectangle, 40 inches long and 5 inches wide, keeping the remaining dough covered until needed. Trim the rectangle as needed, divide the filling equally into 4 portions, and spread ¼ over the surface of the dough, leaving a 1-inch space on all sides. Starting from the top, roll the dough over the filling, enclosing it completely. Cut off 1 inch from both ends and cut the roll into approximately 1-inch pieces, yielding 30 slices. Repeat with the remaining dough and filling.

⑤ Preheat the oven to 375°F.

⑥ Melt the remaining 1 tablespoon butter and brush ten 4-inch tart pans with the butter. Arrange 12 of the slices cut from the roll in a circle, cut-side up, in each pan (it will be a tight squeeze, but it can be done) and sprinkle with grated Parmesan cheese. Set the pans on a baking tray for easier handling and bake 30 to 35 minutes, or until the rounds are golden brown. Invert onto the tray after 15 minutes so that both sides brown. The pasta will be crisp.

Presentation: Heat the sauce and spoon a little in the center of each of 10 warmed plates. Set one of the rounds on the sauce and serve immediately. Pass the remaining sauce in a small bowl.

To prepare ahead: In step 6, arrange the slices in the pans and refrigerate, covered, until needed. Remove from the refrigerator 30 minutes before you are ready to bake the rounds, and continue with the recipe.

SMOKED SALMON RAVIOLI WITH LIME-DILL BUTTER SAUCE

Makes 32 ravioli, serving 4 to 6

MOUSSE

¼ pound smoked salmon, cut into 1-inch pieces

¼ pound fresh salmon, cut into 1-inch pieces

2 teaspoons coarsely chopped fresh dill leaves

1 egg

½ cup chilled heavy cream

½ teaspoon freshly ground white pepper

Salt

Dash of cayenne pepper

¾ pound Regular Pasta Dough (see page 184)

Semolina flour

1 egg, lightly beaten, for egg wash

SAUCE

¾ cup dry white wine

Juice of 1 medium lime, plus additional to taste

1 tablespoon minced shallot

1 cup Chicken Stock, heated (see page 41)

½ cup heavy cream

One does not have to buy center-cut smoked salmon slices for this. The end cuts are perfectly fine since they have a stronger smoky flavor.

1 *Prepare the mousse:* Chill the bowl and blade of a food processor. With a few on/off turns, chop the smoked salmon, fresh salmon, and dill. Add the egg, and with the machine running, pour the cream through the feed tube and process until the mixture is a smooth puree. Transfer to a small bowl and season with pepper, salt, and cayenne to taste. Cover and refrigerate until needed.

2 Cut the pasta dough into 4 pieces. Working with one piece at a time, keep the remaining pieces covered. On a surface dusted with semolina flour, using a pasta machine or by hand, roll out the first piece of dough to a rectangle, about 28 inches long and 6 inches wide, trimming as necessary. Brush with egg wash and, using a heaping teaspoonful of the mousse, place 16 mounds on the dough in two rows, each mound about 1½ inches apart. Roll out the second piece of dough and cover, pressing down around the mounds to secure. With a sharp knife or pizza cutter, cut the ravioli into approximately 3-inch squares, trimming the edges as necessary. Arrange on a tray dusted with semolina flour. Repeat with the remaining dough, egg wash, and mousse. Refrigerate, covered, until needed.

3 While preparing the sauce, bring a large pot of water to a boil with a little olive oil.

(Continued)

6 tablespoons (3
  ounces) unsalted
  butter
¼ cup chopped fresh
  dill leaves
Salt
Freshly ground white
  pepper
½ roasted red pepper,
  cored, peeled,
  seeded, and cut into
  julienne strips

EQUIPMENT

Food processor
Small bowl
Pasta machine and/or
  rolling pin
Pastry brush
Pizza cutter or sharp
  knife
Baking tray
Large pot
Medium saucepan
Strainer
Whisk

④ *Prepare the sauce:* In a medium saucepan, reduce the wine, lime juice, and shallot until ¼ cup liquid remains. Pour in the chicken stock and reduce by half. Pour in the cream and reduce just until the sauce thickens. Strain, pressing down on the shallots to get all the sauce, and return to a clean pan. Whisk in the butter and dill leaves and season with salt and pepper to taste. Keep warm.

⑤ Add a little salt to the pot of boiling water, then the ravioli, and cook for 5 minutes. Drain the ravioli on a clean towel and arrange in the sauce with the julienned peppers. Heat just to the boiling point.

Presentation: Divide the ravioli among 4 or 6 heated plates. Spoon the sauce over and garnish with the peppers and a small sprig of dill, if desired. Serve immediately.

To prepare ahead: Through step 2. The sauce can be prepared in step 4 and reheated over a very low flame. If the sauce thickens too much, thin with a little stock.

DUCK RAVIOLI WITH RED PEPPER SAUCE

Makes 36 ravioli, serving 6 to 8

INGREDIENTS

DUCK MOUSSE
1 teaspoon olive oil
½ medium red bell
   pepper, cored,
   seeded, and minced
8 ounces boned and
   skinned chicken leg,
   cut into 1-inch pieces
6 ounces boned and
   skinned duck meat,
   cut into 1-inch pieces
¼ cup loosely packed
   chopped fresh
   chervil
½ teaspoon salt
½ teaspoon freshly
   ground white pepper
1 egg
1 cup heavy cream

1 pound Herb Pasta
   Dough (see page
   185), cut into 3
   pieces
Semolina flour
1 egg, lightly beaten
   with a little water,
   for egg wash

SAUCE
2 whole red bell
   peppers (about 1
   pound)
1 tablespoon olive oil
2 garlic cloves, crushed

Though I love duck because of its very tasty meat, you can replace it with quail, squab, or pheasant.

1 *Prepare the mousse:* In a small skillet, heat the olive oil. Over medium-high heat, sauté the red pepper, 4 to 5 minutes, stirring occasionally. Cool completely.

2 Chill the bowl and steel blade of the food processor. Combine the chicken and duck meat, chervil, salt, and pepper, and process until chopped. Add the egg and continue to process until pureed. With the motor running, pour the cream through the feed tube and process until the mixture is smooth, scraping down the sides of the bowl as necessary. Transfer to a mixing bowl and fold in the cooled peppers. To test for taste, drop a teaspoonful of the mousse into simmering salted water and cook about 2 minutes. Correct seasoning to taste. Refrigerate, covered, until needed.

3 With a pasta machine or by hand, on a surface dusted lightly with semolina flour, roll out one piece of the pasta dough, keeping the remaining two pieces covered, approximately 42 inches long and 5 inches wide. Cut to even all sides. Brush the dough with egg wash and spoon out 12 mounds of mousse, about 1 teaspoonful each, along the bottom half, spaced 2½ to 3 inches apart. Fold the top half over to cover the mounds and press down around each mound to seal. With a round (about 4-inch) cookie cutter, cut into half moon circles. Sprinkle semolina flour on a baking tray, arrange the ravioli on the tray, and again sprinkle with semolina flour. Repeat this procedure with the remaining pieces of dough, egg wash, and mousse. Refrigerate, covered, until needed.

4 *Prepare the sauce:* Roast the peppers over an open

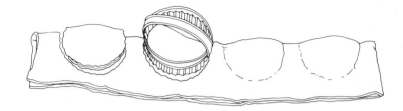

(Continued)
....

2 teaspoons chili
  pepper flakes
2 to 3 plum tomatoes
  (8 ounces), seeded
  and coarsely
  chopped
½ cup Brown Duck
  Stock (see page 42)
1 cup heavy cream
3 tablespoons (1½
  ounces) unsalted
  butter
2 ounces boned and
  skinned duck, cut
  into julienne
Salt
Freshly ground white
  pepper

Chopped fresh herbs
  for garnish

EQUIPMENT

Small skillet
Food processor
Mixing bowl
Pasta machine or
  rolling pin
4-inch round cookie
  cutter
Pastry brush
Baking tray
10-inch skillet
Small skillet
Whisk
Large pot
Slotted spoon

flame or grill. Peel, core, seed, and cut into strips.

5 In a 10-inch skillet, heat the olive oil. Add the garlic cloves and chili pepper flakes and cook 1 to 2 minutes. Do not brown the garlic. Stir in the roasted peppers and sauté 2 or 3 minutes. Add the tomatoes and cook 5 minutes longer, stirring occasionally. Pour in the stock and reduce just until thickened slightly. Pour in the cream, bring to a boil, and simmer 1 or 2 minutes. Scrape into a blender or food processor and puree. Strain into a clean saucepan, pressing down to get as much sauce as possible.

6 Meanwhile, in a small skillet, melt 1 tablespoon butter. Sauté the julienned duck over high heat until cooked on the outside but pink inside, 2 to 3 minutes. Whisk into the sauce with the remaining 2 tablespoons butter and season to taste with salt and pepper.

7 When ready to serve, bring a large pot of water to a boil with a little olive oil. Add salt to the water and then the ravioli. Cook for 5 to 6 minutes. At the same time, heat the sauce over a very low flame. Remove the ravioli with a slotted spoon and drain on a clean towel. Arrange the ravioli in the sauce and simmer for 2 to 3 minutes.

Presentation. Divide the ravioli among large, heated soup bowls. Spoon the sauce over with some of the julienned duck. Sprinkle with chopped herbs and serve immediately.

To prepare ahead: In step 5, strain the sauce into a clean saucepan and continue with the recipe when ready to serve.

WILD MUSHROOM RISOTTO

Serves 4

½ cup peanut oil
½ pound (1 medium)
  onion, minced fine
1 large garlic clove,
  minced
2 cups arborio rice
1 cup dry white wine
2 cups Mushroom
  Stock, heated (see
  page 47)
5 cups Chicken Stock,
  heated (see page 41)
3 tablespoons olive oil
½ pound wild
  mushrooms, stems
  reserved for stock
Salt
¼ cup (1 medium)
  tomato, chopped,
  peeled, and seeded
4 tablespoons (2
  ounces) unsalted
  butter, chilled and
  cut into small pieces
2 ounces (½ cup)
  grated Parmesan
  cheese
Large pinch chopped
  Italian parsley
Freshly ground pepper

EQUIPMENT

Medium saucepan
Medium skillet
Wooden spoon
Baking sheet, optional

Making risotto requires your full attention. Though the rice can be partially cooked in advance and cooled, the finishing process is so precise that the risotto cannot wait for your guests, but rather your guests have to wait for the risotto.

1 In a medium-size heavy saucepan, heat the peanut oil. Over medium-high heat, sauté the onion and garlic just to soften, stirring all the while, 3 to 4 minutes. Add the rice and continue to stir, using a wooden spoon, coating the rice with the oil and onion.

2 Deglaze with the white wine and cook until the liquid is absorbed, stirring often. Pour in enough mushroom and/or chicken stock to cover, about 3 cups, and cook, stirring often, until the liquid is absorbed. (See step 4 under François' Seafood Risotto [page 200] for preparation in advance.)

3 Meanwhile, in a medium skillet, heat the olive oil. If the mushrooms are large, cut them into bite-size pieces and sauté over medium-high heat just to soften, 3 to 4 minutes.

4 Pour 3 cups of stock into the rice, turn the flame to high, and stir in a large pinch of salt and the tomatoes. Stir until almost al dente. Stir in the mushrooms and the remaining 1 cup stock, as necessary. Remember, the risotto should be creamy, not runny. Remove from the flame and vigorously beat in the chilled butter and ¼ cup of the Parmesan cheese until completely dissolved. Stir in the parsley, and season with salt and pepper to taste.

Presentation: Divide among 4 heated plates and serve immediately. Pass the remaining ¼ cup Parmesan cheese.

To prepare ahead: Through step 2, see François' Seafood Risotto.

Françcois' Seafood Risotto with Crisp Ginger

Serves 4

Peanut oil
2 ounces fresh ginger,
  peeled and cut into
  julienne

¾ pound scallops, the
  small white rounded
  protuberances on the
  side removed*
¼ pound shelled
  uncooked shrimp*
⅓ cup olive oil
4 teaspoons chopped
  fresh basil
4 garlic cloves, minced
½ cup peanut oil
½ pound (1 medium)
  onion, minced fine
2 cups arborio rice
1 cup dry white wine
4 cups Fish Stock,
  heated (see page 54)
3 to 4 cups defatted
  Chicken Stock,
  heated (see page 41)

This is the base for any kind of seafood risotto. The fried ginger gives it a delicate oriental flavor.

1 In a medium saucepan, heat 1 inch of oil to 350°F. Fry the ginger until golden, about 3 minutes. Drain and reserve.

2 In a flat dish or bowl, marinate the scallops and shrimp in 2 tablespoons olive oil, the basil, and 3 of the garlic cloves. Refrigerate until needed, turning occasionally. (If the scallops are large, cut them in half, horizontally.)

3 In a medium-size heavy saucepan, heat ½ cup peanut oil. Over medium-high heat, sauté the onion and the remaining garlic clove just to soften, stirring all the while, 3 to 4 minutes. Add the rice and continue to stir with a wooden spoon, coating the rice with the oil and the onion.

4 Deglaze with the wine and cook until the liquid is absorbed, stirring often. Pour in enough chicken and/or fish stock to cover, about 3 cups, and cook, stirring often, until the liquid is absorbed. (You can prepare up to this point earlier in the day. Spread the rice mixture over a baking sheet to cool until serving time. Then scrape the rice back into the saucepan and continue with the recipe.)

5 Meanwhile, in a medium skillet, heat the remaining olive oil. Over high heat, sauté the scallops and shrimp just to color on one side, about 2 minutes. Remove from the pan and reserve.

(Continued)

1 teaspoon salt

¼ cup (1 medium) tomato, chopped, peeled, and seeded

4 tablespoons (2 ounces) unsalted butter, chilled and cut into small pieces

½ cup grated Parmesan cheese

2 to 3 tablespoons chopped fresh Italian parsley

Freshly ground white pepper

EQUIPMENT

Flat dish or bowl
Medium saucepan
Strainer
Wooden spoon
Medium skillet
Baking sheet, optional

6 Pour 3 cups of stock into the rice, turn the flame to high and stir in the salt and the tomatoes. Stir constantly until almost al dente. Add the reserved seafood and the remaining 1 cup stock—the risotto should be creamy, but not runny. (Use the remaining 1 cup of stock only if necessary.)

7 Remove the pan from the flame and vigorously beat the chilled butter and ¼ cup Parmesan cheese into the risotto until completely dissolved. Add the parsley and season with salt and pepper to taste.

Presentation: Divide the risotto among 4 large heated plates, sprinkle with the fried ginger, and serve immediately. Pass the remaining ¼ cup Parmesan cheese.

To prepare ahead: Through step 3.

*You can use only shrimp or only scallops, but I find the combination a little more interesting.

DESSERTS, DOUGHS, AND SAUCES

Apricot Pine Nut Tart

Christmas Apple Pie

Lemon-Lime Tart

Plum-Almond Tart

Individual Macadamia Nut Tarts

Pumpkin Pie with Cranberry Marmalade

Apple and Dried Cherry Turnovers

Peach and Berry Cobbler

The Best-Ever Fruit Cake

Whiskey Fudge Cake

White Chocolate Cheese Cake

Strawberry Shortcake

Butterscotch Pudding

Chocolate Bread Pudding

Three-Chocolate Frozen Mousse

Cinnamon Ice Cream

Milk Chocolate Malt Ice Cream

Crème Frâiche Ice Cream with Strawberry Sauce

Honey Ice Cream with Almond Nougatine

Strawberry Swirl Ice Cream

Apricot-Coconut Macaroons

Chocolate Chip Cookies

Almond Pâte Sucré

Pâte Sucré

Pâte Royal

Puff Pastry

Streusel

Sesame Seed Cups

Hot Fudge Sauce

Chocolate Ripple

Years ago, French food and French pastries were de rigeur at fine dinner parties, and many wonderful American desserts were largely overlooked. These days any restaurant or home cook can be proud of making a great cheesecake or a perfect fruit cobbler. A delicious pumpkin pie in fall or strawberry shortcakes in early summer are true American classics and now you can find them in restaurants from France to Japan.

Only the ripest strawberries or peaches at the peak of their season will do justice to your hard work. When fruits are out of season or in limited supply, you might prefer to make a chocolate fudge cake, a cheesecake, or a nut tart. With the help of a little ice cream freezer (I prefer the electric to the hand-cranked machines), you can make superb ice cream and sorbet combinations by adding different spices and liqueurs.

When planning a menu, always keep in mind that the dessert is also a course of your dinner. And though dessert comes at the very end of the meal, it should be treated as thoughtfully as the first course. Not unlike a theater piece or a movie, dessert should provide the happy ending.

APRICOT PINE NUT TART

Makes one 10-inch tart, serving 8 to 10

INGREDIENTS

1 cup water
8 ounces dried apricots
⅓ cup Grand Marnier
¼ cup orange juice

1 recipe Pâte Sucré (see
    page 235)

1½ cups (9 ounces)
    pine nuts
⅓ cup sugar
4 tablespoons (2
    ounces) unsalted
    butter, at room
    temperature
1 tablespoon finely
    chopped orange peel
2 tablespoons apricot
    jam

EQUIPMENT

Small saucepan
Rolling pin
10-inch tart pan with
    removable bottom
Strainer
10- or 12-inch skillet
½-inch measure (see
    Christmas Apple Pie)
Baking tray
Small bowl
Electric mixer with
    paddle

The intense flavor of dried apricots gives this tart a very distinctive flavor.

❶ *Prepare the filling:* In a small saucepan, combine the water, apricots, Grand Marnier, and orange juice. Bring to a boil, turn off the flame, and let soak for 1 hour.

❷ While the apricots are soaking, roll out the pâte sucré. Divide the dough in half and on a lightly floured surface, roll out one half, about ⅛ inch thick and large enough to line a 10-inch tart pan. Fit into the pan and trim the edges. Add the trimmings to the remaining half of dough. Refrigerate the lined pan until needed.

❸ Roll out the second half to a 10-inch square, evening the sides. Using a ½-inch measure, cut out sixteen ½-inch strips. On the back of a baking tray, weave a lattice pattern (see Christmas Apple Pie, page 206). The strips do not have to be placed too close together. Refrigerate just until slightly firm. Using a 9-inch round, cut out a circle (excess dough can be wrapped and refrigerated or frozen for future use). Refrigerate until needed.

❹ Reserving the apricots in a small bowl, strain the liquid and return to the saucepan. Reduce until 3 tablespoons remain. Cool.

❺ In a 10- or 12-inch skillet (or 2 smaller ones), lightly toast the nuts, stirring constantly and watching carefully to prevent burning. Add ½ cup of nuts and the sugar to the apricots and combine.

❻ Using the paddle of an electric mixer, beat the butter until light and fluffy. Add the cooled liquid and the chopped orange peel and mix just until combined.

(Continued)

7 Preheat the oven to 375°F.

8 *Assemble the tart:* Spread the jam over the bottom of the lined tart pan. Arrange the apricot mixture in the pan, as evenly as possible. Sprinkle the remaining 1 cup of pine nuts over the apricots and top with the butter mixture. Using a wide metal spatula, transfer the latticework circle and place on the filling. Bake until the top crust is golden brown, about 35 minutes. Cool on a rack.

Presentation: Warm slightly before serving and serve with vanilla ice cream or crème anglaise, if desired.

To prepare ahead: Through step 8, reheating at serving time.

CHRISTMAS APPLE PIE

Serves 8 to 10

INGREDIENTS

2 pounds Pâte Sucré or Pâte Royal (see pages 235, 236)

5 pounds (about 10 large) pippin or Granny Smith apples

6 tablespoons (3 ounces) unsalted butter

1 cup sugar

¼ cup plus 1 tablespoon calvados

1 tablespoon brandy

2 tablespoons heavy cream

2 ounces (about ¼ cup) chopped dried prunes

Though we serve this pie at the restaurant during the holiday season, it is much too good to be confined to such a limited period of time. Pippin or Granny Smith apples retain their shape during the cooking process, but must be sautéed first to become tender.

1 *Prepare the crust:* Divide the pastry into two parts, one a little larger than the other. Wrap the larger piece in plastic wrap and reserve. On a lightly floured surface, roll the smaller piece into a round, ⅛ to ¼ inch thick, large enough to overlap a 10 × 2-inch pie plate. Arrange in the pie plate and even with a sharp knife, leaving about a ½-inch overhang. (Add the trimmings to the reserved dough.) Tuck the overhang back under, making a slightly thicker edging. Chill for 30 minutes. If using a glass pie plate, remove from the refrigerator 15 minutes before filling.

(Continued)

1 ½ ounces (about ¼ cup) chopped dried apricots

1 ounce (about ¼ cup) chopped dried figs

1 tablespoon lemon juice

2 teaspoons ground cinnamon

1 teaspoon lemon zest

1 teaspoon orange zest

½ teaspoon freshly grated nutmeg

1 egg white, very lightly whisked

1 ½ tablespoons crystallized sugar*

EQUIPMENT

Plastic wrap

Rolling pin

10- or 12-inch piece of cardboard

Baking pan

2 or 3 large skillets

Small and large bowls

10 × 2-inch pie plate

Pastry brush

2 On a lightly floured surface, roll out the reserved piece of dough into a 12-inch square, about ¼ inch thick. Cut out a piece of cardboard, ½ inch wide and 10 or 12 inches long. Wrap the strip in plastic wrap and use as a guide. With a sharp knife or a pastry cutter, cut the dough into 20 ½-inch strips. Lay 10 strips vertically on the back of a large baking pan, leaving a very small space between strips. Weave a lattice pattern by placing each of the remaining strips over and under horizontally. (It is easier to weave if the dough is not too firm, but it can't be too soft either. If it is too soft, refrigerate for a little while and then continue.) To weave, turn back every other strip of dough (1, 3, 5, etc.), lay a horizontal strip across, as close to the top as possible, and return the turned-back strips to the original length. For the next row, alternate the strips that you turn back (2, 4, 6, etc.) and again place a horizontal strip across, close to the first strip. Repeat this procedure until all the strips are used. Refrigerate just until firm. Using a 9-inch cardboard round, a plate, or a pot cover as a guide, cut out a 9-inch circle of lattice work and refrigerate on the baking pan until needed. (Excess dough can be wrapped and refrigerated or frozen for future use.)

3 *Prepare the filling:* Peel, core, and quarter the apples. Cut into ¼-inch slices. In 2 or 3 large skillets, melt the butter (2 or 3 tablespoons in each skillet, depending upon how many you use) and brown. The butter will have a slightly nutty aroma. Divide the apples, arrange in the pans, and coat with the butter. Sprinkle in the sugar and over medium-high heat, sauté the apples until lightly caramelized and tender, 15 to 20 minutes, turning often so that the apples cook evenly. Pour in 1 tablespoon calvados and the brandy and cook until the alcohol burns off. Pour in the cream and stir through. Transfer and spread over a large baking tray to cool.

4 Preheat the oven to 400°F.

(Continued)

5 Warm the remaining ¼ cup calvados. Combine the chopped prunes, apricots, and figs in a small bowl. Pour the calvados over and let plump.

6 In a large bowl, combine the cooled apples and the plumped dried fruit. Stir in the lemon juice, cinnamon, lemon and orange zests, and nutmeg, and mix well. Spoon the filling into the prepared pie plate. Using a wide spatula, carefully transfer the 9-inch latticework circle and arrange on top of the filling. Brush the latticework with egg white and sprinkle with the crystallized sugar. Bake 30 minutes, turn the oven down to 350°F and bake 35 to 40 minutes longer, until the crust is golden brown. Cool on a rack.

Presentation: Serve warm with Cinnamon Ice Cream (see page 227).

To prepare ahead: Through step 6, reheating at serving time.

*Crystallized sugar, a coarse sugar with larger granules than granulated sugar, is usually sprinkled on certain pastries before baking for a shinier, prettier look. It can be obtained in specialty food shops.

LEMON-LIME TART

Makes one 9-inch tart, serving 8

INGREDIENTS

½ recipe Pâte Sucré (see page 235)
4 whole eggs
4 egg yolks
1 cup plus 2 tablespoons sugar
⅔ cup lemon juice
⅔ cup lime juice
Zest of 2 small lemons
Zest of 2 small limes

Whenever Whoopi Goldberg or Dabney Coleman comes to our restaurant, we know that we have to reserve a quarter of this tart for each of them. Dabney likes it with ice-cold milk, but Whoopi just eats the pie alone.

1 Roll out the pâte sucré to a circle about ¼ inch thick and large enough to slightly overlap a 9-inch metal tart pan. Fit the dough into the pan and trim the edges. Line the bottom and sides of the shell with parchment, or coffee filter papers, or aluminum foil. Fill the lining with dried beans, rice, or aluminum

6 ounces (1 ½ sticks)
soft butter, cut into
small pieces

9-inch tart pan or
ovenproof glass pie
plate
Parchment paper
Pie weights (rice or
dried beans)
Large metal bowl
Whisk
Strainer
Medium bowl
Propane blowtorch*

beans and bake in a preheated 350°F oven 20 to 25 minutes. Cool and remove the beans and the lining. Return the shell to the oven and bake until golden, 5 to 10 minutes longer.

2 In a large metal bowl, whisk together the whole eggs, egg yolks, 1 cup sugar, lemon and lime juice, and zests. Set over simmering water and continue to whisk until the mixture is very thick, about 10 minutes.

3 Turn off the flame and whisk in the butter, a few pieces at a time. (You don't want the mixture to cool down before all the butter is incorporated.) Strain the filling into a bowl. Scrape into the baked tart shell and smooth with a metal spatula. Cool and then refrigerate until firm, 3 to 4 hours, up to overnight.

4 Sprinkle the remaining 2 tablespoons of sugar evenly over the top of the filling. With a propane blowtorch, caramelize the sugar. (This can also be done under the broiler. Place the tart on the broiler tray directly under the flame, watching carefully to prevent burning.) Refrigerate the tart for at least 30 minutes. Or, if desired, eliminate the 2 tablespoons of sugar and arrange circles of raspberries on top of the tart. Sift a little powdered sugar over the berries just before serving.

Presentation: Cut into slices and serve. If you have carmelized the sugar, serve the tart with fresh strawberries or raspberries.

To prepare ahead: Through step 3 or 4.

*A blowtorch can be purchased at most hardware stores. (Follow directions carefully when using the blowtorch.)

PLUM-ALMOND TART

Makes 8 5-inch tarts

INGREDIENTS

½ recipe Almond Pâté
Sucre (see page 234)

FILLING
1 cup almond meal*
½ cup sugar
2 eggs
1 teaspoon lemon zest
1½ pounds (about 10
small) plums
4 teaspoons crystallized
sugar (see page 208)
¼ cup sliced blanched
almonds, optional

Plum Compote (see
Note below)

EQUIPMENT

Rolling pin
5-inch round
Wooden spoon
2 baking trays
Parchment paper
Medium bowl

Note: To make the compote, cut
2 pounds of plums, pitted, into
sections and place in a small
saucepan. Add ½ cup of sugar
and a vanilla bean, split in half
and scraped into the pan. Cook
over a low flame, stirring often
to prevent scorching, until the
plums are very soft and the
compote thickens.

1 Preheat the oven to 350°F.

2 Cut the dough into 8 equal pieces. On a floured surface, lightly flouring your rolling pin, roll out 1 piece of dough to a 5½-inch circle. (The dough breaks easily, but can be pushed together easily as well.) Using a 5-inch round (ring, plate, etc.), cut out a circle and, using a wide spatula, place the circle of dough on a baking pan lined with parchment paper. Repeat with the remaining pieces of dough. Refrigerate for 30 minutes. Then bake until lightly golden, 10 to 12 minutes. Cool.

3 *Prepare the filling:* In a medium bowl, combine the almond meal, sugar, eggs, and lemon zest with a wooden spoon. Set aside.

4 Cut each plum in half and remove the pit. Cut each half into 5 or 6 thin wedges (the number of wedges depends upon the size of the plums).

5 Divide the filling evenly and spread over each tart, leaving a small border around the edges. Arrange the plums in a circular pattern on the filling, sprinkle about ½ teaspoon of crystallized sugar over the plums and place a few sliced almonds in the center, if desired. Bake until the plums are lightly caramelized, about 20 minutes.

Presentation: Place one tart on each of 8 dessert plates. Surround the tart with warm compote and top with a scoop of Cinnamon Ice Cream (see page 227).

To prepare ahead: Through step 5, reheating the tart when ready to serve.

*To make almond meal, grind a scant 1 cup of blanched almonds (about 5 ounces) in a food processor just until fine, being careful that the meal does not turn to paste.

INDIVIDUAL MACADAMIA NUT TARTS

Makes 8 4-inch tarts

INGREDIENTS

1 pound Pâte Sucré
   (see page 235)
2¾ cups light corn
   syrup
1¼ cup brown sugar
6 eggs
3 egg yolks
4½ tablespoons
   unsalted butter
1 vanilla bean, split
   and scraped
1 cup Frangelico
3 cups macadamia nuts
½ pound unsweetened
   shredded coconut

EQUIPMENT

Rolling pin
Parchment paper
Baking tray
8 4 × ½-inch tart pans
Whisk
Large mixing bowl
Small skillet
Ladle

Macadamia nuts can be replaced by pecans, walnuts, cashews, or a combination.

1 Preheat the oven to 375°F.

2 Roll the dough into 2 11-inch squares, place on a parchment paper-lined baking tray, and chill for 20 minutes. Using a 5-inch round (plate, ring, etc.), cut out 8 circles and fit them into 8 4 × ½-inch tart pans. Trim the edges and refrigerate until needed.

3 In a large bowl, combine the corn syrup, sugar, eggs, and egg yolks, and whisk until well mixed.

4 In a small skillet, heat the butter with the vanilla bean over medium heat until the mixture turns golden brown and has a nutty aroma. Scrape into the corn syrup mixture. Stir in the Frangelico.

5 Divide the nuts equally among the tart shells. Ladle the filling over the macadamia nuts.

6 Bake the tarts until the filling feels firm to the touch, about 30 minutes. Remove the tray from the oven and sprinkle the coconut over the top of each tart. Return the tray to the oven and continue to bake the tarts until the coconut turns golden, 10 to 15 minutes longer. Transfer to a rack and let cool.

Presentation: Slide a sharp knife around the sides of each tart and unmold onto individual serving plates, coconut-side up. Serve with ice cream of your choice.

To prepare ahead: Through step 6.

PUMPKIN PIE WITH CRANBERRY MARMALADE

Makes one 10-inch pie, serving 12

INGREDIENTS

12 ounces Pâte Sucré or Pâte Royal (see pages 235, 236)

CRANBERRY MARMALADE

4 tablespoons Sugar Syrup*

1 tablespoon orange zest

2 tablespoons Grand Marnier

1 vanilla bean, split and scraped

1 cinnamon stick or a pinch of ground cinnamon

¼ teaspoon ground nutmeg

8 ounces fresh cranberries

FILLING

2 cups pumpkin puree, preferably made with fresh pumpkin**

1 cup dark brown sugar

1 teaspoon ground ginger

½ teaspoon ground cinnamon

½ teaspoon ground nutmeg

½ teaspoon ground cloves

Pinch of salt

Making your own fresh pumpkin puree may seem to be a needless bother when canned puree is so available, but it is well worth the effort—the taste will tell you that.

1 Preheat the oven to 375°F.

2 Roll out the dough and line a 10 × 1-inch flan ring or a 10-inch shallow pie dish. Trim the edges and refrigerate for 30 minutes. Line with parchment paper and fill with pie weights or beans. Bake 15 minutes, remove the paper and beans, and bake 10 minutes longer.

3 *Meanwhile, prepare the cranberry marmalade:* In a stainless steel saucepan, combine the sugar syrup, orange zest, Grand Marnier, vanilla bean, cinnamon stick, and nutmeg. Bring to a boil, reduce the heat, add the cranberries, and simmer for 3 to 5 minutes, until the berries are softened. Cool and remove the vanilla bean and the cinnamon stick. Spread the mixture in a thin layer over the bottom of the prebaked tart shell.

4 *Prepare the filling:* In a large bowl, combine the pumpkin puree, sugar, ginger, cinnamon, nutmeg, cloves, salt, and pepper. Whisk in the eggs, cream, and bourbon and mix well. Pour into the tart shell.

Pinch of ground white
  pepper
4 eggs, lightly beaten
1½ cups heavy cream
3 tablespoons bourbon

EQUIPMENT

10 × 1-inch flan ring or
  10-inch shallow pie
  dish
Parchment paper
Pie weights or dried
  beans
Stainless steel medium
  saucepan
Large bowl
Whisk

⑤ Bake 35 to 40 minutes, until the filling is firm to the touch.

Presentation: Serve warm with Cinnamon Ice Cream (see page 227) or ice cream of your choice.

To prepare ahead: Through step 5, warming before serving.

*To make Sugar Syrup, combine 3 cups of water and 2¼ cups sugar in a large saucepan. Bring to a boil and, over medium heat, boil until the sugar has dissolved and the mixture is clear, 30 to 40 seconds. Cool and refrigerate in a covered container. Sugar Syrup will keep indefinitely.
**To make fresh pumpkin puree, cut the pumpkin into about 4-inch chunks, remove the seeds, and arrange the pieces on a baking tray. Bake in a preheated 325°F oven until dry, 2½ to 3 hours. Cool and complete the drying-out process for another 3 hours. Scoop out the inside of the pumpkin and puree through a food mill.

APPLE AND DRIED CHERRY TURNOVERS

Makes 16 turnovers

INGREDIENTS

FILLING

2 cups (about ½ pound) dried cherries

1 cup (¼ pound) walnuts

¾ cup water

¼ cup sugar

¼ cup whole fresh cranberries

1 cinnamon stick

1 vanilla bean, split down the center and scraped

Zest of 1 medium orange

Freshly grated nutmeg, to taste

1 tablespoon (½ ounce) unsalted butter

¾ pound apples, peeled, cored, and cut into thin slices

1½ pounds Pâte Sucré* (see page 235)

1 egg, lightly beaten

Crystallized sugar (see page 208)

Dried blueberries or cranberries or raisins can be substituted for the dried cherries. Health food stores generally carry the unsulfured fruits, which I recommend using.

1 *Prepare the filling:* In a 2-quart saucepan, combine the cherries, walnuts, water, sugar, cranberries, cinnamon stick, the vanilla bean and its scrapings, orange zest, and nutmeg. Cook over medium heat until the cherries are plump and tender, 10 to 15 minutes, stirring occasionally. Most of the water will evaporate so watch carefully to avoid burning.

2 Meanwhile, in a medium skillet, melt the butter. Sauté the apples until lightly caramelized and tender, turning as necessary. Stir into the cherry mixture during the last 2 or 3 minutes of cooking. Remove the cinnamon stick and vanilla bean and transfer to a food processor with a steel blade. Puree and scrape into a clean bowl.

3 Cut the pâte sucré in half. Keeping the unused half covered, roll out one piece, on a lightly floured surface, to a 12-inch square, about ¼ inch thick. Using a cookie cutter, cut out six circles, each approximately 4 to 4½ inches in diameter. Reroll the pastry to an 8-inch square and cut out 2 more circles. Repeat with the reserved pastry. (Dip the cookie cutter in flour occasionally to prevent sticking.)

2-quart saucepan
Medium skillet
Food processor
Rolling pin
4- or 4½-inch cookie
    cutter
Pastry brush
Serrated pastry cutter
1 or 2 baking trays
Parchment paper

④ Divide the filling into 16 equal portions, a little more than 1 ounce each. To make the turnovers, place a portion of the filling on a circle of dough, brush egg wash around the edges, fold over the filling, making a semicircle, and gently pinch the edges together. Repeat with the remaining circles of dough, filling, and egg wash. Arrange on 1 or 2 baking trays lined with parchment paper and refrigerate for about 30 minutes.

⑤ Preheat the oven to 350°F.

⑥ Trim the edges of each turnover with a serrated pastry cutter or a larger cookie cutter and brush with egg wash. With a sharp knife, make 2 or 3 slits on top of the turnover and sprinkle with crystallized sugar. Bake 30 to 35 minutes, until the pastry is golden. Cool on a rack.

Presentation: Serve warm with ice cream of your choice.

To prepare ahead: Through step 6, reheating before serving.

*Puff pastry can be used as well. Proceed as above, but do not make the slits on top before baking.

PEACH AND BERRY COBBLER

Serves 12

INGREDIENTS

1 recipe Shortcake (see
    page 221)
Heavy cream
Sugar

FILLING

3 pounds (8 or 9 large)
    ripe peaches
4 cups (2 baskets)
    blackberries,
    blueberries,
    raspberries, or a
    combination
3 tablespoons dark
    brown sugar
3 tablespoons
    all-purpose flour
3 tablespoons lemon
    juice
2 tablespoons peach
    brandy, kirsch, or
    Grand Marnier
½ teaspoon cinnamon
Pinch of freshly grated
    nutmeg
⅓ cup Streusel (see
    page 239)

EQUIPMENT

Baking trays
Parchment paper
Rolling pin
Pastry brush
Large bowl
8½ × 13½ × 2½-inch
    baking dish

One can make apple pie all year round, but this is a recipe that demands ripe, delicious fresh fruit. Make this only when peaches are at their best.

1 *Prepare the shortcakes:* Preheat the oven to 375°F. Line one or two baking trays with parchment paper.

2 Roll out the dough to ½-inch thickness. Cut out 12 2½-inch circles, rerolling the dough as necessary. Arrange the circles on the prepared trays, brush the tops with cream, and sprinkle lightly with sugar. Bake 5 minutes, reduce the oven temperature to 350°F and continue baking 15 to 20 minutes longer, until just lightly golden.

3 *Prepare the filling:* Blanch the peaches, peel, cut in half, and remove the pits. Cut each half into 4 slices and place in a large bowl. Combine with the remaining ingredients, tossing well. Let sit 20 to 30 minutes.

4 Raise the oven temperature to 375°F.

5 Lightly butter an 8½ × 13½ × 2½-inch baking dish. Spoon the fruit into the dish, spreading it evenly. Sprinkle the streusel over and arrange the shortcakes on top (4 each across three rows). Bake 40 minutes, until the shortcakes are nicely browned.

Presentation: Warm the cobbler, if made earlier in the day. Serve with your favorite ice cream or softly whipped cream or just as is with a sprinkling of sifted powdered sugar.

To prepare ahead: Through 5, reheating when ready to serve.

THE BEST-EVER FRUIT CAKE

Makes one 8½ × 4 × 3½-inch loaf

INGREDIENTS

1 cup marsala or
   sauternes
1 cup water
1 cup dark raisins
1 cup dried apricots
1 cup walnuts
½ cup dried pears
½ cup dried figs
½ cup pecans
8 tablespoons (4
   ounces) unsalted
   butter
½ cup sugar
1 teaspoon ground
   cinnamon
¼ teaspoon ground
   cloves
2 cups all-purpose flour
2 teaspoons baking
   soda
½ teaspoon salt

EQUIPMENT

8½ × 4 × 3½-inch loaf
   pan
Medium and small
   saucepans
Small and large mixing
   bowls

You can use any dried fruit that is available and to your taste. At Spago, we use only unsulfured fruit, which can be purchased at health food stores. The recipe can be increased easily to make two, three, or more cakes.

1 Preheat the oven to 350°F. Butter an 8½ × 4 × 3½-inch loaf pan and dust with flour, shaking out any excess. Set aside.

2 In a medium saucepan, combine the marsala, water, raisins, apricots, walnuts, pears, figs, and pecans. Bring to a boil and then simmer until the fruits are tender, about 5 minutes. Let cool. Drain, reserving the liquid, and coarsely chop the fruits and nuts. Transfer to a large bowl with the reserved liquid.

3 In a small saucepan, melt the butter with the sugar, cinnamon, and cloves, stirring occasionally, until the sugar is completely dissolved. Cool.

4 Meanwhile, in a small bowl, sift together the flour, baking soda, and salt. Stir into the melted butter and then scrape into the fruit and nut mixture and combine thoroughly. Don't be afraid to mix with your hands. This is a very thick batter. Scrape into the prepared pan, patting down as necessary to level.

5 Bake until the cake is firm to the touch and nicely browned, 1 hour to 1 hour 10 minutes. Invert onto a parchment-lined rack and let cool. This cake is better when made one or two days before serving. Wrap well.

Presentation: Cut into thin slices and serve. If desired, you can sift powdered sugar over, slice, and serve.

To prepare ahead: Through step 5, this cake, wrapped well, will keep for two or three weeks.

WHISKEY FUDGE CAKE

Makes one 8-inch cake

INGREDIENTS

1 ¼ cups pastry or cake
    flour
1 teaspoon baking soda
10 ½ ounces
    bittersweet
    chocolate, cut into
    small chunks
12 tablespoons (6
    ounces) unsalted
    butter, at room
    temperature
1 ¼ cups sugar
4 eggs, separated
⅓ cup whiskey or
    brandy, warmed
    slightly
1 tablespoon vanilla
    extract
Powdered sugar

EQUIPMENT

Baking tray
Parchment paper
8 × 2 ½-inch ring
8-inch cardboard round
Aluminum foil
Small bowl
Double boiler
Whisk
Electric mixer with
    paddle

I love chocolate cakes that are very dense and need no filling. Cakes like this should either be served at room temperature or a little warm.

1 Preheat the oven to 350°F. Line a baking tray with parchment paper and set an 8 × 2 ½-inch ring* on it. Wrap an 8-inch cardboard round with foil and set aside.

2 In a small bowl, sift together the flour and baking soda. Set aside.

3 In a double boiler or a metal bowl placed over simmering water, melt the chocolate. Keep warm.

4 Meanwhile, with the paddle of an electric mixer, cream the butter until light. Gradually add 1 cup sugar and continue to cream until fluffy. (It is very important that this mixture is light and fluffy.)

5 Beat in the egg yolks, one at a time, the whiskey or brandy, and the vanilla. Stop the machine and scrape in the melted chocolate. Continue to mix until well combined. Remove the bowl from the machine and fold in half the flour mixture. Fold in the remaining flour.

6 With a clean whisk and bowl, whip the egg whites until soft peaks form. Gradually add the remaining ¼ cup of the sugar and continue to whisk until shiny and firm, but not stiff. Stir ¼ of the whites into the batter to lighten, then fold in the remaining whites.

7 Pour the batter into the prepared cake ring and bake for 1 hour. Invert immediately onto the foil-covered cardboard round and run a sharp knife around the sides of the cake, loosening the cake from the ring. *Do not remove the ring from the cake.* Let cool completely on a rack. Then, carefully lift off the ring.

Presentation: Dust the cake with sifted powdered sugar and serve with Crème Frâiche Ice Cream (see page 229) or whipped cream.

To prepare ahead: Through step 7.

*Rings can be purchased at Avery's in Los Angeles or at Bridge Kitchenware in New York (see list of resources).

WHITE CHOCOLATE CHEESE CAKE
Makes one 10-inch cake, serving 8 to 10

INGREDIENTS

½ recipe Pâte Sucré (see page 235)

¾ pound (about 2 medium) red or green delicious apples, peeled, cored, and quartered

4 tablespoons (2 ounces) unsalted butter

⅓ cup sugar

1 ½ pounds cream cheese, at room temperature

¾ cup plus 1 tablespoon sugar

4 eggs

2 teaspoons vanilla

4 ounces white chocolate, melted

This is a particularly rich cake, so cut into small slices and serve with a few fresh strawberries or raspberries.

1 Preheat the oven to 350°F. Pour water about halfway up the sides of a baking dish into which you can set an 8- or 10-inch springform pan,* and bring to a simmer on top of the stove.

2 On a lightly floured surface, roll out the pastry to fit the bottom of a 10-inch nonstick springform pan. Using the bottom as a guide, cut out a circle. Transfer the circle to a pastry sheet and bake until golden, 15 to 20 minutes. Cool, and with a wide spatula, place in the springform pan. Set aside.

3 *Meanwhile, caramelize the apples:* Cut each quarter of apple into 5 or 6 slices, each about ¼ inch thick. In a 10-inch skillet, melt the butter. Add the apples and the sugar and over medium heat, sauté the apples until lightly caramelized, about 15 minutes, stirring occasionally. The apples will be very soft. Spread evenly over the baked crust.

(Continued)

Baking dish large
   enough to hold the
   springform pan
Rolling pin
Pastry sheet
10-inch skillet
Electric mixer with
   paddle
8- or 10-inch nonstick
   springform pan
Aluminum foil

④ Cut the cream cheese into small pieces and in an electric mixer, using the paddle, cream the cheese until smooth. Gradually pour in the sugar and continue to beat until the mixture is not grainy and there are no lumps. Stop the machine occasionally and scrape down the sides and under the cheese. Add the eggs, one at a time, and the vanilla. Scrape in the chocolate and mix just until combined. Pour into the springform pan, on top of the apples. (The filling will only reach about ⅓ up the sides of the pan.) Twist the pan gently to level.

⑤ Wrap foil tightly around the outside of the pan so that water won't seep through and place in the baking dish with simmering water (the water should come halfway up the sides of the 10-inch springform pan). Bake 55 to 60 minutes. The center will still be a little soft, but that's okay. Remove the foil and cool on a rack. Refrigerate until firm, at least 2 hours, up to overnight.

Presentation: Carefully remove the ring around the cheese cake. Serve as is or, if desired, melt 4 ounces of dark chocolate and decorate the top of the cake. To slice, dip a sharp knife into warm water and then cut the cake.

To prepare ahead: Through step 5.

*The cheese cake will come out pure white when baked in a 10-inch pan. However, if you bake it in the 8-inch pan, the top will brown slightly.

STRAWBERRY SHORTCAKE

Serves 10

INGREDIENTS

SHORTCAKE

2¾ cups pastry or cake
flour

¼ cup sugar plus
additional to
sprinkle on top

1 tablespoon plus 1
teaspoon baking
powder

1 teaspoon salt

10 tablespoons (5
ounces) chilled
unsalted butter, cut
into 1-ounce pieces

1 cup heavy cream plus
additional to brush
on top

3 pints fresh
strawberries,
stemmed

2 or 3 tablespoons
sugar

1 tablespoon lemon
juice

2 teaspoons kirsch

1 teaspoon orange zest

Strawberry Swirl Ice
Cream (see page 231)

*Strawberry shortcake is usually prepared with whipped
cream, but I prefer serving it with Strawberry Swirl Ice
Cream. The strawberries surrounding the cakes can be
replaced with blackberries, raspberries, blueberries, or a
combination of all of the above.*

1 *Prepare the shortcake:* Preheat the oven to 375°F.
Line one or two baking trays with parchment paper.

2 In a food processor fitted with the steel blade,
combine the flour, ¼ cup sugar, baking powder, and
salt with a few on/off turns. Add the chilled butter and
process just until combined. With the motor running,
pour the cream through the feed tube, stopping just
before the dough forms a ball.

3 Turn out the dough onto a lightly floured surface
and gently knead, forming a smooth ball. Do not
overwork. Roll out the dough to a round ¾ inch thick.
Using a 3-inch cookie or biscuit cutter, cut out 7
circles. Knead the scraps together, roll, and cut out 3
more circles.

4 Arrange the circles on the prepared baking trays,
brush the tops with cream and sprinkle lightly with
sugar. Bake 5 minutes, reduce the heat to 350°F, and
bake 25 to 30 minutes longer, or until the cakes are
golden and firm to the touch. Cool on a rack.

5 Meanwhile, rinse and drain the strawberries. Cut
each berry into thick slices and toss with the sugar in a
large mixing bowl. Add the lemon juice, kirsch, and
orange zest, and gently mix. Set aside.

6 When ready to serve, split each shortcake in half
and warm slightly.

(Continued)

2 baking pans
Parchment paper
Food processor
Rolling pin
3-inch cookie cutter
Pastry brush
Large mixing bowl

Presentation: For each serving, place the bottom half of the shortcake on a dessert plate. Spoon about 1 cup of ice cream on the cake, arrange a scant cup of strawberries over and around the ice cream, and top with the remaining half of the cake. Serve immediately.

To prepare ahead: Through step 5.

BUTTERSCOTCH PUDDING

Makes 12 ¾-cup servings

INGREDIENTS

12 tablespoons (6 ounces) unsalted butter, cut into small pieces
2½ cups brown sugar
1 vanilla bean, split down the center and scraped
4½ cups milk
2 cups heavy cream
½ cup plus 2 tablespoons cornstarch
½ teaspoon salt
6 egg yolks
1 tablespoon vanilla extract

I remember eating this as a child. My mother used to make this for lunch on Sunday and I always had to have a second helping. Now we serve it at Eureka and it has become one of the most asked-for desserts.

1 In a large, heavy saucepan, over medium heat, melt the butter with the brown sugar and the vanilla bean, stirring occasionally. Cook 3 to 5 minutes to develop the butterscotch flavor.

2 In a medium saucepan, bring the milk and the cream to a boil. Slowly whisk into the butter mixture, whisking well. The mixture may break at this point. If it does, remove from the heat and continue to whisk until it becomes smooth.

3 In a small bowl, combine the cornstarch and the salt. Whisk in some of the hot milk mixture to dissolve the cornstarch, then whisk back into the milk and bring to a boil.

4 In a medium mixing bowl, whisk the egg yolks. Whisk in some of the hot mixture, and then whisk back into the milk. Cook for 30 seconds, stirring all the while. Stir in the vanilla extract and strain through a

Large and medium
saucepans
Whisk
Small and medium
mixing bowls
Fine strainer
12 ¾-cup ramekins

fine strainer. Pour into 12¾-cup ramekins and let cool. Refrigerate, covered, until needed.

Presentation: Pipe whipped cream around the edge of the pudding and place a few raspberries or a strawberry, partially sliced and fanned, in the center.

To prepare ahead: Through step 4. The pudding can be prepared the day before needed.

CHOCOLATE BREAD PUDDING

Makes 8¾-cup servings

CUSTARD
6 ounces bittersweet
chocolate
1½ ounces bitter
chocolate
3 whole eggs
3 egg yolks
½ cup sugar
2 cups half-and-half

SOAKING LIQUID
1½ cups half-and-half
1 cup plus 2
tablespoons sugar
⅓ cup unsweetened
cocoa

8 ½-inch thick slices
brioche

Stainless steel bowl or
double boiler
Large stainless steel
bowl

If the thought of serving chocolate soufflé makes you nervous for fear that it might not be perfect, try this Chocolate Bread Pudding. It is as good as any soufflé and can be prepared in advance.

1 *Prepare the custard:* In a stainless steel bowl or double boiler placed over simmering water, melt the two chocolates.

2 In a large stainless steel bowl, beat the whole eggs and the egg yolks. Gradually whisk in the sugar and beat until fluffy.

3 Meanwhile, in a small saucepan, bring the half-and-half to a rolling boil. Slowly whisk into the egg mixture. Then, whisk in the melted chocolate. Chill over ice and refrigerate, covered, until needed. (This should be prepared the day before so that the custard will thicken.)

4 When ready to prepare the pudding, combine the soaking liquid ingredients in a saucepan and heat until the cocoa is completely dissolved. Cut each slice of bread into two 2-inch circles (16 circles), using a cookie cutter or something similar. Arrange the circles of

....

Whisk
Small and medium
    saucepans
2-inch cookie cutter
Large shallow dish or
    pan
8 ¾-cup custard cups
Slotted spoon
Large baking pan
Sifter or fine strainer

bread in 1 or 2 dishes with sides large enough to hold the circles in one layer. Pour the soaking liquid over and soak well, turning so that the bread absorbs as much liquid as possible.

5 Preheat the oven to 350°F. Butter 8 ¾-cup molds or custard cups.

6 *Prepare the pudding:* Spoon a layer of custard (about 2 ounces) into the bottom of each of the 8 cups. Using a slotted spoon, remove a circle of bread and set in the custard. Spoon over a second layer of custard, a second circle of bread and top with a final layer of custard. Repeat this procedure, filling the remaining cups with custard and bread, and then arrange the cups in a large baking pan. Fill the pan with boiling water, halfway up the sides of the cups. Bake 30 minutes. Cool and refrigerate until needed.

Presentation: Dust the puddings with sifted powdered sugar and pass a bowl of unsweetened whipped cream.

To prepare ahead: Through step 6.

Note: To make 10 ½-cup servings, cut out 20 2-inch circles and continue with recipe as above.

THREE-CHOCOLATE FROZEN MOUSSE

Serves 12

INGREDIENTS

About 2 tablespoons (1
   ounce) unsalted
   butter, melted
12 egg yolks
½ cup sugar

3½ cups heavy cream

WHITE CHOCOLATE MOUSSE

5 ounces white
   chocolate
1½ teaspoons instant
   coffee

MILK CHOCOLATE MOUSSE

5 ounces milk
   chocolate
2½ tablespoons cognac
   or whiskey

DARK CHOCOLATE MOUSSE

5 ounces bittersweet
   chocolate
2½ tablespoons cognac
   or whiskey
Chocolate Ripple (see
   page 242) or Hot
   Fudge Sauce (see
   page 241), at room
   temperature
Edible flowers or
   candied violets,
   optional

This should be prepared one or two days before it is needed. It is a delicate, rich dessert, perfect for that very special dinner party. The mousse is unmolded from dariole cups, but the dessert can also be made in pretty goblets and served directly from the goblet.

1 With the melted butter, brush twelve ¾-cup dariole* cups. Line the bottom of each cup with a circle cut from wax paper** and butter the circles. Arrange the cups on a flat baking tray and set aside.

2 In the large bowl of an electric mixer, using the whisk, whisk together the egg yolks and sugar on high speed until the mixture is pale yellow, almost white, and very thick.

3 Meanwhile, in a medium saucepan, bring 2 cups of cream to a boil. With the mixer on low speed, slowly pour the cream into the egg yolk mixture and continue to whisk until completely incorporated. Divide into three equal portions, about 2 cups each, and refrigerate, covered, until needed.

4 In a clean bowl, with a clean whisk, whip the remaining 1½ cups cream to soft peaks. Refrigerate, covered, until needed. When ready to use, whisk slightly to return to the soft peak stage.

5 Melt the white chocolate in the top of a double boiler or small heat-proof bowl placed over very lightly simmering water. Turn off the heat when the chocolate is almost melted and let the bowl sit over the water to finish melting. Stir occasionally. In a small saucepan, bring one of the egg yolk mixtures (about 2 cups) *just* to a boil, stirring all the while. Strain into a clean bowl of the mixer. With a rubber spatula, scrape in the melted chocolate, add the instant coffee, and with the

(Continued)

EQUIPMENT

Wax paper
12 dariole cups
Electric mixer with 2
  bowls and whisk
Baking tray
Measuring cups
Medium and small
  saucepan
Fine-mesh strainer
Double boiler or small
  metal bowl and small
  saucepan
Pitcher

whisk, whisk until the bottom of the bowl feels cool to the touch. Refrigerate, covered, about 30 minutes. Remove from the refrigerator and fold in ⅓ (about 1 cup) of the softly whipped cream. For easier pouring, transfer to a pitcher and divide among the 12 dariole cups (about ¼ cup in each). Place in the freezer for at least 2 hours to set.

6 Repeat step 5 using the milk chocolate and the cognac or whiskey. Remove the tray of cups from the freezer and divide the milk chocolate mixture among the cups, pouring over the white chocolate. Return to the freezer for at least 2 more hours.

7 For the dark chocolate, repeat step 5, but with one exception. At the point when the bowl feels cool to the touch, do not refrigerate, just fold in the softly whipped cream and continue with the recipe.

Presentation: Remove the tray from the freezer and run a sharp knife around the mousse, as close to the sides of the cup as possible. Turn the cups upside down onto a flat surface, tap the tops a few times, and unmold. Remove the circles of wax paper and, with a small metal spatula, smooth the sides of the mousse. Pour a little of the chocolate sauce on each of 12 dessert plates and place one mousse in the center. Decorate the top with a small edible flower or a candied violet, if desired.

To prepare ahead: Through step 7. This can be prepared 2 days ahead and kept frozen until needed.

*Dariole cups can usually be purchased in shops that carry gourmet kitchen equipment. However, if not available, you might be able to use large demitasse cups or water glasses. They should be approximately 2¾ inches wide and 2¾ inches deep.
**To cut out the circles, fold a piece of wax paper, about 11 × 14 inches, in half one way (11 × 7), then in half the other way (5½ × 7). Using the bottom of one of the cups as a guide, draw 3 circles on the folded paper. Cut out the circles, completely through the folded paper, and you will have 12 circles. Trim as necessary.

CINNAMON ICE CREAM

Makes about 1 ½ quarts

INGREDIENTS

2 cups heavy cream
2 cups milk
2 cinnamon sticks
8 egg yolks
½ cup sugar

EQUIPMENT

Medium-size heavy
  saucepan
Large mixing bowl
Whisk or rotary beater
Wooden spoon
Fine strainer
Ice-cream maker

Ice cream makes a wonderful ending to a meal, whether served alone or with hot apple pie or as a filling for our shortcakes. The recipes are quite simple to prepare, but an ice-cream maker, no matter how modest or how sophisticated, will give you a smoother texture.

1 In a medium-size heavy saucepan, bring the cream, milk, and cinnamon sticks to a boil. Turn off the flame, cover, and let steep for 20 minutes.

2 In a large bowl, using a whisk or a rotary beater, whip the egg yolks. Gradually whisk in the sugar until thoroughly combined. Slowly whisk the hot cream mixture into the egg yolks and return to the saucepan. Over low heat, stirring constantly with a wooden spoon, cook until the mixture heavily coats the back of the spoon. Return to the bowl and cool over ice cubes and cold water.

3 Strain into a clean bowl and freeze in an ice-cream maker according to the manufacturer's directions. Scrape into a large container and freeze, covered, until needed.

To prepare ahead: Through step 3 (see Milk Chocolate Malt Ice Cream).

MILK CHOCOLATE MALT ICE CREAM

Makes about 1 ½ quarts

2 cups milk
2 cups heavy cream
8 egg yolks
10 ounces milk
    chocolate, broken or
    cut into small
    chunks
½ cup Horlicks malt
    powder

Large stainless steel
    saucepan
Large and small
    stainless steel mixing
    bowls
Wooden spoon
Whisk
Fine strainer
Ice-cream maker

1 In a large heavy saucepan, combine the milk and cream and bring to a boil.

2 In a large stainless steel mixing bowl, whisk the egg yolks. Gradually pour the heated liquid into the bowl, whisking all the while. Return to the saucepan and cook over medium heat, stirring occasionally, until the mixture coats the back of a wooden spoon.

3 Meanwhile, in a small stainless steel bowl or the top of a double boiler set over barely simmering water, melt the chocolate. Whisk into the heated milk mixture. Remove 1 cup of liquid and dissolve the malt powder in it. Return to the saucepan and mix well. Strain into a large mixing bowl and chill over ice cubes and cold water.

4 Freeze in an ice-cream maker according to manufacturer's instructions.

Presentation: Place a scoop of ice cream on a large Chocolate Chip Cookie (see page 233) and serve immediately. You may want to pass around Hot Fudge Sauce (see page 241) or warmed Chocolate Ripple (see page 242).

To prepare ahead: Through step 3, refrigerating, covered, overnight and freezing a few hours before serving. Or through step 4. Remove the ice cream from the freezer and place in the refrigerator about 15 minutes before you are going to serve it.

CRÈME FRAÎCHE ICE CREAM WITH STRAWBERRY SAUCE

Makes about 1 ½ quarts

INGREDIENTS

10 egg yolks
⅓ cup sugar
1 quart crème fraîche*

EQUIPMENT

Large stainless steel
  bowl
Whisk
Fine strainer
Ice-cream maker

1 In a large stainless steel bowl, whisk the egg yolks. Gradually whisk in the sugar and then the crème fraîche until well combined and smooth.

2 Strain and freeze in an ice-cream maker according to manufacturer's instructions.

Presentation: Arrange 2 scoops of ice cream in a serving dish. Spoon strawberry sauce (recipe follows) over and serve immediately.

To prepare ahead: Through step 2 (see Milk Chocolate Malt Ice Cream).

*If you cannot buy crème fraîche, you can make your own. For each cup of crème fraîche, stir 2 tablespoons of buttermilk into 1 cup of heavy cream. Let sit at room temperature until the mixture thickens, usually overnight. Scrape into a container, cover, and refrigerate until needed.

STRAWBERRY SAUCE

INGREDIENTS

2 boxes fresh
  strawberries,
  stemmed and thinly
  sliced
¼ cup sugar
Juice of ½ large lemon

1 In a small bowl, combine all the ingredients and gently toss to combine well. Cover and refrigerate for 1 hour before using.

HONEY ICE CREAM WITH ALMOND NOUGATINE

Makes about 1 quart

INGREDIENTS

2 cups heavy cream
1 cup milk
4 egg yolks
½ to ¾ cup honey,
　clover or orange
Almond Nougatine
　(recipe follows)
Sesame Seed Cups (see
　page 240)

EQUIPMENT

Large heavy saucepan
Whisk
Stainless steel bowl
Wooden spoon
Fine strainer
Ice-cream maker

1 In a large heavy saucepan, bring the cream and milk to a boil. In a large stainless steel bowl, whisk the egg yolks. Gradually pour the heated liquid into the bowl, whisking all the while. Return to the saucepan and cook over medium heat, stirring with a wooden spoon, until the mixture coats the back of the spoon.

2 Remove from the heat and stir in the honey to taste. Transfer to a clean bowl and chill over ice cubes and cold water. Strain.

3 Freeze in an ice-cream maker according to manufacturer's instructions. Just before the ice cream is completely set, stir in the nougatine, and continue to churn for a few minutes longer.

Presentation: Set a large scoop of the ice cream in a sesame seed cup. Spoon some warm Chocolate Ripple (see page 242) over and serve immediately.

To prepare ahead: Through step 2, refrigerating, covered, until ready to churn in the ice-cream machine. Or through step 3 (see Milk Chocolate Malt Ice Cream).

ALMOND NOUGATINE

INGREDIENTS

½ cup sugar
⅓ cup sliced blanched
　almonds

1 Brush a small baking sheet with vegetable oil and set aside.

2 In a medium-size heavy saucepan, cook the sugar over high heat until it turns a caramel color. Stir in the almonds and cook 1 or 2 minutes longer. Pour out onto the prepared pan in a very thin layer and let harden. Cool.

Medium-size heavy
  saucepan
Wooden spoon
Small baking sheet

3 When completely set, scrape the nougatine onto a chopping board with a heavy spatula. Cut or chop into small bits. Store in an airtight container until ready to use.

To prepare ahead: Through step 3.

STRAWBERRY SWIRL ICE CREAM

Makes about 2 quarts

STRAWBERRY
COMPOTE
6 boxes strawberries,
  stemmed and wiped
  clean
3 cups sugar
¼ cup lemon juice
1 vanilla bean, split in
  half and scraped

ICE CREAM BASE
2 cups heavy cream
2 cups milk
1 vanilla bean, split in
  half and scraped
8 egg yolks
½ cup sugar

4-quart saucepan
Medium saucepan
Large mixing bowl
Whisk or rotary beater
Wooden spoon
Fine strainer
Ice-cream maker

1 *Prepare the compote:* In a wide 4-quart saucepan, combine all the compote ingredients and stir through. Cook over a medium-high flame until the liquid begins to thicken, about 45 minutes, stirring occasionally. Lower the flame and cook 15 minutes longer, continuing to stir. Watch carefully during the last 15 minutes to prevent scorching. You should have about 6 cups of compote. Cool.

2 *Meanwhile, prepare the base:* In a medium saucepan, bring the cream, milk, and vanilla bean to a boil. In a large bowl, using a whisk or a rotary beater, whip the egg yolks. Gradually whisk in the sugar until thoroughly combined. Slowly whisk in the hot cream mixture and return to the saucepan. Over low heat, stirring constantly with a wooden spoon, cook until the mixture heavily coats the back of the spoon. Return to the bowl and cool over ice. Strain into a clean bowl and freeze in an ice-cream maker according to manufacturer's directions.

3 Scrape half the ice cream into a large container and swirl 2 cups of the strawberry compote through. Repeat with the remaining half of the ice cream and 2 more cups of compote. Freeze, covered, until needed.

Presentation: Place a large scoop of ice cream on a chilled serving dish. Top with strawberry compote.

To prepare ahead: Through step 3 (see Milk Chocolate Malt Ice Cream, page 228).

APRICOT-COCONUT MACAROONS

Makes 24 to 26 macaroons

INGREDIENTS

3 ounces (½ cup
  packed) dried
  apricots, each cut
  into 3 or 4 pieces
½ cup water
¾ cup plus 1
  tablespoon sugar
11 ounces (4½ cups)
  unsweetened
  shredded coconut
3 egg whites

EQUIPMENT

1 or 2 baking sheets
Parchment paper
Small saucepan
Food processor
Electric mixer with
  paddle

The addition of apricots keeps the macaroons moist and gives them a great flavor. At Spago, we serve these at the end of our Passover dinner.

1 Preheat the oven to 350°F. Line 1 or 2 baking sheets with parchment paper.

2 In a small saucepan, combine the apricots, water, and 1 tablespoon sugar. Over medium heat, poach the apricots until tender and about 1 tablespoon of water remains. Cool slightly and transfer to a food processor fitted with the steel blade.

3 Add the remaining ¾ cup sugar, the egg whites, and ½ cup coconut and process until the apricots are pureed. (Start with on/off turns and then let the machine run.) Transfer to the large bowl of an electric mixer fitted with the paddle and add the remaining 4 cups of coconut. On medium speed, beat until the coconut is well combined. Stop the machine and check the texture—the mixture should hold together when pinched. Continue to mix if necessary.

4 Using your hands, form and pinch together 24 to 26 mounds of macaroons, each about 2 ounces. Arrange on prepared pans, 1 to 2 inches apart. Bake until the tops are well browned, 15 to 20 minutes. Cool on a rack and store in an airtight container.

To prepare ahead: Through step 4.

CHOCOLATE CHIP COOKIES

Makes 12 large cookies or 36 small cookies

INGREDIENTS

1 cup walnuts or
  pecans
1 ¾ cups cake or pastry
  flour
½ teaspoon salt
6 ounces (1 ½ sticks)
  unsalted butter, at
  room temperature
¾ cup brown sugar
½ cup white sugar
½ teaspoon baking
  soda
2 teaspoons warm
  water
1 egg
1 teaspoon vanilla
1 cup chocolate chips

EQUIPMENT

2 or 3 baking trays
Parchment paper
Sifter
Electric mixer with
  paddle
Cup or small bowl
Rack

Small or large, these cookies are delicious. At home, when I want to make a more elaborate dessert, I just put a scoop of ice cream between 2 cookies and serve ice-cream sandwiches.

1 Preheat the oven to 375°F.

2 Arrange the nuts on a baking tray and toast 12 to 15 minutes, turning occasionally. Cool and chop coarsely. Set aside.

3 Sift together the flour and salt. Set aside.

4 In an electric mixer, using the paddle, cream the butter until light and fluffy. On low speed, gradually pour in the brown and white sugars. Turn speed up and beat until well combined.

5 In a cup or small bowl, dissolve the baking soda in the warm water and pour into the machine. Add the egg and vanilla and mix until blended. With the motor off, sprinkle the nuts, chocolate chips and last of all the flour around the blade. On low to medium speed, mix just until the flour is incorporated.

6 Turn out of the bowl, wrap in plastic wrap, and chill until firm. With lightly floured hands, shape the dough into 12 equal balls,* about 3 ounces each, and arrange on parchment-lined baking trays, 3 inches apart. Flatten each ball slightly and bake 20 to 22 minutes, until golden brown. Let the cookies cool slightly on the baking tray, then transfer to a rack to finish cooling.

To prepare ahead: Through step 6, storing in an airtight container.

*To make smaller cookies, divide the dough into 36 balls, about 1 ounce each, and proceed as above, arranging them about 2 inches apart and baking 15 to 18 minutes.

ALMOND PÂTE SUCRÉ

Makes about 2¼ pounds

¾ cup (about 4
   ounces) whole
   unblanched almonds
3⅓ cups sifted
   all-purpose flour
12 ounces (1½ cups)
   unsalted butter, cut
   into small pieces
1 cup sugar
1 egg
½ teaspoon lemon zest

Baking pan
Food processor
Electric mixer with
   paddle
Plastic wrap

Any leftover dough can be rolled into a log, cut into ¼-inch slices and baked in a preheated 350°F oven until golden, 10 to 12 minutes. Toasted hazelnuts can be substituted for the almonds, if desired.

1 Preheat oven to 375°F.

2 Spread the nuts on a baking tray and toast until golden, 12 to 15 minutes. Cool and coarsely grind in a food processor fitted with a steel blade. Do not grind too fine. Transfer to a medium bowl and combine with the flour. Set aside.

3 In an electric mixer, using the paddle, combine the butter and sugar until light and fluffy. Add the egg and the zest. Add the flour-nut mixture and mix just to combine. Turn out onto a lightly floured surface and knead into a ball. Flatten the ball, making a small round, and wrap in plastic wrap. Refrigerate for at least 2 hours, or until needed.

To prepare ahead: Through step 3, the dough can be cut in half, wrapped, and refrigerated or frozen. If freezing, defrost, wrapped, in the refrigerator.

PÂTE SUCRÉ

Makes 1 ½ pounds or two 9-inch tart shells

INGREDIENTS

2⅓ cups cake or pastry
   flour
⅓ cup sugar
½ pound (2 sticks)
   unsalted butter,
   chilled, cut into
   small pieces
2 egg yolks
1 or 2 tablespoons
   heavy cream

EQUIPMENT

Food processor
Small bowl
Plastic wrap

Always make the pastry dough hours before using it, preferably the day before. You will find the dough much easier to work with. Quantities can be increased as desired, and then divided into portions for freezing. Just remember to wrap carefully and seal well before freezing.

1 In a food processor fitted with the steel blade, combine the flour and sugar. Add the butter and process until the texture resembles fine meal.

2 In a small bowl, whisk together the yolks and 1 tablespoon of the cream. Scrape into the machine and process until a ball begins to form, using the additional tablespoon of cream, if necessary. Remove the dough from the machine, and on a lightly floured surface, press down into a circle. Wrap in plastic wrap and refrigerate for at least 1 hour.

3 Use as needed.

To prepare ahead: Through step 2, the pâte sucre can be cut into portions, wrapped well, and frozen.

PÂTE ROYAL

Makes 2 pounds

INGREDIENTS

3½ cups (1 pound)
   pastry flour, sifted
2 tablespoons ground
   cinnamon
1 tablespoon sugar
1 tablespoon orange
   zest
½ teaspoon salt
¾ pound (3 sticks)
   unsalted butter,
   chilled, cut into
   small pieces
4 egg yolks
¼ cup heavy cream

EQUIPMENT

Food processor
Small bowl
Whisk
Plastic wrap

1 In a food processor fitted with the steel blade, combine the flour, cinnamon, sugar, orange zest, and salt. Add the butter and process until the mixture resembles fine meal.

2 In a small bowl, whisk together the egg yolks and cream. With the machine running, pour through the feed tube and process until the dough just comes together.

3 On a lightly floured board, pat into a circle or a rectangle. Wrap in plastic wrap and refrigerate until firm, about two hours. Use as needed.

To prepare ahead: Through step 3, the dough can be wrapped well and frozen in 1-pound packages, or as desired.

PUFF PASTRY

Makes 3 pounds

INGREDIENTS

DÉTREMPE
1¾ cups pastry flour
1¾ cups all-purpose
    flour
½ teaspoon salt
½ pound plus 5
    tablespoons unsalted
    butter, chilled and
    cut into small pieces
1 to 1¼ cups chilled
    water

BUTTER BLOCK
¾ pound plus 5
    tablespoons unsalted
    butter

EQUIPMENT

Food processor
Heavy rolling pin,
    preferably ball
    bearing
White linen napkin

If pastry flour is not available, use only all-purpose flour. Puff pastry freezes well, so you can make this well ahead of when you may need it, cut into portions and frozen. This can be used for savory as well as sweet pastries.

1 *Prepare the détrempe:* Measure 1¼ cups water and refrigerate until well chilled.

2 In a food processor fitted with the steel blade, combine the pastry flour, all-purpose flour, and salt with a few on/off turns. Arrange the small pieces of butter evenly around the blade and process until the texture resembles fine meal. (Turn the machine off while checking on texture.)

3 With the machine running, pour the chilled water through the feed tube just until a ball forms. (The amount of water needed depends upon the water content of the butter. Start with 1 cup and add the remaining ¼ cup if necessary.) Turn out onto a lightly floured surface, shape into a round, and score with a sharp knife. Wrap securely in plastic wrap and refrigerate overnight.

4 *Prepare the butter block:* Arrange the butter into as much of a square as possible. Wrap in a clean white linen napkin to absorb excess moisture in the butter. With a heavy rolling pin, pound the butter to form an 8-inch square, about 1 inch thick. Even the sides as necessary with the rolling pin. Refrigerate overnight.

5 Remove the détrempe and the butter block from the refrigerator to bring to room temperature before using (about ½ hour in warm weather or in a warm kitchen; 1½ hours in cold weather). Both should have the same texture before rolling.

(Continued)

6 Lightly flour your work surface and rolling pin. Roll out the détrempe to an 18-inch square. Remove the butter from the napkin and set in the middle of the détrempe. Fold 2 opposite sides over to meet in the center of the butter. If the overlapping ends are too thick, level by lightly moving the rolling pin over the ends. Even the 2 remaining opposite ends and fold to meet in the center, stretching as necessary until the seams come together.

7 Roll out the pastry to a rectangle, about 12 × 18 inches. Starting with the 12-inch side, fold the dough into thirds. Turn the dough so that the seam is on your right and again roll out to the same size rectangle, sprinkling the work surface and dough with flour as necessary to prevent sticking. Using a large, dry pastry brush, brush away excess flour *before* and *after* folding. Using the rolling pin, even the pastry as it is being rolled. Press two indentations in the dough with your knuckles, to remind you of the number of turns you have made, and wrap securely in plastic wrap. (You have just completed two turns.) Refrigerate for 4 hours, up to overnight.

8 Remove the pastry from the refrigerator and let soften slightly before rolling. With the seam on your right, again complete two turns. Press four indentations in the dough, rewrap well, and refrigerate for 2 hours. Again, let the dough soften slightly and roll one more time to complete five turns. At this point, your pastry can be cut, wrapped, and frozen for future use. When cutting, cut the dough lengthwise. Remove the pastry from the freezer and refrigerate overnight.

To prepare ahead: Through step 8.

STREUSEL

Makes 1 ¾ cups

INGREDIENTS

¼ cup (2 ounces) unblanched whole almonds
⅓ cup pastry flour
2 tablespoons brown sugar
2 tablespoons white sugar
1 ½ teaspoons ground cinnamon
¾ teaspoon freshly grated nutmeg
Pinch of ground cardamon
4 tablespoons (2 ounces) unsalted butter, chilled and cut into small pieces
⅓ cup quick oats

EQUIPMENT

Baking tray
Food processor
Small bowl

Streusel will keep very well. You can refrigerate it in a covered container for up to one month or you can freeze it for up to three months. Streusel can replace pastry as a covering for pie.

1 Preheat oven to 350°F.

2 Arrange almonds on a baking tray and toast 15 to 18 minutes, turning occasionally with a spatula. Cool. Chop coarsely and set aside.

3 In a food processor fitted with the steel blade, combine the flour, the brown and white sugars, cinnamon, nutmeg, and cardamon with on/off turns. Add the butter and process just until the mixture comes together.

4 Transfer to a small bowl and stir in the oats and almonds. Refrigerate, covered, until needed. This will keep 2 to 3 weeks, refrigerated, but can be frozen and will keep 2 to 3 months.

To prepare ahead: Through step 4.

Sesame Seed Cups

Makes 10 to 12 cups

INGREDIENTS

1 ¼ cups sesame seeds
¾ cup sugar
¾ cup (4 to 5) egg
  whites
3 tablespoons (1 ½
  ounces) unsalted
  butter, melted
1 tablespoon sifted
  all-purpose flour
½ teaspoon sesame oil,
  optional
Milk

EQUIPMENT

Medium bowl
Whisk
Fork
2 nonstick baking trays
2 ½- to 3-inch mold

This is the Chinois version of the almond tuille or cup. You can use this batter to make ice-cream cones, wrapping the circles around a wooden cone-shaped object, which can be purchased in specialty food shops.

1 In a medium bowl, whisk together all the ingredients, except the milk, until well combined. Let rest at least 30 minutes, up to overnight, refrigerated and covered.

2 Preheat the oven to 350°F.

3 Using a 2-tablespoon measure, spoon some of the batter onto a nonstick baking sheet. Dip a fork into the milk and, using the back of the tines, gently pat the batter, spreading it into a very thin circle, about 6 to 8 inches in diameter. (The milk will prevent the sugar from sticking to the fork.) You should be able to make 2 or 3 circles on an 11 × 15-inch baking sheet, spaced about 2 ½ inches apart.

4 Bake 8 to 10 minutes, until golden brown. Remove the pan from the oven and *immediately* shape over a 2 ½- to 3-inch bowl or mold, forming a free-form cup. Let harden. (You may want to start by making 1 or 2 at a time—the cookie crisps very quickly and can crack.)

To prepare ahead: Through step 4.

Note: Cool pans between use to prevent circles from spreading too much; the hotter the pan, the more the circle will spread.

HOT FUDGE SAUCE

Makes about 4½ cups

15 ounces bittersweet
chocolate, cut into
small pieces
½ cup sugar
1 cup light corn syrup
1 cup plus 2
tablespoons water
1½ cups unsweetened
cocoa powder
1½ tablespoons instant
coffee
6 tablespoons cognac
or brandy

Small metal bowl
Large saucepan

1 In a small stainless steel bowl, over barely
simmering water, melt the chocolate. Turn off the heat
and let stand over the warm water until ready to use.

2 Meanwhile, in a large saucepan, combine the sugar,
corn syrup, water, cocoa, and instant coffee and bring
to a boil. Simmer for 1 or 2 minutes, stirring constantly
to prevent burning on the bottom. When the surface is
covered with bubbles, remove from the heat and whisk
in the melted chocolate. Reduce, over low heat, until
the mixture is as thick and sticky as you like. Stir in
the cognac and cool slightly before using.

To prepare ahead: through 2. When needed, reheat
over simmering water until liquid.

Note: Refrigerated, covered, the sauce will last two to
three months.

CHOCOLATE RIPPLE

Makes 3 ½ to 4 cups

INGREDIENTS

1 ⅔ cups water
1 cup sugar
½ cup light corn syrup
1 ½ cups unsweetened
    cocoa
4 ounces bittersweet
    chocolate, cut into
    small pieces

EQUIPMENT

Medium saucepan

At Spago, we layer this through our vanilla ice cream for the ripple effect, but it also can be used as a sauce.

1 In a medium saucepan, combine the water, sugar, and corn syrup. Bring to a boil and simmer until the sugar dissolves completely. Remove from the heat, stir in the cocoa, and whisk until smooth. Add the chocolate and, over low heat, stir until the chocolate melts. Simmer for 2 to 3 minutes. Strain and cool.

2 Pour into a jar and refrigerate, covered, until needed.

To prepare ahead: Through step 2, reheating as desired over a low flame. This will keep 2 to 3 months.

EQUIPMENT

Lots of modern gadgets save time and effort, but they should be used for the right jobs. A food processor will produce a wonderful fish mousse, but only a food mill will make a good vegetable puree. An electric can opener would collect lots of dust in my kitchen—I only open cans of pet food. For many years, I have used an electric knife to cut salmon en croute or beef Wellington since a conventional knife would crumble the crust or mash the fish. But an electric knife is useless when it comes to chopping onions or mincing parsley.

My favorite kitchen tool is also the most useful—a stainless steel mandoline. With this one tool, you can slice vegetables into a variety of shapes and forms—juliennes, french fries, or vegetable chips. A basic set of good sharp knives is indispensable when used properly. Keep your good chef's knife for vegetables and meat, your cleaver to chop bones, and use a screwdriver to fix door handles (I ruined many of my mother's knives for lack of a screwdriver).

Many serious home cooks think they need a set of copper pots, which are very expensive, don't improve the taste of the food, and are difficult to clean. The type of cookware you use depends upon what you are preparing. A nonstick pan is magic for sautéing, with very little oil needed. For sauces and soups and stocks, I use only stainless steel or other nonreactive metal. Heavy cast iron skillets are fine, but you must have a very hot stove and good ventilation.

I have compiled a list of items useful in the kitchen. You must be the best judge of what will be helpful to you in your kitchen.

Knives
   Paring knife
   10-inch chef's knife
   Serrated bread knife
   Small cleaver
   Boning knife
Hardwood chopping
   boards
Sharpening stone
Kitchen shears
Vegetable peeler
Citrus zester
Four-sided grater
Nutmeg grater
Melon baller
Mandoline
Pastry cutter
Pizza cutter

Ravioli cutter
Bamboo skewers
Flat spatula
Offset spatula
Rubber spatula
Stir-fry spatula
Griddle spatula
Wooden spoons,
   variety of sizes
Perforated spoon
Ladles
Ice-cream scoop
Tongs, 9½ and
   12½ inch
Chef's fork
Balloon whisk
Sauce whisk
Electric mixer

Pepper mill
Manual pasta
    machine, optional
Ice-cream machine,
    manual or electric
Food mill
Food processor
Chinois (fine-mesh
    cone-shaped strainer)
Sifter
Colander, for draining
    pasta, etc.
Rolling pin
Pots and pans, stainless
    steel and nonstick
    surface

Griddle
Waffle iron
Pastry brushes
Pizza stone, optional
Baking pans, preferably
    nonstick surface
Tart pans, different sizes
Pastry bags and
    assorted tips
Mixing bowls,
    stainless steel
Parchment paper

GLOSSARY OF COOKING TECHNIQUES AND TERMS

To better understand recipes, an explanation of cooking terms and techniques is sometimes necessary. Practicing the techniques described below is essential, for only with practice will you be able to master them.

BATONNETS—To cut food into batonnets, first cut into ⅛-inch thick slices, and then cut the slices into ⅛-inch strips, about 2 inches long.

BLANCHING and REFRESHING VEGETABLES—Lower food to be blanched into boiling water and cook briefly, just to soften, then transfer to a bowl of cold water to refresh. To blanch garlic, place peeled garlic into a fine strainer and lower into the boiling water for one or two minutes. Blanching will soften and also decrease the strong taste of the garlic.

BRUNOISE—To cut vegetables into brunoise, cut the julienne strips into small dice.

CONCASSE—Roughly chopped foods.

DEGLAZE—To deglaze a pan, a small amount of liquid (wine, stock, cream, or water) is poured into the pan *after* the cooked meat, fish, or poultry is removed from a sauté or roasting pan and the grease poured off. The browned particles are scraped up with a wooden spoon and incorporated into the liquid as it cooks, giving flavor to the final sauce.

DÉTREMPE—Technical term meaning a mixture of flour and water to be used in the preparation of pastries.

JULIENNE—To cut into matchstick-size strips. Make a stack of ⅛-inch slices, and then cut downward at ⅛-inch intervals.

MANDOLINE—French slicing tool, indispensable in a professional kitchen. It is used to cut thin slices, fancy waffled slices, julienned strips.

MINCE—To cut food into tiny dice.

MIREPOIX—A combination of onion, carrots, and celery, cut into cubes and used to flavor stocks and sauces.

POACH—To gently cook food in a small amount of simmering liquid.

REDUCE—To cook liquid, uncovered, over high heat, in order to thicken the consistency, decreasing the amount of liquid and increasing the flavor.

SAUTÉ—To cook food, over high heat, in a small amount of fat or oil, turning as necessary. Food also can be sautéed in a nonstick pan, using no oil or fat.

SIMMER—To heat liquid until small bubbles form on the surface. Low to medium heat is used to maintain the simmer.

STIR FRY—To cook food in a small amount of oil, generally over high heat, stirring frequently during the cooking process.

SWEAT—To cook vegetables, often onions, shallots, or leeks, in butter or oil over low heat until translucent and glossy, without changing the color.

WATER BATH (Bain-Marie)—Used in professional kitchens, this is used to cook food over simmering water (on top of the stove) or in a hot water bath (in the oven). The first method requires nothing more than a metal bowl set over a saucepan or a double boiler, used to keep sauces warm or for melting chocolate. The second method consists of a smaller pan, filled with the food to be cooked, set into a larger pan, filled with enough simmering water to come halfway up the sides of the smaller pan.

RESOURCES FOR
FOOD AND EQUIPMENT

Resources with asterisk will send a free catalog upon request.

American Spoon Food*
P.O. Box 566
Petroskey, MI 49770
800-222-5886
*Flours, preserves, dried
berries, nuts, and honeys*

Avery Services
905 E. Second Street
Los Angeles, CA 9001
213-624-7832
*Gourmet cookware, small
and large appliances*

Bridge Kitchenware*
214 E. 52nd Street
New York, NY 10022
212-688-4220
Gourmet cookware

Chef's Catalog*
3005 N. Clark Street
Chicago, IL 60657
312-327-5210
*Gourmet cookware,
small appliances*

Dean & Deluca*
560 Broadway
New York, NY 10017
212-431-1691
*Specialty foods and
gourmet cookware*

Kitchen Bazaar
1098 Taft Street
Rockville, MD 20850-1308
301-424-4880
*Gourmet cookware
For $3.00, a one-year subscription
to a newsletter with sale items.*

Kitchen Supply Co.*
209 S. Lombard
Oak Park, IL 60302
708-383-5990
*Kitchen gadgets, pizza-baking
stones, pizza-making equipment*

Kozlowski Farms*
5566 Gravenstein Highway
Forestville, CA 95436
707-887-2104
Preserves, syrups, jams, jellies

La Cuisine Classique
439 Decatur
New Orleans, LA 70130
504-524-0068
Gourmet cookware

Oriental Pantry*
423 Great Road
Acton, MA 01720
508-263-6922
*Bamboo kitchen tools, steamers,
stir-fry cookware, and accessories*

Peppercorn Gourmet
  1235 Pearl St.
  Boulder, CO 80302
  303-449-5847
*Oriental and gourmet cookware,
pizza-baking stones, gourmet foods*

San Francisco Herb Co.*
  250 14th Street
  San Francisco, CA 94103
  800-227-4330
Herbs, spices

S. E. Rykoff Co.*
  P.O. Box 21467
  Market Street Station
  Los Angeles, CA 90021
  800-421-9873
Specialty foods, gourmet cookware

The Spice Market*
  664 Bergen Street
  Brooklyn, NY 11238
  718-636-6300
*Herbs, spices, seasonings
(Minimum purchase is $50.00)*

Sur La Table
  Pike Place Market
  84 Pine Street
  Seattle, WA 98101
  800-243-0852
Gourmet cookware

Williams-Sonoma*
  P.O. Box 7546
  San Francisco, CA 94120
  415-421-4242
Specialty foods, gourmet cookware

Zabar's*
  2245 Broadway
  New York, NY 10024
  212-787-2000
*Specialty foods, gourmet
cookware, small appliances*

Index

H

Halibut with Tomatoes and Sweet
   Peppers, 70
Ham Hash Topped with
   Guacamole, 162–163
Hash
   Corned Beef, 166–167
   topped with Guacamole,
      162–163
Herbed Croutons, 52
Herb Mustard, 140
Herb Pasta Dough, 185
Honey Ice Cream with Almond
   Nougatine, 230–231
Hot Fudge Sauce, 241
Huckleberry Sauce, 85

I

Ice cream
   Cinnamon, 227
   Crème Fraîche, with Strawberry
      Sauce, 229
   Honey, with Almond Nougatine,
      230–231
   Milk Chocolate Malt, 228
   Sesame Seed Cups for, 240
   Strawberry Swirl, 231
Italian Parsley Oil, 52
Italian-style Pickled Eggplant,
   124–125

J

Jalapeño peppers
   Cream, 50–51
   Sauce, 17
   Spicy Cinnamon-Chili Paste, 141
Jams and marmalades
   Cranberry Marmalade, 212
   Strawberry Jam, 151
Juice, Postrio Fresh
   Tomato-Vegetable, 150

L

Lamb
   Black Bean Chili, 106–107
   Braised Moroccan, 89–90
   Leg, with Black Bean Ragout, 88
   Meatballs, on Creamy Mashed
      Potatoes with Brown Onions,
      90–91
   Meatballs, in Golden Lentil
      Soup, 48–49
Lasagna, Chicken, 189–190
Lemon-Butter Sauce, 36–37
Lemon-Lime Tart, 208–209
Lentils, Soup with Lamb
   Meatballs, 48–49
Liver
   Calves', 98–99
   Calves', with Pancetta Sauce,
      99–100

Duck, with Cabbage and Green
Onion, 13
Duck, Pâté, 10–12
marinade for, 10
Lobster
Salad, 36
Stock, 45

M

Macadamia Nut Tarts, Individual,
211
Macaroons, Apricot Coconut, 232
Mandarin Noodles with Sauteed
Tenderloin and Vegetables,
93–94
Marinade(s)
beef, 3
chicken, 4, 180
liver, 10
quail, 83
seafood, 5
Marmalades. *See* Jams and
marmalades
Meatballs, Lamb, 48–49, 90–91
Meat Loaf on Vegetable Puree with
Mushroom Sauce, 91–93
Mexican Pizza, 181
Middle-Eastern-style Pickled
Eggplant, 125
Milk Chocolate Malt Ice Cream,
227

Mint Vinaigrette, 4
Mousse
Spinach-Ricotta, in Pasta
Rounds, 193–194
Three-Chocolate Frozen,
225–226
Mushroom(s)
Sauce, 92
Sauce, Pancetta, 99–100
Sauce, Spicy, 86–87
Stir-fried Vegetables, 113
Stock, 47
Wild, Angel Hair Pasta with,
187
Wild, Risotto, 199
Mustard
Chinese, 139
Herb, 140
Vinaigrette, 34

N

Nougatine, Almond, 230–231

O

Oil(s)
Basil, 53, 58
Chili, 145
Chili and Garlic, 179–180
Italian Parsley, 52

Puff Pastry, 237–238
   Goat Cheese and Black Olives
      in, 6–7
Pumpkin
   Pie with Cranberry Marmalade,
      212–213
   Puree, 80, 88
Puree
   Celery Root, 66–67, 114
   Potato, 98–99
   Pumpkin, 80, 88
   Vegetable, 92–93, 111

Q

Quail
   marinade for, 83
   with Persimmon Relish, 31
   with Pineapple and Green
      Onion, 83–84
   with Wild Rice Risotto, 81–82
Quesadilla Eureka, 94–96

R

Radicchio, Minced Garlic Chicken
   in, 32–33
Ragout, Black Bean, 88, 116
Ratatouille, 122

Ravioli
   Duck, with Red Pepper Sauce,
      197–198
   Smoked Salmon, with Lime-Dill
      Butter Sauce, 195–196
   Three-Cheese, 191–192
Red Bell Pepper Sauce, 28
Red Snapper
   with New Potato Crust and Red
      Onion Sauce, 67–68
   with Spring Vegetable
      Vinaigrette, 21–22
Red Wine Sauce, 104–105
Relish
   Persimmon, 31
   Red Bell Pepper, 165
   Spiced Cranberry, 143
Rib Sauce, 136
Risotto
   Seafood, with Crisp Ginger,
      200–201
   Wild Mushroom, 199
   Wild Rice, Grilled Quail with,
      81–82

S

Salad(s)
   Calamari, with Potato Strings,
      20–21
   Chino Chopped Vegetable,
      34–35

About the Author

WOLFGANG PUCK began his formal chef's training in Austria at age fourteen. He continued his apprenticeship at L'Ousteau de Baumanière in Provence and further developed his culinary creativity at Hôtel de Paris in Monaco and Maxim's in Paris, both world-renowned three-star restaurants. Shortly after his arrival in the United States in 1973, he drew crowds to Los Angeles's Ma Maison, where he was chef and part owner. He now owns five spectacular restaurants in California, each one a fantastic creation designed by his wife and partner, Barbara Lazaroff. Spago, their first adventure in restaurateuring, has been a Los Angeles phenomenon since it opened in 1982. Their second restaurant, Chinois on Main, opened in 1983 and features inventive and interpretive Chinese-French cuisine. San Francisco is graced with Postrio, whose menus are inspired by the local Italian and Asian communities. In 1990 the Puck-Lazaroff duo opened Eureka Brewery and Restaurant, where Puck serves up his celebrated pizzas along with homemade breads and charcuterie. Their latest adventure, opened in August 1991, is Granita, which offers Puck's interpretation of the flavors and dishes of the Mediterranean.

In addition to *Adventures in the Kitchen*, Wolfgang Puck is the author of *The Wolfgang Puck Cookbook* and *Wolfgang Puck's Modern French Cooking*. He resides in Los Angeles with his wife and their son, Cameron.